Abstracts of Lancaster County, PA, DEED RECORDS, Volume III (BOOKS W, X, Y, Z)

Including the areas now comprising Dauphin and Lebanon counties

Deeds Recorded 1779-1786

Compiled by

Edward N. Wevodau

Published by
Closson Press
Apollo, PA

Published by
Closson Press
1935 Sampson Dr, Apollo, PA 15613
http://www.clossonpress.com
Library of Congress Control Number 2002108684
ISBN# 155856425X
First Printing

While church and probate records steal the headlines in genealogical circles, the more earthy deed records have equal significance. An experienced Pennsylvania genealogist rejoices with the discovery that his ancestors owned property. Through careful study of the land, much can be gleaned about its residents.

This volume is the third in an occasional series of early Lancaster County deed abstracts. I greatly admire R. Thomas Mayhill's *Lancaster County, Pennsylvania, Deed Abstracts and Oaths of Allegiance (Revised Edition), Deed Books 'A' Through 'M', 1729 Through ca1770.* This seminal work is, in a word, THOROUGH. I chose to base my abstracts on this work, but—due to time constraints—I could not include the same detailed information as Mr. Mayhill. Thus, I did not abstract certain elements. In deciding what information to abstract, I chose to include information that would help a researcher identify a familial connection. I operated under the assumption that, once a person identified a possible match, they would then order the full text of the deed.

For sundry reasons, those living in outlying areas often did not bring their deeds to Lancaster to be recorded. Though far from scientific, I would estimate that, at most, 60 percent of all land transfers prior to 1800 were recorded—and the figure could be much lower. Nonetheless, there is hope: After describing the tract to be conveyed, deeds give the prior history of the property. If the land had not been patented, the history normally begins with the warrant; otherwise, the history begins with the patent. From that starting point, the deed briefly denotes all transfers of the property up to the present. Thus, previously unrecorded deeds can be unearthed. For this reason, it is especially important to abstract early deed records, as critical information about a family may be found in a place one would never think to look.

Information of Genealogical Value That May Be Found in Deeds:
--Occupation and place of residence.
--Name of spouse at a given point in time.
--Marriages.
--Parent-Child relationships.
--References to other court records, often with cited locations.
--Lists of heirs.
--Family migrations.
--Arrival/departure in and from a particular area.

Deeds also contain a wealth of other information, varying in genealogical importance. For temporal reasons, I did not abstract them. They are as follows:

Elements Not Abstracted:

1. Adjacent Landowners: In describing the property to be conveyed, adjacent property owners are almost always listed. This information has great significance, as neighbors often were relatives. Also, they sometimes reveal conveyances of neighboring property (e.g., land formerly of Chad Leinaweaver but now of Jeff Wachtman). Ultimately, I chose not to include this information because the great influx of names would clog the index.
2. Date of Recording: Deeds were recorded months to years to decades after being executed. While the deeds in this volume may range from 1712 to 1789, all deeds were recorded between 1774 and 1789. Often, the earlier deeds were recorded because the same land (or part thereof) had been more recently transferred; the old deed was simply brought in with the new to be recorded at the courthouse. Thus, in a series of 10 pages, one might see the entire history of a particular piece of property over a span of 70 years. Since the date of recording has minimal value, I chose not to include this information.

3. Justices: The deed had to be affirmed before a judge. I have not abstracted this information since it has no genealogical value.
4. Affirmations: If a deed was recorded eight months after being executed, then a participant or witness had to affirm its veracity before a judge. Usually, I did not abstract this information; however, please be advised that affirmations can sometimes contain significant clues. For example, the affirmation may note that a grantor or grantee has died or removed from the area. Also, the affirmation can sometimes take place decades after the date of the instrument. If I saw clear significance, then I did abstract this information.
5. Metes & Bounds: Along with adjacent landowners, the property description typically includes the survey metes and measures. With this information, a researcher can draw the property to scale. For those interested, I recommend Neal Otto Hively's *How to Plot Land Surveys: A Basic Primer for Drawing Deeds, Surveys, and Other Land Descriptions*.
6. Monetary Sums: The land value may reveal something important about the grantor and/or grantee's financial situation. Also, the sum—if an unusually low figure—may indicate a familial relationship between grantor and grantee.
7. German Signatures & Marks: If a person signed their name in German script, then it is usually noted on the record. Foolishly, I did not include this information in my abstracts. I suppose that, to me, the German names are clear and distinct from their English-speaking counterparts. Furthermore, the record notes whether the grantor signed or made his or her mark. This information may be of value, although it appears the majority of marks were the uniform "X".

Basic Steps to Land Possession in Pennsylvania:

As a proprietary colony, the Penn family owned all the land in Pennsylvania. For their own profit and benefit, they sold parcels of this land to settlers. To acquire land, a settler followed these basic steps:

1. Application: An informal oral or written request, made before the Land Commission, to purchase a certain amount of land.

2. Warrant: Once the land commission approved the application, the secretary gave a written order to survey a certain amount of land to the applicant. This document gives the amount of land, location, price, and terms of sale.

3. Survey: Days to months to years later, the settler hired a surveyor, who visited the claimed property to measure and mark the same. The survey was then returned to the land office. Often, the survey found the claimed property to contain more land than allowed by the warrant (e.g., the survey finds the property to contain 90 acres, but the warrant was only for 50 acres). As one might guess, this "overplus land" was not free—before the proprietors divested full ownership of the property to the warrantee, he had to make restitution at an agreed upon price.

4. Patent: With a patent, the proprietors formally conveyed legal title to the land described in the return of survey (subject to certain conditions) to the applicant. To receive a patent, the landowner had to pay the remainder of the purchase price. Often, the warrantee and the patentee were different persons. The right to the property could be transferred at any time in the process.

PLEASE! A goldmine of information lies buried in Pennsylvania patent records. Since deed histories begin with the patent, many land transfers prior to the patent are omitted. However, many of them can be found in the actual patent records. The patent record begins with the warrant and often cites all (if any) land transfers from that point. From my own research, I find that patents prior to 1785 normally include such transfers, but later patents generally refer to "sundry conveyances". Patent abstracts are a worthy and important project for someone!

Suggestion for further research: The ultimate source for information about land records in Pennsylvania is Donna Bingham Munger's *Pennsylvania Land Records: A History and Guide for Research.*

Important Factors to Consider:

1. The boundaries of Lancaster County have changed significantly since the county's formation in 1729. The following counties, with their date of incorporation, were originally a part of Lancaster:

York County, 1749
Cumberland County, 1750
Dauphin County, 1785
Lebanon County (taken out of Dauphin County), 1813

Perhaps more appropriately, this volume should be entitled *Abstracts of Lancaster, Lebanon, and Dauphin County Deeds*, as a large number of deeds pertain to lands in modern-day Lebanon and Dauphin counties.

2. Original Records: The original deed went to the grantee. At the time of recording, a copy of the deed was transcribed by hand into the Lancaster County deed books. Beginning in the 1930's, some of these handwritten deed books were replaced by new, typed versions. The microfilmed records I used to create these abstracts are usually the typed transcriptions. Thus, think of these abstracts as a copy of a copy of a copy of a copy. No—you shouldn't expect any errors [sarcastic laughter].

The Basic Deed Abstract:

(1.) R118: (2.) John Hochstetter, yeoman, & his wife Catharine; Joseph Hochstetter, yeoman, & his wife Ann; Barbara Stutsman, widow (all of Berks County); and Christian Hochstetter, yeoman, & his wife Barbara of Lancaster County (3.) enf-rel.to (4.) John Nafftzger, yeoman, of Lancaster County

(5.) 150a Lebanon tp.: (6.) HISTORY: Same tract pat. 29 Apr 1767 to Peter Benedict (Ref. PB AA-8-275). On 7 Apr 1772, Peter Benedict & his wife Elizabeth released the same to the said Christian Hochstetter. On 2 Mar 1775, Christian Hochstetter & his wife Barbara granted the same to John Hochstetter, yeoman, of Berks County. Said John Hochstetter died intestate, leaving a widow named Anna and issue four children, to wit, the above grantors (John, Joseph, Barbara, & Christian).

(7.) 17 Feb 1776: (8.) Christian Hertzler & Jacob Yotter

1. Volume and Page. The earliest deed books have been given letters for identification purposes (to wit, A-Z, with A being the earliest). After Book Z, the letters are doubled (AA, BB, CC, etc.). The number given is the page number. Thus, Deed R118 may be found in Deed Book R, page 118.

2. Grantor: The grantor(s) is always listed first. The following details, if provided, are given in this order: Name, occupation, spouse, place of residence. IMPORTANT: The wife had a one-third right to her husband's real estate. Thus, if land is conveyed, the spouse will be identified. One should assume that a male grantor is either unmarried or a widower if he conveys land by himself. Exception to the rule: Water rights or privileges—presumably since no land is exchanged. IMPORTANT: If the person resided in Lancaster County, then I only list the township [if given].

Also, I did not include the state in which they resided unless they lived in a state other than Pennsylvania..

3. Type of Transfer. Quite frankly, I don't understand the difference between granting, releasing, enfeoffing, or release-enfeoffing a piece of property. To me, one guy simply sells the land to another. But, in following Mayhill, I have chosen to denote what kind of transaction is taking place. The following types of transfers are found on the record, with the abbreviations I use in parentheses:

    a. ASSIGNMENT (assign[s] to): [Assignor] has granted, bargained, sold, assigned, and set over by these presents and doth grant, bargain, sell, assign and set over to [assignee].
    b. RELEASE (rel.to): [Grantor] released and confirmed and by these presents doth grant, bargain, sell, alien, release and confirm to the said [grantee]
    c. ENFEOFFMENT (enf.to): [Grantor] hath granted, bargained, sold, aliened, enfeoffed and confirmed and by these presents do grant, bargain, sell, alien, enfeoff and confirm to [grantee]
    d. GRANT (gr.to): [Grantor] doth grant, bargain, and sell to [grantee]
    e. QUIT CLAIM (quitclaim.to): [Grantor] hath devised, released, and forever quit claimed and by these presents devise, release, and quit claim to [grantee]
    f. ENFEOFF AND RELEASE (enf-rel.to): [Grantor] grant, bargain, sell, alien, enfeoff, release, and confirm to [grantee]
    g. MORTGAGE (mort.to): [Mortgager] doth acquit, release, and discharge to [Mortgagee]. He [mortgager] hath granted, bargained, sold, aliened, released and confirmed and by these presents doth grant, bargain, sell, alien, release and confirm unto [mortgagee]...*property description*...providing always nevertheless and it is the only true intent and meaning of these presents: and the second parties that I the said [mortgagor] heirs, Executive and Administrators do and shall will and truly pay of cause to be paid unto [mortgagee] etc. the sum of (--) with lawful interest for the same.

4. Grantee(s): The following details, if given, are provided: Name, occupation, place of residence. IMPORTANT: Unlike the male grantor, a male grantee will not have his wife identified because he is acquiring rather than selling property. The wife gains her one-third right after her husband acquires the property—thus she does not have to give her consent for the transaction to take place.

5. Property: The record normally contains a detailed description of the property to be conveyed. I simply identify the amount of land in acres (a.) and perches (p.), with the location by township [if given]. All land in these abstracts was located within the boundaries of Lancaster County as of the date of the instrument. [Exception: If two properties are transferred by the same instrument, one could be located outside of the county boundaries. This situation requires that the deed also be recorded in the other county in which the land is located.]

6. History: If the land has been patented, the history begins there. If the land has not been patented, the history normally begins with the original warrantee. For patents, I have included the specific reference given in the record; e.g., "Same tract pat. 29 Apr 1767 to Peter Benedict (Ref. PB AA-8-275)". To find the patent, locate Patent Book AA, Volume 8, page 275. The history given in the patent starts with the original warrantee. Patent records (as well as warrant records) are available on microfilm at the Pennsylvania State Archives in Harrisburg. For a nominal fee, copies can be requested via mail. The same patent records can also be ordered at any LDS Family History Center. Lancaster County Deeds may also make reference to previous indentures recorded in Lancaster. "Ref. Deed Q56" simply means that the previously stated transfer was recorded in

Deed Book Q, page 56. WARNING: I have not verified the references. Be advised that that due to transcriptions completed since the original recording, the pagination may be slightly (or grossly) off the mark.

7. Date of Instrument: The deed was signed and executed on this date. This date is quite different from the date of recording, which marks the time when the deed was entered into the Lancaster County record books. This date has great significance, as it often verifies marital status and residence at a fixed point in time.

8. Witnesses: Deeds had two witnesses who could—if necessary--later verify that the transaction legally took place. Often, these men and women were neighbors, family, or prominent individuals. To simplify the index, I have created a two-letter symbol for frequent witnesses.

Basic Types of Eighteenth Century Records found in Lancaster Deed Books:

1. Conveyance: The most common type of deed found on the record. One party sells certain property to another party.

2. Sheriff's Deeds: The country sheriff received orders from a court—usually the Court of Common Pleas—to seize the property of a convicted debtor. If the debtor could not satisfy his creditors within a space of seven years, then the court ordered the sheriff to auction the property to the highest bidder at a public sale. Once the court approved the sale, the sheriff wrote and executed a deed. Sheriff's deeds usually contain three or four references to specific court dates; however, these abstracts only include the first date given. Descendants should consult the original deed for further details.

   N18: John Barr, Esq., the High Sheriff of Lancaster County, gr.to George Ross, Esq.
   --Three tracts totaling 562a in Lampeter tp.: HISTORY: On 11 May 1765, the Court of Common Pleas ordered the sheriff to seized the real estate of Jacob Downer, yeoman, of Lampeter tp., for debts owing to Isaac Whitelock & Benjamin Davis. The sheriff seized the following properties: (1.) three tracts in Lampeter tp. totaling 500a, (2.) 190a Manheim tp., & (3.) 700a Donegal tp. [on which the town of May Town is erected], the latter including a ferry across the Susquehanna River. On 19 Jan last, the sheriff sold the three tracts in Lampeter tp. (to wit, 106a, 200a, & 200a) at public vendue to George Ross, attorney, of Lancaster Borough. A resurvey of the properties has since found them to contain a total of 562a.
   6 Feb 1767: E. Biddle, Richard Peters, Jr., William Bowsman, & JM

3. Quitclaim: Ah! The crown jewel of deed records. In a quitclaim, a person gives up all right, claim, title, and interest to a particular piece of property. Usually, the person is an heir of a deceased freeholder and therefore retains a claim to the property. By legal means, the property becomes vested in one specific heir; however, s/he must pay the other heirs their equal shares. In a quitclaim, the heir or heirs acknowledge that they have received their full share of the property and therefore *quit* any further *claim* thereto. Now, why are these records the crown jewel? Since they deal with heirs, they often link parent to child. Further, the child's marital status and physical location are given at a specific point in time. These records often prove migrations and verify marriages.

   N84: Balser Shelhorn & his wife Mary, Henry Good & his wife Christina, Abraham Kassel & his wife Catharine (the said Mary, Christina, & Catharine being daughters of John Martin Amweg, deceased, late of Rapho tp., yeoman) quitclaim to John Stouffer
   --Two tracts: (1.) 140a Rapho tp. & (2.) 5-½ a. Rapho tp.: HISTORY: Said John Martin Amweg died seized of both properties. By his last will & testament dated 16 May 1768, he bequeathed the same to his son-in-law John Stouffer, who was intermarried to his daughter Barbara—they to pay the above-named heirs their equal share.
   28 Aug 1769: MH & JH

4. Articles of Agreement: As the name suggests, this type of record is an agreement between two or more parties. Most agreements are between parent and child, with the latter receiving special bequests in exchange for caring and providing for their elderly parents. Also, these records may include the rare marriage contract. Please be advised that, unless the matter of agreement has genealogical value, I am quite succinct.

N137: Agreement between John Killhoffer of Manor tp. and John Stoner, yeoman, of Hempfield tp.
--The two parties own adjacent tracts. A milldam erected on John Stoner's property has resulted in parts of John Killhoffer's property being overflowed. With this indenture, the parties resolve the issue.
21 Nov 1769: MH & JH

5. Water Rights: Water powered eighteenth-century mills, and ditches carried water to fields and meadows. Without water, land was worthless. Thus, numerous deeds involve the granting of water rights or privileges. Since a river or stream ran across multiple properties, the settlers often had to compromise on its usage. A person who built a dam on his property had to forge agreements with his neighbors whose water supply had been affected by the dam. A person without an adequate water source on his property had to make an agreement with his neighbor to dig a ditch (or watercourse) connecting a stream on his neighbor's property to his own land. And so on. While containing little genealogical value, these indentures often contain useful descriptions of the properties.

O133: Joseph Long, yeoman, of Rapho tp. rel.to Abraham Long of Warwick tp.
Water rights: HISTORY: Both are sharers in part of the estate of John Long of Manheim tp., whose property lyeth on the Shickasalunga Creek. Said John Long has granted a part of the property to Joseph Long which is convenient to dam.
19 June 1764: John Long & James Fulton

6. Power of Attorney: For divers reasons (usually due to location), a person may have to appoint an attorney to carry out business matters. While most of these records pertain to Philadelphia residents who had entered into mortgage agreements with Lancaster County residents, a small but significant number involve persons from overseas or in other states and provinces in North America.

P102: Amos Strettell of Philadelphia appoints Mathias Slough of Lancaster County as his attorney to acknowledge satisfaction of the "within mortgage" [not identified].
28 Jan 1771: James Barker & James Kerr

7. Mortgage Deed: Just like today, prospective landowners usually had to borrow money in order to meet the asking price for a desired piece of property. In a mortgage deed, the grantor has already borrowed a certain sum from the grantee. As a pledge of his faithfulness to repay that money, the grantor mortgages part or all of his property, such that if he fails to repay the borrowed principal with interest, the grantee takes legal right to the mortgaged land. In most cases, a notation in the side margin identifies when the mortgage was satisfied. These notations have significance as they clearly indicate if the mortgager and mortgagee were living or deceased.

P159: Philip Shertzer, shoemaker, & his wife Catharine of Manor tp. mort.to Henry Funck, Jr., miller, of same

--Two five-acre lots (#19 and #24) in Millersburg, Manor tp.: HISTORY: On 28 Aug 1767, Francis Sanderson & his wife Margaret sold lot #19 to Philip Shertzer. On 28 Nov 1770, Philip Frick & his wife Margaret sold lot #24 to Philip Shertzer.
28 Mar 1772: Melchior Dunckell & Jacob Immel
--Henry Funck, Jr., ack.sat. 4 Apr 1777.

Commonly Used Abbreviations:

a.----acre(s)
ack.sat.----acknowledged satisfaction
adm.----administrator
decd.----deceased
enf.to----enfeoffed to
enf-rel.to----enfeoffed & released
f-ly----formerly
CB ----Commissioners Book
gr.to----grant(s) to
Lan.bor.----Lancaster Borough
Lan.Co.----Lancaster County
MD----Maryland
mort.to----mortgaged to
NJ----New Jersey
p.----perch(es)
pat.----patented
Phil.----Philadelphia
PB----Patent Book
Ref. ----Reference
rel.to----released to
SHF----Sheriff
VA----Virginia
war.----warranted

SPECIAL ADVISEMENT: All last names are spelled exactly as given on the record [although I omitted alternate variations within a single record, favoring the most common form]; however, I sometimes altered first names to fit a standardized spelling [e,g., Catharine, Catherine, Catharina, & Chatharine, etc. are all Catherine.] Furthermore, I always use the standard spelling of all townships. Lastly, Lancaster (as in the town, borough, or city) is always Lancaster Borough. Why? Thinking long-term, I believe this approach simplifies the search capabilities on CD-ROMS. Also, for my own research, if I wish to pull all the deeds for Caernarvon tp., then I can without difficulty.

Good luck in your search!

ENW, February 2004

Index to Frequent Witnesses in Lancaster County Deeds

To simplify the index, I have created codes for frequent witnesses. In general, these individuals were either attorneys or prominent men. Their appearance rarely has genealogical significance. Be advised that there may be a junior or senior. For example, Casper Shaffner, Sr., and Casper Shaffner, Jr., witnessed numerous deeds. If identified, I included junior or senior in the abstract [e.g., CS Jr. or GR Sr.]; however, I used the same code for each.

AH = Adam Hubley
AN = Adam Nees
AR = Adam Reigart
AS = Abraham Shoemaker
ASK = Adam Simon Kuhn
CJ = Caleb Johnson
CM = Charles Morse
CRW = Christopher Wegman
CS = Casper Shaffner
CW = Casper Weitzel
DS = David Stout
DW = David Watson
EA = Esther Atlee
EG = Everard Gruber
EM = Eberhart Michael
ES = Elizabeth Shaffner
ESH = Edward Shippen
EW = Elias Wood
FK = Frederick Kuhn
GR = George Ross
HD = Henry Dehuff
HR = Henry Ream
IK = Isaac Kagey
IS = Isaac Sanders
JB = James Bickham
JE = John Ewing
JH = John Hubley
JHZ = Jerome Heintzelman
JJ = John Jones
JJACK = James Jacks
JJH = John J. Henry
JK = Jacob Kagey
JM = J. Moore
JMO = John Moore
JMR = John Miller
JPD = John Philip Dehaas
JR = John Reily
JT = John Thome
JY = Jasper Yeates
LW = Ludwig Weiss
MH = Michael Hubley
MJ = Martha Johnson
MM = Mary Michael
MN = Margaret Nees
MS = Mathias Slough
PG = Philip Gloninger
PH = Peter Hoofnagle
PIV = Paul Isaac Voto
PM = Philip Marsteller
PMR = Peter Miller
SH = Stewart Herbert
SS = Samuel Steel
WA = Will Atlee
WB = William Bausman
WC = William Clemm
WCA = William Campbell
WF = William Feltman
WH = William Henry
WJ = William Jevon
ZD = Zaccheus Davies

Abstracts of Lancaster County Deed Book W

W1: James Moor, yeoman, of Drumore tp. mort.to James Morrison, yeoman, of same
--Plantation in Drumore tp.: HISTORY: Same tract acquired by James Moor in accordance with his late father's last will & testament, dated 30 June 1750.
27 Feb 1782: Thomas _________ [omitted]
--James Morrison ack.sat. 11 May 1786.

W2: John Faustenauer, yeoman, & his wife Matlena of Earl tp. mort.to Martin Bowman, yeoman, of same
49 ½ a. Earl tp.: HISTORY: It being composed of parcels from two tracts: (1.) Five acres taken from a larger 91-acre tract patented to John Beck, who granted part thereof to John Faustenauer, and (2.) 44 ½ acres taken from a larger 94-acre tract patented to Andreas Weise. Said Andreas Weise granted the same to Christian Eckstein. Said Christian Eckstein granted the same to Samuel Seligley, who granted part thereof to John Faustenauer.
5 May (also given as January) 1782: Anne Davis & ZD
--By a Power of Attorney (Ref. Deed HH-510), Peter Hoofnagle ack.sat. 29 Apr 1791.

W3: John Crawford & George Martin, both of Colerain tp., mort.to John Baird of same
--Plantation in Colerain tp.: HISTORY: Same tract that said John Baird & his wife Agnes granted on equal date herewith to John Crawford & George Martin.
31 Jan 1782: HISTORY: Thomas Whiteside & Abraham Whiteside
--John Baird ack.sat. 3 Mar 1792.

W5: Ludwig Meyer, tavernkeeper, of Manchester tp., York County, mort.to Major William Bailey of York Town, York County
--Lot on Market & Cumberland streets in the town of Lebanon: HISTORY: Not given.
--13 Mar 1782: William Bailey ack.sat. 7 Nov 1782.

W7: David Musselman, yeoman, & his wife Barbara of Hempfield tp. mort.to John Hopson, merchant, and Christopher Reigart, innkeeper, both of Lancaster Borough
194a Hempfield tp.: HISTORY: Not given.
--18 May 1782: Godleb Youngmann & CS
--John Hopson & Adam Reigart [the executor of Christopher Reigart] ack.sat. 15 Mar 1784.

W9: William Moore & his wife Jean of Londonderry tp. mort.to William Brisben of Newton tp., Cumberland County
--Their undivided fourth part of 150a Londonderry tp.: HISTORY: Not given.
15 Feb 1782: Timothy Green & John Ramage.
--By a Power of Attorney (Ref. Deed HH-519), James Campbell ack.sat. 6 May 1794.

W11: William Querll, yeoman, & his wife Lydia of Drumore tp. mort.to Stephen Collins, merchant, of Philadelphia
--Three tracts: (1.) 100a Drumore tp., (2.) 25a Drumore tp., and (3.) 83a Drumore tp. [being contiguous to the latter tract]

1. HISTORY: Same tract that John Marshall, the executor of James Marshall, granted 3 Aug 1778 to William Querll.
2. HISTORY: Same tract that James Patterson & his wife Mary granted 25 Oct 1779 to William Querll.
3. HISTORY: Same tract that James Patterson & his wife Mary granted 25 Oct 1779 to William Querll.

--12 Jul 1782: Miers Fisher & Samuel W. Fisher

W12: Anthony Long, yeoman, & his wife Esther of Lebanon tp. mort.to Nicholas Brightbill, yeoman, of same
209a Lebanon tp.: HISTORY: Not given.
--17 Jul 1782: Hannes Wilhelm & JT
--Nicholas Brighbill ack.sat. 8 Aug 1787.

W14: Michael Philipi & his wife Elizabeth of Paxton tp. mort.to Isaac Harrison of Hanover tp.
--Two tracts: (1.) 150 ¾ a. Paxton tp. and (2.) 112 ½ a. Paxton tp.: HISTORY: Same tracts pat. 23 Jan 1775 to James Finey. On 16 Dec 1770, by his two separate indentures, James Finey granted the same to James Finey, Jr. On 7 Feb 1779, James Finey, Jr., granted the same to Isaac Harrison. On 1 May 1779, Isaac Harrison granted the same to Michael Philipi.
30 Jul 1782: Joseph Green & John Gilchrist the younger

W15: Robert Craig, yeoman, & his wife Jean of Donegal tp. mort.to Melchior Brennemen, yeoman, of Lancaster County
228a Donegal tp.: HISTORY: Not given.
--20 May 1782: James Bayley & John Haldmon
--Melchior Brennemen ack.sat. 18 Jul 1789.

W17: Daniel Keiler (or Keyler), taylor, & his wife Sibilla of Lancaster Borough mort.to Andrew Bausman, stiller, of Lancaster tp.
--Lot #298 on Water St. in Lancaster Borough: HISTORY: Same lot that Henry George & his wife Anna Maria granted on even date herewith to Daniel Keiler.
29 Mar 1782: Henrig George & CS
--Andrew Bausman ack.sat. 7 Apr 1787.

W19: Christopher Ort, mason, of Conestoga tp. mort.to Henry Resh & Adam Gochenauer, yeomen, both of same
50a Conestoga tp.: HISTORY: Not given.
--24 Aug 1782: Henrich Gochenauer & EG
--Henry Resh & Adam Gochenauer ack.sat. 23 Aug 1790.

W21: John Bower, yeoman, of Strasburg tp. mort.to Christian Good of Conestoga tp.
--His right, title, & claim to 229 ½ a. Upper Paxton tp.: HISTORY: Not given.
--21 Sep 1782: CJ & JK

W22: Adam Litzeberger, yeoman, of Manor tp. mort.to Martin Bare & Jacob Mayer [the executors of John Bare, late of Conestoga tp.]
61 ½ a. Manor tp.: HISTORY: Same tract that Abraham Miller & his wife Mary granted 13 May 1782 to Adam Litzeberger, adjoining the land of Christian Kendrick, which had originally been part of the same larger tract.
13 May 1782: ES & CS
--Martin Bare ack.sat. 13 June 1786.

W24: John Hamilton, yeoman, & his wife Mary of Lancaster Borough mort.to Daniel Keeport (or Keenport) & David Hess, yeomen, both of Conestoga tp.
--Two lots in Lancaster Borough: (1.) Lot #125 on Queen St. and (2.) Lot #96 on Queen St.: HISTORY: Not given.
10 Sep 1782: CJ & MH
--Daniel Keeport & David Hess ack.sat. 18 Mar 1797.

W25: Abraham Buchwalter, miller, of Lampeter tp. mort.to Moses Brinton, yeoman, of Leacock tp.
125a Lampeter tp.: HISTORY: Same tract that Joseph Buchwalter & his wife Barbara granted 23 Feb 1747 to Abraham Buchwalter.
3 May 1782: ES & CS

--Moses Brinton ack.sat. 28 Apr 1784.

W27: Isaac Mayer, blacksmith, of Warwick tp. mort.to John Shrantz & Jacob Erb, Jr., yeomen, both of same
--3a Warwick tp.: HISTORY: Not given. The said John Shrantz & Jacob Erb co-signed a bond with Isaac Mayer dated 10 Mar 1781 and given to John Widder of Warwick tp. As the bond is the lawful debt of Isaac Mayer only, this mortgage is given to indemnify Shrantz & Erb from suffering any personal loss.
15 June 1782: AN & Christian Meier
--Jacob Erb, Jr., ack.sat. 13 June 1789.

W28: George Fackler (or Fagler), yeoman, of Paxton tp. mort.to Nicholas Waln & Mordecai Lewis, both of Philadelphia
375a Paxton tp.: HISTORY: Not given.
--10 Oct 1782: Isaac Milnor & John Todd, Jr.
--By a Power of Attorney (Ref. Deed F-3-534, given by Nicholas Waln, the surviving mortgagee), Adam Reigart, Jr., ack.sat. 22 Apr 1802.

W30: Sims Chambers, yeoman, & his wife Mary of Mount Joy tp. mort.to David Chambers, yeoman, of same
222a Mount Joy tp.: HISTORY: Not given, but—as part of the agreement--Sims Chambers is to provide for the said David Chambers & his wife Mary for the rest of their natural lives.
12 Apr 1782: Timothy Green & JT
--By a Power of Attorney, John W. Kittera ack.sat. 15 Apr 1793.

W32: John Evans, yeoman, & his wife Hannah of Earl tp. mort.to James Keimer, yeoman, of same
156a Earl tp.: HISTORY: Not given, but subject to several legacies to be paid in accordance with the last will & testament of Philip Evans, late of Chester County, yeoman.
17 Jul 1782: Martin Bowman, William Smith, Phillip Rolf [German], & ZD
--Sarah Keemer, Thomas May, & James Keemer [the executors of James Keemer] ack.sat. 25 May 1784.

W33: Jacob Cassel, yeoman, & his wife Elizabeth of Rapho tp. mort.to Abraham Cassel of same, Henry Buchwalter of Lampeter tp., & Christian Swarr of Hempfield tp.
--123a Rapho tp.: HISTORY: Not given.
8 Jan 1783: J.F. Yeates & Matthew McAllister
--Abraham Cassel, Henry Buchwalter, & Christian Swarr ack.sat. 7 June 1784.

W35: George Hoke, Jr., yeoman, & his wife Margaret of Lebanon tp. mort.to Michael Tice, yeoman, of same
--Two contiguous tracts: (1.) 98a, 96p Lebanon tp. and (2.) 100a Lebanon tp.: HISTORY: Not given, but Michael Tice is security for George Hoke in an obligation with Jacob Graff, clockmaker, of the town of Lebanon.
2 Nov 1782: JT & Anna Maria Thome
--Michael Tice ack.sat. 12 Nov 1800.

W38: Michael Reinhart, skinner, & his wife Margaret of Lancaster Borough mort.to Adam Reigart, innkeeper, of same
--Half lot on Vine St. in Lancaster Borough: HISTORY: Same half lot that Jacob Urich & his wife Catharine granted 30 Nov last to Michael Reinhart.
4 Jan 1783: ES & CS
--Adam Reigart ack.sat. 20 Dec 1793.

W40: Henry Bushman, yeoman, of Strasburg tp. mort.to Paul Trout, yeoman, of same
45a, 34p Strasburg tp.: HISTORY: Same tract that John Miller & his wife Elizabeth granted 4 Feb 1782 to Henry Bushman (Ref. Deed U98).
1 Nov 1782: John Carpenter & EG

W42: Daniel Fetter, the younger, cooper, of Lancaster Borough mort.to Benjamin Bowman, yeoman, of Cocalico tp.

--Half lot on Queen St. in Lancaster Borough: HISTORY: Same half lot that John Mourer granted 16 Nov 1782 to Daniel Fetter.

23 Nov 1782: ES & CS

--Benjamin Bowman ack.sat. 13 May 1785.

W43: John Spore & his wife Mary of Lancaster Borough mort.to Wendel Gilbert of Warwick tp.

--Lot on Queen St. in Lancaster Borough: HISTORY: Same lot that Henry Small granted 11 Aug 1777 to John Spore.

28 Feb 1783: Anthony Seyfert Jr. & Anthony Seyfert

W45: Andrew Rehm (or Rihm), yeoman, of Cocalico tp. mort.to Samuel Miles & William Wistar, merchants, both of Philadelphia

62 ½ a. Cocalico tp.: HISTORY: Same tract that Eberhard Rehm & his wife Elizabeth granted 15 Feb 1759 to his son Andrew Rehm.

16 Jan 1783: Elizabeth Miller & Peter Miller

--By a Power of Attorney (Ref. Deed W357), Andrew Rehm ack.sat. 27 Oct 1785.

W47: Samuel Morrison of Upper Paxton tp. mort.to Joseph Little of same

200a Upper Paxton tp.: HISTORY: Same tract war. 27 Jan 1775 to Benjamin Walker but now in the possession of said Samuel Morrison.

20 Jan 1783: Joshua Elder & Richard McCalister

W49: Christian Eckenrode, yeoman, & his wife Catharine of Mount Joy tp. mort.to Henry Eckenrode, yeoman, of same

--Three tracts: (1.) 55 ¾ a., 30p Mount Joy tp.; (2.) 26 ½ a., 28p Mount Joy tp.; and (3.) 23 ½ a., 16p Mount Joy tp.: HISTORY: Same tracts that said Henry Eckenrode & his wife Elizabeth granted on even date herewith to Christian Eckenrode.

30 Nov 1782: James Bayley & Johannes Shuirnizer

--Henry Eckenrode ack.sat. 9 Apr 1789.

W51: Joseph Eckenrode, yeoman, & his wife Therisia of Mount Joy tp. mort.to Henry Eckenrode, yeoman, of same

121 ¼ a. Mount Joy tp.: HISTORY: Same tract that said Henry Eckenrode & his wife Elizabeth granted on even date herewith to the said Joseph Eckenrode.

30 Nov 1782: Henry Eckenrode ack.sat. 8 Sep 1786.

W53: Valentine Wiland, yeoman, of Donegal tp. mort.to John Wiland, yeoman, of same

105a Donegal tp.: HISTORY: Same tract surveyed to John Wittmer in pursuance of a warrant. Said John Wittmer granted the same to George Smith, who granted the same to Valentine Wiland.

31 Mar 1783: C. Frederick Oberlander & John Spade

--John Wiland ack.sat. 2 Mar 1785.

W54: Benjamin Mishey, yeoman, of Rapho tp. mort.to Samuel Miles & William Wistar, merchants, both of Philadelphia

169a Rapho tp.: HISTORY: Same tract pat. 1 May 1770 to Benjamin Mishey (Ref. PB AA-11-298).

--7 Apr 1783: William Ralston & PMR

--By a Power of Attorney (Ref. Deed W317), Christian Herr ack.sat. 13 June 1785.

W56: Daniel Hahn, yeoman, of Earl tp. mort.to Philip Fasnacht, wheelwright, of same

112 ¾ a. Brecknock tp.: HISTORY: On 9 May 1777, Jacob Shirk granted the same to Christian Eckstein. On 19 Mar 1779, Christian Eckstein granted the same to Philip Fasnacht. [End of history—incomplete or error?]

30 Nov 1782: Johannes Arndt & Michael Franssz
--Philip Fasnacht ack.sat. 30 Jul 1789.

W57: John Weiland, yeoman, of Donegal tp. mort.to John Nissly, Jr., yeoman, of same
120 ½ a. Donegal tp.: HISTORY: Not given.
--28 Apr 1783: Mabbeick Marrel & CS
--John Nissly, Jr., ack.sat. 17 Feb 1785.

W59: John Gall, shoemaker, & his wife Elizabeth of Derry tp. mort.to James Porter, Thomas Walker, & William Mitchel, yeomen, all of Hanover tp.
--Lot #14 in Frederick Town in Derry tp.: HISTORY: Not given.
26 Nov 1782: Timothy Green & Robert Fremong
--James Porter ack.sat. 13 Sep 1784.

W60: John Thompson & his wife Margaret of Hanover tp. mort.to John Robison of same
133a Hanover tp.: HISTORY: Same tract that Jacob Brunner & his wife Mary granted on equal date herewith to John Thompson.
22 Apr 1783: Robert Boal & James McCreigh

W61: John Wunderlich, yeoman, & his wife Elizabeth of Lebanon tp. mort.to George Wampler, yeoman, of same
300a Lebanon tp.: HISTORY: Same tract war. 5 Mar 1749 to Ulrich Stephen. Said Ulrich Stephen died intestate leaving issue several children. On 3 Sep 1765, the Orphans Court confirmed his real estate to his eldest son Michael Stephen. On 7 Mar 1767, Michael Stephen & his wife Catharine granted the 300a tract to the said George Wampler. On equal date herewith, George Wampler & his wife Elizabeth granted the same to John Wunderlich.
10 May 1783: Thomas Clark & Daniel Wunderlich
--By a Power of Attorney (Ref. Deed ZZ-___), George Killinger ack.sat. 11 Oct 1798.

W62b: George Deitrich & his wife Dorothea of Earl tp. mort.to Peter Diller, yeoman, of same
--24a, 66p Earl tp.: HISTORY: Same tract that Martin Bowman & his wife Elizabeth granted 12 May 1772 to George Deitrich.
26 Sep 1782: Catharine Vonkenen & Barbara Vonkenen
--Peter Diller ack.sat. 25 May 1784.

W64: Henry Oyman, yeoman, of Lampeter tp. mort.to Christian Rohrer, yeoman, of same
--Lot #3 in Hains Town in Lampeter tp., containing three acres: HISTORY: Same lot that Salome Hains granted 1 Apr 1783 to Henry Oyman.
5 May 1783: MJ & Benjamin Johnson
--Christian Rohrer ack.sat. 17 May 1796.

W65: John Hart, yeoman, & his wife Anna of Martic tp. mort.to Jacob Huber, yeoman, of same
--Five tracts: (1.) 120a Martic tp., (2.) 200a Martic tp., (3.) 100a Martic tp., (4.) 50a Martic tp., and (5.) 3a Martic tp.: HISTORY: Same five tracts that Peter Albright & his wife Mary and Henry Cryder & his wife Magdalena granted 4 May 1779 to John Hart.
8 Mar 1783: John Hoober & Matthias Lora
--Jacob Huber ack.sat. 4 June 1805.

W67: Henry Bushman, yeoman, of Strasburg tp. mort.to Abraham Hare, miller, of same & Henry Eckman, yeoman, of Lampeter tp.
42a, 28p Strasburg tp.: HISTORY: Same tract that John Miller & his wife Elizabeth granted 1 June 1780 to Henry Bushman.
1 Apr 1783: Martin Kendig & EG

W69: Peter Schwartzwalter (or Schwartzenwalder), yeoman, of Earl tp. mort.to Henry Keppele, merchant, of Philadelphia

12a, 100p Earl tp.: HISTORY: Same tract that Christian Schwartzenwalder granted 26 Oct 1781 to said Peter Schwartzenwalder.

28 May 1783: PMR & William Fusselberg

W70: Jacob Muhleisen, yeoman, of Derry tp. mort.to Henry Sneider, yeoman, of Warwick tp.

186 ½ a. Derry tp. [being the total of two contiguous tracts]: HISTORY: Same tract that said Henry Sneider & his wife granted on the day before the date of these presents to Jacob Muhleisen.

15 May 1783: Conrad Fehder & CS

--Henry Sneider ack.sat. 17 Aug 1792.

W72: Ludwig Huber, yeoman, of Londonderry tp. mort.to Christopher Ulrich, yeoman, of Lebanon tp.

220a Londonderry tp.: HISTORY: Not given.

--14 Mar 1783: Anna Maria Thome & JT

--Christopher Ulrich ack.sat. 24 May 1787.

W73: Jacob Hain, yeoman, of Heidelberg tp. mort.to Leonard Illig (or Ihlich), yeoman, of same

70a Heidelberg tp.: HISTORY: Not given.

12 Apr 1783: Anna Maria Thome & JT

W74: John Myer, yeoman, of Lebanon tp. mort.to Abraham Ebersole, Sr., yeoman, of same

213a Lebanon tp.: HISTORY: Same tract pat. 18 Jan 1768 to John Kreeker (or Kreeger). On 4 Dec 1770, John Kreeker & his wife Margaret granted the same to Abraham Ebersole. On equal date herewith, Abraham Ebersole granted the same to John Myer.

29 Apr 1783: George Reinoll & JT

W76: Isaac Martin, yeoman, & his wife Susanna of Manor tp. mort.to Christian Baughman, yeoman, of same

139 ½ a. Manor tp.: HISTORY: Same tract that said Christian Baughman & Peter Whittmer [the executors of Jacob Martin, late of Manor tp.] granted on equal date herewith to Isaac Martin.

7 May 1783: CJ & Frederick Ziegler

--Christian Baughman ack.sat. 12 May 1784.

W78: Michael Shaffet, yeoman, & his wife Catharine of Donegal tp. mort.to Nicholas Ricksecker, shoemaker, of same

128a Donegal tp.: HISTORY: Not given.

--6 June 1783: James Bayley & Thomas Bayley

W80: Jacob Fester assigns to Adam Witman, merchant, of the town of Reading in Berks County

--"the within indenture of mortgage" concerning a 54a, 70p tract: HISTORY: The mortgage was given by Frederick Piper.

11 June 1776: Henrich Meyer & Collinson Read

W80: John Becker of Bethel tp. mort.to Jacob Plank, saddler, of same

--Lot #55 on Walnut St. in Jones's Town in Bethel tp.: HISTORY: Not given.

10 Jan 1783: Sara Jones & Samuel Jones

--By a Power of Attorney (Ref. Deed F-3-509), Philip Youngblood ack.sat. 16 Mar 1802.

W81: John Creamer (or Kreamer), cooper, & his wife _______ [omitted] of Strasburg tp. mort.to Salome Hains, widow, of Lampeter tp.

--Lot #12 in Hains Town in Lampeter tp., containing four acres: HISTORY: Not given.

1 Apr 1783: JK & IK

--By decree, the Court of Common Pleas ack.sat. 18 Aug 1934 (Ref. Mortgage Book 372, page 366).

W82: Rudolph Sheaffer, yeoman, of Earl tp. mort.to John Showalder, yeoman, of same

178a Earl tp.: HISTORY: Not given.

--18 June 1783: John Evans & ZD

W84: Jacob Snevely, yeoman, & his wife Elizabeth of Leacock tp. mort.to Moses Brinton (or Branton), yeoman, of same

140 ½ a. Leacock tp.: HISTORY: Same tract that James Hamilton & his wife Catharine granted 17 May 1782 to Jacob Snevely.

16 May 1783: WH & CJ

--John Whitehill, the assignee of Joseph Whitehill, who was the assignee of Joseph Brinton & William Brinton [the executors of Moses Brinton], ack.sat. 18 May 1794.

W85: Abraham Brown, mason, & his wife Magdalena of Lancaster Borough mort.to Philip Arnold, yeoman, of the town of Manheim

--Lot on Water St. in Lancaster Borough: HISTORY: Not given.

4 Aug 1783: ES & CS

--Philip Arnold ack.sat. 5 Apr 1786.

W87: Peter Good, yeoman, & his wife Christina of Brecknock tp. mort.to Jacob Snider, yeoman, of Earl tp.

104a Brecknock tp.: HISTORY: Part of two larger tracts pat. 16 Jan 1764 to Jacob Good. On 22 Nov 1766, Jacob Good & his wife Susanna granted "the same" to Peter Good.

10 Apr 1783: John W. Kittera & Josiah Kittera

W88: Thomas Miles, yeoman, & his wife Ann of Drumore tp. mort.to James Griben (or Gribin), taylor, of same

181 ½ a. Drumore tp.: HISTORY: Same tract that Andrew Dunbar granted 28 Apr 1778 to Thomas Miles. The deed further makes reference to a deed dated 4 Apr 1763 in which Henry Cougil granted certain land to Andrew Dunbar—probably the same tract as given in this indenture.

15 Mar 1783: James A. White, Rosanna Irwin, & Moses Irwin

W90: James Douglass of Salisbury tp. mort.to Caleb Way, innkeeper, of West Caln tp., Chester County

--Two adjoining tracts: (1.) 100a Salisbury tp. and (2.) 90a Salisbury tp.: HISTORY: Same tracts pat. 10 Jan 1752 to Edward Douglass (Ref. PB A-17-45). By his last will & testament, Edward Douglass devised the same to his son James Douglass (the party hereto).

7 Aug 1783: Andrew Caldwell & Joseph Ash

--Caleb Way ack.sat. 13 Apr 1790.

W91: Gregory Farmer, yeoman, of Martic tp. mort.to Christian Shenck, yeoman, of same

--Two adjoining tracts: (1.) 80a Martic tp. and (2.) 200a Martic tp.

HISTORY: Same tract that Robert Reed granted 1 Apr 1772 to Gregory Farmer.

HISTORY: Same tract that John Stevenson granted 16 Sep 1777 to Gregory Farmer.

--9 Aug 1783: ES & CS

--Christian Shenck ack.sat. 19 Dec 1791.

W93: Henry Geiger, tanner, & his wife Susanna of Lancaster Borough mort.to John Burkholder, yeoman, of Lampeter tp.

--Half lot on King St. in Lancaster Borough: HISTORY: Same half lot that John Dehuff, by his last will & testament, devised to his daughter Susanna, who later married the said Henry Geiger. [Both parties above are bound to Nicholas Miller, but it is the only proper debt of Henry Geiger. This indenture serves to indemnify John Burkholder from suffering any personal loss.]

16 Aug 1783: ES & CS

--David Burkholder, the only son & heir of John Burkholder, deceased, ack.sat. 22 June 1808.

W95: John Gennet, yeoman, of Manor tp. mort.to Henry Miller, yeoman, of same
--Lot #71 in the town of Millersburg in Manor tp.: HISTORY: Not given.
22 Aug 1783: Henry Miller ack.sat. 6 May 1784.

W96: Christian Berg, yeoman, & his wife Elizabeth of Manor tp. mort.to Isaac Long, yeoman, of Manheim tp.
150a, 44p Manor tp.: HISTORY: Same tract that John Kendig & his wife Mary granted 17 June last to Christian Berg (Ref. Deed U434).
23 Aug 1783: Jacob Berg & Lewis Lauman
--Isaac Long ack.sat. 24 Aug 1792.

W98: Martin Waggoner, yeoman, & his wife Charlotta of the town of Lebanon mort.to Christopher Seiler & Henry Seiler, yeoman [the executors of Christopher Kinsel, yeoman, late of Lebanon tp.]
--Two contiguous lots in the town of Lebanon, numbered 128 and 131 in the town plan: HISTORY: Not given.
20 June 1783: Christoff Einbich & JT

W100: John Longenecker, yeoman, of Lampeter tp. mort.to Abraham Longenecker, John Witmer, & Jacob Hartman, all of same [the executors of David Longenecker]
75a Lampeter tp.: HISTORY: Same tract that the above-named executors granted 1 May 1781 to John Longenecker.
27 Aug 1783: WH & CS Jr.
--Abraham Longenecker, John Witmer, & Jacob Hartman ack.sat. 10 Apr 1787.

W102: Jacob Eyer, miller, of Lebanon tp. mort.to Peter Grubb, Sr., ironmaster, of Warwick tp.
200a Lebanon tp.: HISTORY: Not given, but the tract adjoins the town of Annwill, commonly called Miller's Town.
11 Nov 1783: JT & Anna Maria Thome
--Peter Grubb ack.sat. 7 Dec 1785.

W103: John Derflinger, yeoman, of Rapho tp. mort.to Henry Eckenrode, yeoman, of Mount Joy tp.
--Lot #117 on Charlotte Street and Outlot #12 in the town of Manheim: HISTORY: Not given.
26 Nov 1783: Jacob Krug & CS
--Henry Eckenrode ack.sat. 4 Aug 1790.

W105: John Shiffer, yeoman, of Cocalico tp. mort.to Samuel Miles & William Wistar, merchants, both of Philadelphia
--Three contiguous tracts: (1.) 28 ¾ a. Cocalico tp., (2.) 107a Cocalico tp. [excepting 22a previously granted to Mathias Riem], and (3.) 32a Cocalico tp.: HISTORY: Same three tracts that Abraham Riehm & his wife Anna Maria granted 14 May last to John Shiffer (Ref. Deed W618 [sic]).
23 Oct 1783: PMR
--Samuel Miles & William Wistar ack.sat. 25 Sep 1793.

W108: John Cromwell (or Crowwell?), yeoman, of Conestoga tp. mort.to Jacob Mehnert, yeoman, of same
40a Conestoga tp.: HISTORY: Same tract that Henry Miller & his wife Mary granted 7 Mar 1777 to John Cromwell.
29 Nov 1783: Christian Stauffer & CS
--Jacob Mehnert ack.sat. 21 May 1785.

W110: Martin Spickler, yeoman, of Warwick tp. mort.to Michael Spickler, Christian Spickler, & John Sumy [the latter the guardian of Frederick Spickler, Peter Spickler, & Justina Spickler], all of Lancaster County
153a, 30p Warwick tp.: HISTORY: Not given.
--17 Jul 1783: Martin Gross & CS

--Michael Spicker ack.sat. 2 Mar 1802; John Summy ack.sat. 4 Dec 1802; Christian Spickler ack.sat. 26 Oct 1803. [Note: See the following indenture.]

W113: John Spickler, yeoman, & his wife Mary of Warwick tp. mort.to Margaret Spickler, Joseph Huber, Nicholas Spickler, & John Sumy [the latter the guardian of Simon Spickler & Jacob Spickler], all of Lancaster County

--Three tracts: (1.) 107a Warwick tp., (2.) 27a, 130p Warwick tp., and (3.) 2a, 120p Warwick tp.: HISTORY: Not given.

17 Jul 1783: Martin Gross & CS

--John Summy ack.sat. 27 Nov 1793; Margaret Spicker & Nicholas Spickler ack.sat. 7 Nov 1795; Joseph Huber ack.sat. 15 Aug 1796.

W116: Henry Carpenter, tanner, of Lampeter tp. mort.to John Carpenter & John Hare, yeomen, both of Strasburg tp.

--His undivided third part of three tracts in Lampeter tp.: HISTORY: By his last will & testament dated 2 Dec 1772, Jacob Carpenter devised his three plantations in Lampeter tp. to his three sons, to wit, Henry Carpenter [the party hereto], Martin Carpenter, & Jacob Carpenter—subject to the widow Magdalena's dower.

1 Nov 1783: John Feree & EG

--John Carpenter ack.sat. 4 May 1791; by a decree dated 2 Apr 1943, the Court of Common Pleas cleared the property of the mortgage (Ref. Mortgage Book 465, page 216).

W118: Everard Gruber, yeoman, of the Village of Strasburg mort.to John Carpenter, yeoman, of Strasburg tp.

1a, 5p lot on Main St. in the Village of Strasburg: HISTORY: Not given.

--26 Nov 1783: Abraham Carpenter & John Smith, Jr.

--John Carpenter ack.sat. 12 Nov 1784.

W120: Henry Stuber, druggist, & his wife Catharine of Lancaster Borough mort.to Townsend Speakman, druggist, of Philadelphia

--Three lots in Musser's Town, numbered 12, 13, and 14 in the town plan: HISTORY: Same lots that Nicholas Miller & his wife Margaret granted 19 June 1778 to Henry Stuber.

23 Dec 1783: HD & CJ

W121: William McCandles, yeoman, of Leacock tp. mort.to John Brisben of Lampeter tp.

--Sundry items & livestock.

30 Dec 1783: John Shaffner & CS

W123: John Bitzer of Earl tp. assigns to John Mohler of Cocalico tp.

--"the within mortgage": HISTORY: See Deed P492.

2 Jan 1784: Daniel Bollinger & David Grove

W123: Christian Kurtz, yeoman, & his wife Dorothea of Manheim tp. mort.to William Parr & Henry Dering, gentleman, of Lancaster Borough

104a, 159p Manheim tp.: HISTORY: Not given.

--12 Jan 1784: MH & CS

--Henry Dering ack.sat. 20 Sep 1794; by decree, the Court of Common Pleas ack.sat. 16 Dec 1938 (Ref. Mortgage Book 419, page 393).

W125: Jacob Lindy, distiller, & his wife Mary of Lancaster Borough mort.to James Jacks, Esq., & James Bickham, yeoman, both of same

--Half lot & distillery on Duke St. in Lancaster Borough: HISTORY: Same half lot that Philip Brem granted 18 June 1781 to Jacob Lindy but "remaining in the hands of Anthony Syfert".

10 Dec 1783: PG & WH

--James Jacks ack.sat. 11 Aug 1784.

W127: Christian Lehr of Lancaster Borough mort.to Christopher Heger & Francis Heger, butchers, of Lancaster Borough

--Lot on Queen St. in Lancaster Borough: HISTORY: Same lot that Christopher Heger & his wife Catharine and Francis Heger & his wife Margaret granted on equal date herewith to Christian Lehr.

7 Oct 1783: HD & CS

W129: Jonathan Hudson, yeoman, of Caernarvon tp. mort.to Moses Brinton, yeoman, of Leacock tp.

100a Caernarvon tp.: HISTORY: Part of a larger tract pat. 1 Sep 1739 to George Hudson (Ref. PB A-9-86). By his last will & testament, George Hudson devised the larger tract to his son Nicholas. By his last will & testament, Nicholas Hudson devised 100a to his son Jonathan [the party hereto].

24 Nov 1783: John Watson & Terrens Duffey

--William Brinton & Joseph Brinton, the executors of Moses Brinton, ack.sat. 20 Aug 1794.

W131: Elijah Hudson, yeoman, of Caernarvon tp. mort.to Moses Brinton, yeoman, of Leacock tp.

100a Caernarvon tp.: HISTORY: Part of a larger tract pat. 1 Sep 1739 to George Hudson (Ref. PB A-9-86). By his last will & testament, George Hudson devised the larger tract to his son Nicholas. By his last will & testament, Nicholas Hudson devised 100a to his son Elijah [the party hereto].

24 Nov 1783: John Watson & Terrens Duffey

--Moses Brinton ack.sat. 1 Jul 1785.

W133: Andrew Betz (or Petz), yeoman, & his wife Catharine of Warwick tp. mort.to Abraham Reist, yeoman, of same

86a, 9p Warwick tp.: HISTORY: Not given.

--_____ [omitted] 1784: George Klein & CS

--Abraham Reist ack.sat. 29 May 1799.

W134: Christian Wenditz, tobacconist, of the Village of Strasburg mort.to Benjamin Graff & Jacob Eshleman, yeoman, of same

--Two contiguous lots in the Village of Strasburg: (1.) two acres on Main St. and (2.) another two acres on Main St.: HISTORY: Not given.

18 Aug 1783: EG & Christiana Gruber

--Benjamin Graff & Jacob Eshleman ack.sat. 16 Mar 1787.

W136: Jacob Flubacher, carpenter, & his wife Barbara of Lancaster Borough mort.to Peter Bier (or Beer), shoemaker, of same

--Half lot on Prince St. in Lancaster Borough: HISTORY: Not given.

23 Oct 1783: John Shaffner & CS

--Peter Bier ack.sat. 17 May 1790.

W138: Valentin Kress, shoemaker, of Manor tp. mort.to John David Frank, doctor of physick, of same

10a Manor tp.: HISTORY: Part of 134a, 50p pat. 17 Apr 1762 to Michael Kaufman (Ref. PB AA-3-170). On 21 Jul 1778, Michael Kaufman & his wife Catharine granted 20a to Christian Hare. On 11 Jul 1782, Christian Hare & his wife Mary granted 10a to John David Frank (Ref. Deed X212). On 21 Feb 1784, John David Frank & his wife Catharine granted the same to Valentine Kress.

24 Feb 1784: JJACK & PG

--James Jacks, the assignee of John David Frank, ack.sat. 25 May 1790.

W141: John Shonouer (or Shonover), yeoman, of Bethel tp. mort.to Jacob Fetherhaff of same

--Lot #145 in the town of Fredericksburg in Bethel tp.: HISTORY: Same lot that Sheriff James Webb seized and granted 11 June 1768 to Bernard Faber. On 22 Aug 1774, Bernard Faber & his wife Catharine assigned the same to John Groh. On 6 Jan 1776, John Groh assigned the same to Philipp Fehring. On 7 Apr 1779, Philipp Fehring & his wife Catharine assigned the same to Bernhart Hower. On 6 Apr 1782, Bernhart

Hower & his wife Catharine granted the same to Henry Snevely [the party hereto—sic—incomplete or in error?].

30 Oct 1783: Baltser Faldhaft & Jacob Eppracht

W143: John Longenecker (or Longacre), yeoman, of Strasburg tp. mort.to Jacob Ricksaker, yeoman, of Manheim tp.

125a Manheim tp.: HISTORY: Same tract that said Jacob Ricksaker & his wife Elizabeth granted on even date herewith to John Longenecker.

27 Feb 1784: Bentz Hirschi & Daniel Franck

--Jacob Ricksaker ack.sat. 10 Dec 1792.

W146: Adam Stoneking of Lancaster County mort.to James Patton & John Haugentobler, both of same

3a, 80p Hempfield tp.: HISTORY: Part of 219a pat. 7 Feb 1760 to George Smith (Ref. PB A-20-486). On 29 June 1767, George Smith granted 3a, 80p to John Geiger. On 10 Mar 1779, John Geiger & his wife Anna granted the same to Adam Stoneking.

21 Feb 1784: Johannes Neucomet & H. Davis

W148: James McConnel, yeoman, of Drumore tp. mort.to Adam Kindig, yeoman, of Conestoga tp.

208a, 128p in Drumore & Colerain tps.: HISTORY: Same tract that Joseph Miller & James Kirkpatrick granted 27 Feb 1775 to James McConnel.

8 Mar 1784: John Kuntz & CS

--Adam Kindig ack.sat. 6 May 1789.

W150: Jacob Kittle, yeoman, of Bethel tp. mort.to Henry Humberger, yeoman, of Lebanon tp.

150a Lebanon tp.: HISTORY: Part of 180a Lebanon tp. war. 9 Aug 1738 to Leonard Teininger. On 17 Feb 1741, Leonard Teininger granted the same to Henry Funk. On 11 Aug 1748, Henry Funk granted the same to Peter Smith—however, the instrument was imperfect and the right to the land became vested in Peter Eshelman. To better confirm the property in his him, Henry Funk released the same on 12 Mar 1762 to said Peter Eshelman. On 28 Apr 1775, Peter Eshelman & his wife Elizabeth granted the same to said Henry Humberger. On 19 Mar 1784, Henry Humberger & his wife Catharine granted 150a to Jacob Kittle.

20 Mar 1784: Thomas Clark & Johannes Dubs

--Immediately following this indenture of mortgage, Henry Humberger assigns the same to Peter Klubb & John Haine. They all ack.sat. 25 Jan 1787.

W155: Jacob Boyer, yeoman, of Martic tp. mort.to Peter Miller, yeoman, of same

79a Martic tp.: HISTORY: Same tract that Henry Boyer (or Bayer) & his wife Mary granted 13 Nov 1782 to Jacob Boyer.

2 Mar 1784: CS Jr. & CS

--Peter Miller ack.sat. 30 Apr 1785.

W156: Peter Klubb (or Klop), the younger, & John Heain (or Han), yeomen, of Heidelberg tp., Berks County assigns to Henry Humberger

--Certain bonds: HISTORY: See Deed W150. Said Henry Humberger stood indebted to Peter Eshelman, yeoman, of Lebanon tp., with the said Peter Klubb & John Heain as his security. However, with Henry Humberger about to depart the state, he assigned the bonds due to him from one Jacob Kettle over to Peter Klubb & John Heain. They took the money from Jacob Kettle and paid off the debts owed to Peter Eshelman. It was understood at the time of agreement that when Henry Humberger returned, the bonds would be assigned back over to him.

--Agreement dated 25 Mar 1784, witnessed by George Musser & WA.

--Re-conveyance of bonds to Henry Humberger confirmed on 25 Jan 1787 by James Jacks.

W158: James Moore, yeoman, of Drumore tp. mort.to James Morrison, yeoman, of same

50a Drumore tp.: HISTORY: By her last will & testament dated 9 May 1777, Margaret Moore devised the same tract to her son James Moore [the party hereto].

1 Oct 1783: James Moore & John Toy
--James Morrison ack.sat. 11 May 1786.

W160: Walter Robison, yeoman, of Fawn tp., York County mort.to Samuel Morrison of Drumore tp.

246a Drumore tp.: HISTORY: Same tract acquired by two separate indentures dated 8 Apr 1777: (1.) from John Caldwell of Martic tp. [the executor of William Buchanon, late of Drumore tp. and (2.) from James Buchanon.

14 Nov 1783: William Webb, Agnes Irwin, & Moses Irwin

W162: John Linch, yeoman, of Mount Joy tp. mort.to Daniel Smith, yeoman, of Donegal tp.

143 ½ a. in Donegal & Mount Joy tps.: HISTORY: Same tract that Philip Negly & his wife Elizabeth granted 30 Jan 1777 to John Linch (Ref. Deed R290).

8 Apr 1784: CS Jr. & CS
--Daniel Smith ack.sat. 22 June 1785.

W164: George Cummins (or Commins), yeoman, & his wife Susanna of Manheim tp. mort.to John Swaar, yeoman, of same

6a, 29p Manheim tp.: HISTORY: Part of 183a that Henry Landis & his wife Margaret granted 28 Feb 1782 to John Musser & Abraham Witmer (Ref. Deed Q668). On 10 Feb 1783, John Musser & his wife Sarah & Abraham Witmer & his wife Mary granted 6a, 29p to George Cummins.

15 Apr 1784: HD & JH
--John Swaar ack.sat. 3 Feb 1786.

W166: Jacob Bare, yeoman, of Cocalico tp. mort.to Peter Zimmerman, yeoman, of same

362 ½ a. Cocalico tp.: HISTORY: Same tract that Peter Zimmerman & his wife Ann granted 5 Feb 1781 to Jacob Bare. [Contains a detail agreement: Said Peter Zimmerman & his wife will reside on the property for the rest of their natural lives.]

5 Apr 1784: George Adam Frantz & AN

--By a Power of Attorney from David Bricker, the executor of George Wolfard, who was the surviving executor of Peter Zimmerman [Ref. Letter of Attorney Book #2, page 90], Peter Martin ack.sat. 25 May 1821.

W169: John Reigart & his wife Elizabeth of Hanover tp. mort.to Adam Weiss of same

139a Hanover tp.: HISTORY: Same tract that said Adam Weiss & his wife Eve granted 4 Oct 1782 to John Reigart.

19 Apr 1784: Richard Dearmond & James McCreight
--Richard Dearmond, the assignee of Adam Weiss, ack.sat. 17 Apr 1793.

W170: George Ross, Esq., of Lancaster Borough mort.to John Witmer, the younger, of Philadelphia

--Three tracts: (1.) 125a Lampeter tp., (2.) 145a Lampeter tp., including a gristmill, and (3.) all yearly rent charges in right of said George Ross in the town of Millersburg in Manor tp.

1. HISTORY: Same tract that Benjamin Graff granted 20 Oct 1778 to said John Witmer. On 23 Apr 1781, John Witmer & his wife Mary granted the same to George Ross with the understanding that George Ross would satisfy a debt that said John Witmer owed to the said Benjamin Graff of Lampeter tp. [sureties for John Witmer were Abraham Witmer & Henry Witmer].
2. HISTORY: Not given.
3. HISTORY: Same yearly rent charges that Sheriff Frederick Stone seized and then granted 8 Sep 1773 to George Ross.

--4 Dec 1783: MH & JH
--John Witmer, Jr., ack.sat. 3 Dec 1790.

W173: Conrad Haas (or Hass), yeoman, & his wife Veronica of Cocalico tp. ack.sat. & rel.to the Executors of Jacob Shonauer

--Two tracts in Cocalico tp.: (1.) 114a Cocalico tp. and (2.) 46 ½ a. Cocalico tp.: HISTORY: Both tracts are formerly part of the estate of Abraham Shonauer, late of Cocalico tp., deceased. His executors, John Graff & Jacob Erb, granted the said two tracts to Jacob Shonauer. On 14 Oct 1762, Jacob Shonauer & his wife Magdalena mortgaged the same tracts to the said executors (Ref. Deed H87). By that agreement, Jacob Shonauer agreed to pay the balance one week after the death of Ursula Shonauer, the widow of John Shonauer. // Both the said Ursula Shonauer and Jacob Shonauer are deceased. The said Abraham Shonauer left issue but two daughters, the said Veronica wife of Conrad Haas and Ursula wife of Philipp Reffort, to whom his entire estate descended. Now, with this indenture, Conrad Haas & his wife Veronica acknowledge that the debt owed to the estate of Abraham Shonauer has been satisfied.

20 Nov 1783: JJ & AN

W174: Philipp Reffert & his wife Ursula ack.sat. & rel.to the Executors of Jacob Shonauer

--Two tracts in Cocalico tp.: (1.) 114a Cocalico tp. and (2.) 46 ½ a. Cocalico tp.: HISTORY: See the preceding deed.

21 Nov 1783: C. North & Conrad Hass

W176: Henry Hambright, tanner, of Earl tp. mort.to John Sherck, yeoman, of same

31a, 117p Earl tp.: HISTORY: Not given.

--13 Apr 1784: Jacob Weber & Johannes Dorrel

--John Sherck ack.sat. 5 Nov 1788.

W177: James Knox, yeoman, of Leacock tp. mort.to Moses Brinton, yeoman, of same

139a Leacock tp.: HISTORY: Same tract that John Woods & his wife Jane granted 15 Feb 1779 to James Knox (Ref. Deed U612)—excepting a 10a parcel.

28 4mo. 1784: JJH & WH, Jr.

--Robert Moore, the assignee of the executors of Moses Brinton, ack.sat. 13 June 1801.

W179: William Wistar (for himself & also for Samuel Miles) appoints Adam Reigard, innholder, of Lancaster Borough as his lawful attorney to ack.sat. for a mortgage given by John Shiffer (Ref. Deed T75).

12 Nov 1783: John Wistar & PMR

W180: Adam Seitz, stiller, of Lampeter tp. mort.to Peter Huber, yeoman, of Warwick tp.

--Sundry items: HISTORY: To be held in the possession of Peter Huber until Adam Seitz returns from Germany.

20 May 1783: Peter Huber, Jr., & Joseph Huber

W180: Andrew Adam Lutz, butcher, & his wife Catharine of Lancaster Borough mort.to Henry Leghler of same

--Half lot on Orange St. in Lancaster Borough: HISTORY: Same half lot that Charles Klug & his wife Susanna granted 2 May 1778 to Andrew Adam Lutz.

20 Feb 1784: Jonas Metzger & CS

--Casper Fortnee, the executor of William Bush, who was the assignee of Henry Lechler, ack.sat. 18 June 1788.

W182: Henry Weaver, yeoman, of Caernarvon tp. mort.to John Brackbill & Benjamin Brackbill [the administrators of George Weaver, late of same]

156a Caernarvon tp.: HISTORY: Not given.

--13 Dec 1784: Henry Slaymaker & Faithful Slaymaker

--John Neaff & Jacob Neaff, the assignees of John Brackbill & Benjamin Brackbill (Ref. Deed HH-602), ack.sat. 13 June 1795.

W184: Nathaniel Hantsch (or Hauntch), locksmith, of Lancaster Borough mort.to Charles Boyd, cooper, of same

--Lot on Orange St. in Lancaster Borough: HISTORY: Same lot that David Miller granted 21 Oct 1783 to Nathaniel Hantsch.

11 May 1784: Jonas Metzger & CS

--Andrew Bausman, the assignee of ________ [omitted], ack.sat. 19 Dec 1804.

W186: Christian Pflieger, shoemaker, of Lancaster Borough mort.to John Grush & Henry Dehuff [the executors of George Shench, late of Lancaster Borough]

--Lot on Middle St. in Lancaster Borough: HISTORY: Same lot that said John Grush & his wife Mary and Henry Dehuff, & Peter Fetter granted on even date herewith to Christian Pflieger.

14 May 1784: John Shaffner & CS

--John Grush & Henry Dehuff ack.sat. 2 Feb 1794.

W187: Michael Kremer, cooper, & his wife Elizabeth of Lancaster Borough mort.to John Kremer, yeoman, of Manor tp.

--Half lot on Queen St. in Lancaster Borough: HISTORY: Same half lot that Philip Rayer & his wife Elizabeth granted 26 May 1784 to Michael Kremer.

28 May 1784: John Shaffner & CS

--John Kremer ack.sat. 24 Jul 1787.

W189: Abraham Herr, yeoman, & his wife Elizabeth of Mount Joy tp. mort.to Christian Brand, yeoman, of Mount Joy tp.

197a in Mount Joy & Rapho tps.: HISTORY: It being part of two tracts that Samuel Patterson granted 10 Dec 1783 to Abraham Herr.

27 May 1784: CJ & MJ

--Christian Brand ack.sat. 21 Nov 1785.

W191: Adam Shitz (or Shutz), yeoman, & his wife Mary of Leacock tp. mort.to George Kline, yeoman, of Manheim tp.

150a Manheim tp.: HISTORY: Same tract that George Kline & his wife Christina granted on even date herewith to Adam Shitz.

5 May 1785: CJ & MH

--Michael Kleine [the administrator of George Kleine] ack.sat. 4 May 1810.

W193: Peter Hess, yeoman, & his wife Susanna of Donegal tp. mort.to Isaac Rihm, yeoman, of same

162 ½ a. Donegal tp. [called Bowerton]: HISTORY: Not given.

--10 Apr 1784: John Shaffner & CS

--Isaac Rihm ack.sat. 25 May 1789.

W195: Michael Deibler, yeoman, & his wife Anna Maria of Upper Paxton tp. mort.to Arthur Taggart of Donegal tp.

400a Upper Paxton tp., in the Wickonisco Valley: HISTORY: Same tract pat. 21 Mar 1774 to Arthur Taggart (Ref. PB AA-14-196). –No further history.

21 June 1784: J.J. Henry & Thomas Edwards

W197: Roger Hartley, blacksmith, of Martic tp. mort.to Patrick Campble, cordwinder, of same

--All the lands that said Patrick Campble granted 15 Nov 1782 to Roger Hartley.

16 Apr 1784: Thomas Clark & John Caldwell

--In side margin: "Satisfied . . . on the assignment given to Abraham Miller" (Ref. Deed ZZ-405).

W198: Benjamin Hartley, blacksmith, of Martic tp. mort.to Patrick Campble, cordwinder, of same

--All the lands in Martic tp. that Benjamin Hartley holds by an indenture dated 8 Apr 1784 from Roger Hartley.

16 Apr 1784: Thomas Clark & John Caldwell

W200: Philip Beck of Cocalico tp. [the eldest son of Jacob Beck, yeoman, deceased, late of same] mort.to Elizabeth Beck, spinster, of same

--His share of three undivided tracts in Cocalico tp. totaling 296a, 146p: HISTORY: Said Jacob Beck died intestate seized in possession of 296a, 146p Cocalico tp., leaving issue several children, including the said Philip Beck & Elizabeth Beck [the parties hereto].

8 Mar 1784: James Wright & Conrad Laub

W202: John Boham, yeoman, of Lampeter tp. mort.to Michael Wither of Strasburg tp.

4a Lampeter tp.: HISTORY: Same tract that Salome Hains granted 1 Apr 1783 to John Boham.

--17 Jul 1784: HD & CJ

--Michael Wither ack.sat. 24 Sep 1787.

W203: George Stone (or Stein), yeoman, of Earl tp. mort.to Leonard Stone, yeoman, of same

180a Earl tp. [excepting about 60a previously granted to sundry persons]: HISTORY: Not given.

--19 Jul 1784: David Dieffinderffer & JJ

--George Stone & John Stone [the administrators of Leonard Stone] ack.sat. 6 Oct 1790.

W206: Jacob Stone, yeoman, of Earl tp. mort.to Leonard Stone, yeoman, of same

54a Earl tp.: HISTORY: Same tract that Leonard Stone granted on even date herewith to Jacob Stone.

--19 Jul 1784: David Dieffinderffer & JJ

--George Stone & John Stone [the administrators of Leonard Stone] ack.sat. 31 Aug 1792.

W208: Jacob Rowland, yeoman, of Earl tp. mort.to Elizabeth Rowland, spinster, of same

--His undivided share of 149a Earl tp.: HISTORY: Late the estate of Joseph Rowland, deceased.

5 June 1784: Susanna Jones & JJ

--Elizabeth Rowland (or Rohland) ack.sat. 2 Mar 1785.

W209: Nartz Zwecker, yeoman, of Earl tp. mort.to Jacob Weaver, Jr., yeoman, of same

37a, 50p Caernarvon tp., including a gristmill & sawmill: HISTORY: Not given.

--16 Mar 1784: PH & CS

W211: Michael Kantner, blacksmith, & John Kantner, yeoman, both of Tulpehocken tp., Berks County mort.to John Bishop, gentleman, of Exeter tp., Berks County

194a Heidelberg tp.: HISTORY: Not given.

--6 Apr 1784: James Biddle & James Scull

--By a Power of Attorney (Ref. Deed OO-___), Jonas Eckert ack.sat. 26 Nov 1793.

W214: Daniel Benezet appoints Andrew Capp, yeoman, of Heidelberg tp. as his lawful attorney to ack.sat. for a mortgage dated 26 Nov 1776 (Ref. Deed T254).

24 May 1784: Henry Pratt & Arthur Forac

W214: Robert Grahams of Colerain tp. mort.to John Craig of Sadsbury tp. & Robert Alexander of Little Britain tp.

192a, 105p Sadsbury tp.: HISTORY: Late the estate of John Craig, deceased, late of Sadsbury tp. On 6 Mar 1784, his executors, the said John Craig & Robert Alexander [the parties hereto], granted the said tract to Robert Grahams.

9 Apr 1784: Thomas Whiteside & Abraham Whiteside

--John Craig ack.sat. 29 Nov 1796.

W217: Joseph Simon, merchant, of Lancaster Borough assigns to James Webb, the younger
--"the within mortgage": HISTORY: Not further information, but reference is made to a decision by the Court of Common Pleas dated 15 Aug 1783, in which Joseph Simon was the plaintiff and James Webb the defendant.
10 Aug 1784: JJACK & George Moore

W218: Thomas Smith, ironmaster, rel.to Joseph Simon, merchant, of Lancaster Borough
--Certain sum of money: HISTORY: On equal date herewith, Joseph Simons entered into an obligation with Thomas Smith to one Benedict Eshelman. As it is the only proper debts of Thomas Smith, this indenture indemnifies Joseph Simons from suffering any personal loss.
15 Aug 1765: John Henry & L. Andrew Levy

W219: Joseph Simon, merchant, of Lancaster Borough, assigns to James Webb, the younger
--"the within bond or obligation of and from Thomas Smith for his debt unto the said James Webb the younger": HISTORY: This act is in pursuance of a Court of Common Pleas decision rendered 15 Aug 1783. See Deed W217 for additional information.
3 June 1783: JJACK & George Moore

W220: Hugh Wilson of Colerain tp. mort.to Samuel McClellan & John Patterson, both of same [the executors of Thomas Wilson, late of Lancaster County]
231a Colerain tp.: HISTORY: Same tract that Thomas Wilson granted 31 Jan 1781 to Hugh Wilson.
--29 Jul 1784: Thomas Whiteside & Abraham Whiteside
--Samuel McClellan & John Patterson ack.sat. 16 Nov 1797.

W223: Henry Steinbring, yeoman, of Earl tp. mort.to Martin Road, taylor, of same
--House & lot in the Village of New Holland and other sundry items: HISTORY: Not given.
22 May 1784: Mary McConnell & James McConnell
--Martin Road ack.sat. 24 Apr 1788.

W223: John Hans, yeoman, & his wife Mariana of Lancaster County mort.to Andrew Hoover, Philipp Brown, & Nicholas Liebrich, all of the Province of Pennsylvania
180a Warwick tp.: HISTORY: Not given.
--17 Apr 1784: William Smith, Martin Gross, & Matthew Hoffer

W225: Christian Frantz & Jacob Frantz, yeomen, both of Cocalico tp. mort.to Michael Frantz, yeoman, of same
--Two adjoining tracts: (1.) 32a Cocalico tp. and (2.) ¾ a. Cocalico tp.: HISTORY: Not given.
1 May 1784: Jacob Gibbel & AN
--Michael Frantz ack.sat. 5 Nov 1785.

W227: William Hunter, tanner, of Londonderry tp. mort.to William Sawyer, Sr., yeoman, of Lancaster County
211a Londonderry tp.: HISTORY: Not given.
--9 Aug 1784: Henrich Licht & JT
--Benjamin Sawyer [the surviving administrator of William Sawyer with the will annexed] ack.sat. 7 Jul 1786.

W229: James Purdy, yeoman, of Martic tp. mort.to Patrick Campble, cordwinder, of same
100a Martic tp.: HISTORY: Same tract that said Patrick Campble granted on even date herewith to James Purdy.
4 Sep 1784: HD & John Caldwell

W231: Nicholas Ensminger & Alexander Kroh (or Crow) ack.sat. for a mortgage dated sometime in December 1767, given by Paul Gemberling to the said Nicholas Ensminger, Alexander Crow, George

Gardner, & Jacob Gemberling. The latter four men had co-signed a bond with Paul Gemberling given to Michael Gross of Lancaster. However, as it was the only proper debt of Paul Gemberling, he mortgaged his house & lot on Market Square in the town of Heidelberg to the said Ensminger, Crow, Gardner, & Jacob Gemberling to ensure that they would not suffer any personal loss. [Said George Gardner is now deceased—his executor is George Gardner.]

30 Aug 1784: Nicholas Schope & Samuel King

W232: David Hays (or Hayse), schoolmaster, & his wife Mary of Derry tp. mort.to James Porter, Thomas Walker, & William Mitchell, all of Hanover tp.

--Lot #14 in Frederick Town in Derry tp.: HISTORY: Not given.

31 Aug 1784: Jacob Cook & William McCormick

--James Porter ack.sat. 10 June 1786.

W233: Jacob Kauffman, yeoman, & his wife Magdalena of Manor tp. mort.to Andrew Kauffman, yeoman, of Hempfield tp.

49 ½ a. Manor tp.: HISTORY: Not given. // Said Jacob & Andrew Kauffman are both bound to Michael Shenck, Andrew Kauffman, John Shenck, & John Newcomet; however, it is the only proper debt of Jacob Kauffman. This indenture serves to indemnify Andrew Kauffman.

10 Sep 1784: Barbara Kauffman & CS

--Andrew Kauffman ack.sat. 30 Mar 1793.

W237: Peter Weidner, yeoman, & his wife Margaret of Paxton tp. mort.to Joseph Flori (or Flory), Sr., yeoman, of same

--Lot #29 in Middletown in Paxton tp.: HISTORY: Same lot that John Meyer & his wife Christina granted 28 Dec 1773 to Peter Weidner.

16 Sep 1784: Jacob Cook & Jane Hamilton

W239: John Swift & Joseph Swift of Philadelphia appoints Jasper Yeates, Esq., as their lawful attorney to ack.sat. for a mortgage given by James Willson of Paxton tp. (Ref. Deed M475).

22 May 1784: Andrew Berryhill & George Swift

W239: Joseph Swift, merchant, of Philadelphia appoints Jasper Yeates, Esq., as his lawful attorney to ack.sat. for a mortgage given by Andrew Berryhill of Paxton tp. (Ref. Deed T19).

22 May 1784: Andrew Berryhill & George Swift

W240: James Bickham of Lancaster Borough assigns to George Bickham of Philadelphia

--The yearly rent profits of two messuages in Lancaster Borough, one on King St. now in the tenure of Charles Hamilton and the other on Duke St. now in the tenure of James Jacks. George Bickham is to receive the yearly rent profits until the debt owed to him by the said James Bickham is satisfied. [Said George Bickham had paid off the debts that James Bickham owed to the estate of William West, late of Philadelphia, deceased.]

6 Oct 1784: Charles Syng, John Cook, & Philip Frey

W241: Andrew Keifer (or Kufter), yeoman, of Hanover tp. mort.to George Hook (or Hoke), Jr., yeoman, of Lebanon tp.

202a Hanover tp.: HISTORY: Part of 400a Hanover tp. war. 8 June 1749 to Thomas McCormick. On 12 May 1750, Thomas McCormick & his wife Elizabeth granted the same to Jacob Huber, ironmaster, of Lancaster County. On 15 June 1759, Jacob Huber assigned the same to Frederick Leasore & Jacob Weidman. On 15 Nov 1764, Frederick Leasore & Jacob Weidman granted on equal moiety thereof to Jacob Foght. On 19 May 1766, Jacob Foght & his wife Barbara granted their moiety (or 202a) to Christian Gish. On 25 Oct 1782, Christian Gish & his wife Soviea granted the same to said George Hook, Jr. On 18 Dec 1782, George Hook, Jr., & his wife Barbara granted the same to Andrew Keifer.

29 May 1784: Thomas Clark & Johannes Dubs

--George Hook, Jr., ack.sat. 28 June 1809.

W244: Philip Marsteller, yeoman, of Lebanon mort.to Samuel Miles & William Wistar, merchants, of Philadelphia

--Lot on Market St. in the town of Lebanon: HISTORY: Same lot that Christopher Wegman granted 2 June 1764 to Philip Marsteller.

7 Jul 1784: Reuben Haines & Daniel Wistar

--By a Power of Attorney (Ref. Deed W426), John Hubley ack.sat. 10 June 1786.

W246: John Miller & Henry Miller, yeomen, both of Cocalico tp. mort.to Daniel Bollinger & Peter Reyer, yeomen, both of same [the executors of Tobias Miller, yeoman, late of same]

--Three tracts: (1.) 96 ¾ a. Cocalico tp., (2.) 12a, 68p Cocalico tp., and (3.) 25a Cocalico tp.: HISTORY: Same three tracts that the said executors, by the directions of Tobias Miller's last will & testament, granted on equal date herewith to John Miller & Henry Miller.

1 Oct 1784: Joseph Heffly & Bernhard Feather

--Daniel Bollinger & Peter Reyer ack.sat. 4 Apr 1785.

W249: David Brown & Henry Carpenter of Strasburg tp. mort.to Elizabeth Seager of Lampeter tp.

6a Lampeter tp.: HISTORY: Same tract that Elizabeth Seager granted on equal date herewith to David Brown & Henry Carpenter.

4 May 1784: Michael Wither & Henrich Kindig

--Elizabeth Seager ack.sat. 28 Jan 1788.

W251: Francis Smith (or Frantz Smitt) of Lampeter tp. mort.to Elizabeth Seeger (or Seger) of same

6a Lampeter tp.: HISTORY: Same tract that Elizabeth Seeger granted on equal date herewith to Francis Smith.

4 May 1784: Emma Widder & Michael Wither

W252: John Boham, yeoman, of Lampeter tp. mort.to Elizabeth Seiger (or Seager) of same

6a Lampeter tp.: HISTORY: Same that that Elizabeth Seiger granted on equal date herewith to John Boham.

4 May 1784: CJ & Michael Wither

--Elizabeth Seiger ack.sat. 19 Nov 1787.

W254: John Fowler, yeoman, & his wife Salome of Lampeter tp. mort.to Michael Wither (or Widder), yeoman, of Strasburg tp.

6a Lampeter tp.: HISTORY: Same tract that Elizabeth Seiger granted 4 May 1784 to John Fowler.

--3 Nov 1784: Joseph Bowman & Henrich Kindig

--Michael Wither ack.sat. 2 Feb 1787.

W256: Frederick Carper (or Corper), yeoman, of Heidelberg tp. mort.to John McCallon, yeoman, of Hanover tp.

244a Londonderry tp.: HISTORY: Not given.

--17 Sep 1784: PM & JT

--John McCallon ack.sat. 12 Apr 1802.

W258: Christian Lambach, yeoman, of Warwick tp. mort.to Christian Stouffer of same [the guardian of Philip Lambach & Christina Lambach, the minor children of Philip Lambach, deceased]

113a, 156p Warwick tp.: HISTORY: Not given.

--7 Dec 1784: CS Jr. & CS

--Christian Stouffer ack.sat. 4 Apr 1785.

W259: Peter Eby, Jr., & his wife Mary of Leacock tp. mort.to Peter Eby, Sr., of same

93 ¾ a., 30p Leacock tp.: HISTORY: Same tract that said Peter Eby, Sr., & his wife Barbara granted on equal date herewith to Peter Eby, Jr.

29 June 1784: John Eaby & EC
--Peter Eby, Sr., ack.sat. 25 May 1792.

W261: Samuel Eby & his wife Elizabeth of Leacock tp. mort.to Peter Eby of same
87a, 97p Leacock tp.: HISTORY: Same tract that said Peter Eby & his wife Barbara granted on equal date herewith to Samuel Eby.
29 June 1784: John Eaby & EC
--Peter Eby, Sr., ack.sat. 25 May 1792.

W263: Andrew Surerus (or Surearus), yeoman, of Martic tp. mort.to Abraham Kagey & Christian Shank of same [the executors of Abraham Kagey, the elder, late of same]
--Two tracts totaling 12a, 24p: (1.) 10a, 126p Martic tp. and (2.) 1a, 58p Martic tp.: HISTORY: Same two tracts that Abraham Kagey, the elder, in his lifetime, agreed to sell to Andrew Surerus. On equal date herewith, the said executors fulfilled that agreement and executed a deed good for the same.
20 Dec 1784: JJACK & Richard Kagey
--Abraham Kagey & Christian Shank ack.sat. 3 Apr 1786.

W265: Godlip Eberman, clockmaker, of Lancaster Borough mort.to Michael Lightner (or Litener) of Chamberstown in Franklin County
--Lot on King St. in Lancaster Borough: HISTORY: Not given.
3 Jan 1785: CS Jr. & CS
--Anna Wither [the widow & administratrix of George Wither] ack.sat. 5 Sep 1799 [see the following assignment].

W267: Michael Lightner assigns the "within mortgage" to George Widder of Warwick tp.
3 Jan 1785: CS & CS Jr.

W267: Frederick Druckenmiller, yeoman, & his wife Louisa of Rapho tp. mort.to Valentine Greiner, yeoman, of Warwick tp. and Mathias Long, yeoman, of Rapho tp.
--Their right, claim, title, & interest to the real estate of Peter Gudelius: HISTORY: By his last will & testament, Peter Gudelius, late of Rapho tp., devised his real estate to his children, including the said Louisa wife of Frederick Druckenmiller.
13 Jan 1785: Lewis Lauman, Jr., & PG
--Valentine Greiner & Mathias Long ack.sat. 10 Jan 1799.

W269: Henry Landis, yeoman, & his wife Elizabeth of Hempfield tp. mort.to John Huber, yeoman, of same & Rudolph Hare, yeoman, of Manor tp.
--Their right, claim, title & interest to the real estate of Benjamin Hershey, late of Hempfield tp.: HISTORY: Said Benjamin Hershey died intestate leaving issue several children, including the said Elizabeth wife of Henry Landis.
22 Jan 1785: JJACK & Lewis Lauman, Jr.
--John Huber & Rudolph Hare ack.sat. 9 Aug 1793.

W271: George Loyer (or Leier, or Lawyer), yeoman, of Heidelberg tp. mort.to John Frantz, yeoman, of Bethel tp., Berks County
81a Heidelberg tp.: HISTORY: Not given.
--2 Oct 1784: Henry Weber & Nicholas Valede [German]
--John Frantz ack.sat. 24 Nov 1785.

W273: Christian Romig, yeoman, of Earl tp. mort.to Christian Bowman, stonecutter, of Cocalico tp.
10a Earl tp.: HISTORY: Not given.
--27 Jan 1785: PG & Lewis Lauman, Jr.
--Christian Bowman ack.sat. 28 Mar 1791.

W274: Adonijah Matthews, merchant, of Greenbrier County, Virginia, mort.to Jeremiah Warder, Jeremiah Parker, & Richard Parker, merchants, all of Philadelphia

--Two tracts: (1.) 480a in Greenbrier County, VA, and (2.) 13 lots in or near the town of Lebanon

1. HISTORY: Same tract purchased by Valentine Yorkham. The right to the same was later assigned to Adonijah Matthews.
2. HISTORY: Acquired as follows:
   a. On 22 May 1784, Philipp Fernsler, yeoman, & his wife Christina of the town of Lebanon granted six outlots near the said town to Adonijah Matthews.
   b. On 30 Dec 1783, Christopher Wegman, merchant, & his wife Margaretha of Philadelphia granted three lots in the town of Lebanon to Thomas Atkinson. On _____ [date omitted], Thomas Atkinson & his wife Jane assigned the same to Adonijah Matthews.
   c. Adam Orth, Esq. [the executor of Peter Kucker, late of Lebanon tp.] granted two lots in the town of Lebanon to the said Thomas Atkinson, who later assigned the same to Adonijah Matthews.
   d. On 30 June 1761, Peter Koocher & his wife Barbara granted one lot in the town of Lebanon to Frederick Lutz. By sundry conveyances, the lot is now in the possession of Adonijah Matthews.
   e. On 31 Oct 1765, the Reverend Casper Stoever & his wife Maria Catharine granted one lot in the town of Lebanon to the said Philipp Fernsler. By sundry conveyances, the lot is now in the possession of Adonijah Matthews.

--29 Jul 1784: Richard Gardiner & Jesse Leedom

W276: Christian Lambach, yeoman, of Warwick tp. mort.to Elizabeth Klick, widow, of same

64a Warwick tp.: HISTORY: Same tract that David Hilton granted 1 Feb 1764 to Christian Lambach.

--7 Feb 1785: CS Jr. & CS

--By a Power of Attorney (Ref. Deed W483), Johannes Bauer ack.sat. on 23 Dec 1786 from Joseph Gingrich [the administrator of Christian Lambach, deceased]

W278: Michael Grub, cooper, & his wife Barbara of Lancaster Borough mort.to Henry Gross, innkeeper, of same

--Half lot on Prince St. in Lancaster Borough: HISTORY: Same half lot that Henry Dering & his wife Mary granted 12 Jan 1784 to Michael Grub.

17 Feb 1785: John Shaffner & CS

--Henry Gross ack.sat. 19 Oct 1790.

W280: Joseph White states the following: On 23 Jul 1767 he and his mother Elizabeth White granted 195a Drumore tp. to Thomas McConnel. On the same date, said Thomas McConnel mortgaged the same premises to the said Elizabeth White (Ref. Deed M228). Said Elizabeth White has since died. // Her son Joseph now acknowledges that the said mortgaged was satisfied prior to her death.

17 Feb 1785: Sworn by Joseph White before James Jacks.

W280: Jacob Conrad, yeoman, of Manheim tp. mort.to James Jacks, Esq., of Lancaster Borough

102a Manheim tp.: HISTORY: Part of a larger tract patented to Martin Weybright, who died intestate seized in possession of the same. The Orphans Court confirmed his real estate to his eldest son Martin. On 12 June 1779, Martin Weybright granted 102a Manheim tp. to Jacob Conrad.

12 Mar 1785: PG & Alexander Lowrey

--Philip Gloninger, the assignee of James Jacks, ack.sat. 22 May 1790.

W282: Jacob Miller & his wife Ketran of Hanover tp. mort.to Felix Landes, Jr., of Paxton tp.

141 ½ a. Hanover tp.: HISTORY: Same tract that Martha Swan & Alexander Swan [surname also given as Levan] granted 24 June last to Jacob Miller.

23 Feb 1785: Timothy Green & Mary Green

W284: Anna Cryder (or Criter), widow, of Lampeter tp. mort.to Fronica Hare, Benjamin Graff, John Brachbill, & Christian Hare, all of Lancaster County [the executors of Christian Hare, yeoman, late of Lampeter tp.]

95a Lampeter tp.: HISTORY: Not given.

--7 Mar 1785: Martin Mollinger & EG

--Fronica Hare, John Brachbill, & Christian Hare ack.sat. 9 Aug 1791.

W285: Leckey Murray, doctor of physick, & his wife Elizabeth of Lancaster Borough mort.to Christopher Marshal, gentleman, of Philadelphia

302a Upper Paxton tp., in Armstrong's Valley: HISTORY: Same tract pat. 7 May 1783 to Leckey Murray (Ref. Patent Book #2).

21 Mar 1785: JJACK & L. Andrew Levy

W287: Nathan Evans, yeoman, & his wife Mary of Caernarvon tp. mort.to Joshua Evans, tanner, of same and Thomas Parry, yeoman, of Union tp. in "Barches County" in Pennsylvania [the executors of John Davies, Jr.]

--Two tracts: (1.) 130a Earl tp. and (2.) 133a Earl tp.: HISTORY: The "greater part thereof" being part of 200a Earl tp. pat. 5 Feb 1753 to John Evans (Ref. PB A-17-254). On 9 Nov 1753, John Evans & his wife Ann granted the same [excepting one acre previously granted to the said Joshua Evans & 152 perches granted to James Douglass] to Nathan Evans (Ref. Deed G287). Said Nathan Evans granted two acres to Lewis Wilmin, one acre to Jacob Fox, and one acre & seventy-two perches to James Evans; however, he died intestate pertaining to the residue, leaving issue two sons, Evan Evans and Nathan Evans [the party hereto]. By agreement, the residue of this tract and others contiguous to it were divided among the heirs. On 4 Aug 1782, said Evan Evans & his wife Jane granted their equal share to said Nathan Evans (Ref. Deed L22 [sic]—perhaps meant to be Deed Book Z).

1 Dec 1784: James Evans, James Evans, Jr., & William Boyd

--Joshua Evans ack.sat. 7 May 1790.

W290: Jacob Showalter, yeoman, & his wife Magdalena of Cocalico tp. mort.to Andrew Wisler, yeoman, of Warwick tp.

128a Cocalico tp.: HISTORY: Same tract that Christian Showalter & his wife Barbara granted 16 Mar 1784 to Jacob Showalter.

29 Mar 1785: James Porter & William Ritchey

--Andrew Wisler ack.sat. 11 Apr 1789.

W291: Sarah McClintock [the executor of Abraham McClintock] appoints George Wolf as her lawful attorney to ack.sat. for a mortgage given by William Kirkwood to the said Sarah McClintock & John Camble.

28 Mar 1785: John Wilson & David Steel

W292: John Grow (or Groh) of the town of Manheim mort.to George Hatz of same

--Three lots in the town of Manheim, numbered 290, 291, and 292 in the town plan: HISTORY: Not given.

9 Apr 1785: William Smith & N. Ceasy

W294: Susanna Hausser (or Houser), widow, of Lebanon tp. mort.to Jacob Light, yeoman, of same

4 ¾ a. Lebanon tp.: HISTORY: Not given.

--14 Dec 1784: Jacob Rossle & JT

W295: James Galt of Earl tp. mort.to Sarah Keimer, Thomas May, Thomas Keimer, & James Keimer [the executors of James Keimer, late of Earl tp.]

211a Earl tp.: HISTORY: Same tract that David Morgan granted to the said James Galt.

--14 Apr 1785: EC & William Smith

--Sarah Keimer (or Keemer), the surviving executor, ack.sat. 6 Oct 1800.

W297: Joshua Chamberlain & Jonas Chamberlain, tanners, and William Chamberlain, yeoman, all of Sadsbury tp. mort.to Moses Brinton, yeoman, of Leacock tp.

145 ½ a. Sadsbury tp. [partly in Chester and partly in Lancaster counties]: HISTORY: Same tract pat. 24 June 1738 to Jonas Chamberlain (Ref. PB A-1-92). By his last will & testament, Jonas Chamberlain bequeathed the same tract to his sons, the said Joshua, Jonas, & William [the parties hereto].

13 Apr 1785: Henry Slaymaker & Hannah Slaymaker

--William Brinton, the surviving executor of Moses Brinton, ack.sat. 23 Aug 1809.

W299: John Noseman, yeoman, of Rapho tp. mort.to William Bousman & John Bousman, yeomen, both of Lancaster Borough, and Gabriel Hiester, yeoman, of Bern tp. in Berks County

--Lot #22 in the town of Manheim containing 9a, 123p: HISTORY: Same lot that said William Bousman, John Bousman, & Gabriel Hiester and his wife Elizabeth granted on equal date herewith to John Noseman.

4 May 1785: Frederick Nauman & PG

--William Bousman, John Bousman, & Gabriel Hiester ack.sat. 23 Feb 1797.

W301: Jacob Keiser of Salisbury tp. mort.to John Hopkins

153a Salisbury tp.: HISTORY: Same tract pat. 9 Jan 1752 to Neil McNeighton (Ref. PB A-16-40). On 25 May 1755, Neil McNeighton & his wife Elizabeth granted the same to Isaac Richardson. On 7 Jan 1764, Isaac Richardson & his wife Alice granted the same to Peter Sensnich. On 3 Feb 1767, Peter Sensnich & his wife Ursula granted the same to Jacob Keiser (Ref. Deed Q183).

18 Mar 1785: Samuel J. Atlee & WA

--John Hopkins ack.sat. 3 Jan 1801.

W303: George Grebe, yeoman, of Rapho tp. mort.to Martin Shuch of same

17 ½ a. Rapho tp.: HISTORY: Not given.

--22 Mar 1785: John Shaffner & CS

--Martin Shuch ack.sat. 10 Feb 1791.

W305: Henry Kagey assigns to Christian Hess of Cocalico tp.

--"the within indenture of mortgage": HISTORY: Mortgage given by John Mosser to said Henry Kagey (Ref. Deed M380).

29 May 1773: John Brackbill & John Ferree

W306: Casper Sherck, yeoman, & his wife Ann of Earl tp. mort.to Henry Zercher (or Lercher?) of Conestoga tp.

39a, 82p Conestoga tp., including a gristmill & sawmill: HISTORY: Same tract that said Henry Zercher granted on equal date herewith to Casper Sherck.

--19 May 1785: CS & CS Jr.

--Henry Zercher ack.sat. 22 Aug 1789.

W308: William Flick, blue dyer, & his wife Catharine of Lancaster Borough mort.to Jacob Eideneier, yeoman, of same

--Half lot on Prince St. in Lancaster Borough: HISTORY: Not given.

20 May 1785: Daniel Franck & CS

--Jacob Eideneier ack.sat. 3 Sep 1785.

W309: David Kenig, cooper, & his wife Charlotte of Lancaster Borough mort.to Jacob Metzger & Melchior Rudisill, both of Lancaster Borough

--Lot on King St. in Lancaster Borough: HISTORY: Same lot that George Metzger granted 11 Jan 1785 to Daniel Kenig.

11 Jan 1785: CS & CS Jr.

--Jacob Metzger & Melchior Rudisill ack.sat. 7 Feb 1804.

W311: Nathaniel Torbet of Leacock tp. mort.to William Porter of same
201a Leacock tp.: HISTORY: Not given.
--1 June 1785: Alexander McCay & Samuel Turbett
--William Porter ack.sat. 8 June 1790.

W313: Christian Hess of Conestoga tp. appoints his brother Samuel Hess of same as his lawful attorney to ack.sat. for the following mortgage: On 28 May 1768, John Musser mortgaged 208a Conestoga tp. to Henry Kagey (Ref. Deed M380). On 29 May 1773, Henry Kagey assigned the mortgage over to Christian Hess (Ref. Deed W305).
4 June 1785: Adam Goghenour & Henry Hess

W314: Luke Romer, yeoman, & his wife Elizabeth of Lampeter tp. mort.to Henry Christ, yeoman, of same
6a Lampeter tp.: HISTORY: Same lot that Elizabeth Seger granted 4 May 1784 to Luke Romer (Ref. Deed Z433).
4 June 1785: Johannes Stouffer & CS
--Henry Christ ack.sat. 28 May 1791.

W316: Peter Hederick, yeoman, of Hanover tp. appoints his friend Adam Orth as his lawful attorney to ack.sat. for the following mortgage: On 31 May 1769, Thomas Coppenhaver mortgaged 137a Hanover tp. to Peter Hederick (Ref. Deed O162).
12 Jan 1784: P. Marsteller

W317: Samuel Miles & William Wister, merchants, of Philadelphia appoints Christian Herr, yeoman, of Mount Joy tp. as their lawful attorney to ack.sat. for the following mortgage: Benjamin Mishy of Rapho tp. mortgaged 169a Rapho tp. to Samuel Miles & William Wister (Ref. Deed W54).
11 May 1785: Daniel Freehauff & George Douglass, Jr.

W317: Jacob Huber, yeoman, & his wife Barbara of Earl tp. mort.to his father John Huber, yeoman, of same
238a Earl tp.: HISTORY: Same tract that David Davis & his wife Jean granted 2 June 1762 to Meredith Darlington [excepting 12 acres previously granted to William Douglass & three-quarters of an acre previously granted to the Presbyterian congregation]. On 17 Dec 1768, Meredith Darlington granted the same to John Huber. On equal date herewith, John Huber granted the same to his son Jacob.
1 May 1784: Samuel Carpenter & John McConnaughy
--John Huber ack.sat. 7 June 1788 [partially obscured—hard to read]

W320: Adam Hart, turner, of Lancaster Borough mort.to Richard Henry, innkeeper, of same
--Half lot on Church St. in Adams Town in Lancaster Borough: HISTORY: Not given.
21 Jul 1785: John Griner & PG
--Richard Henry ack.sat. 7 Aug 1792.

W322: John Black (of Swartz), Jr., of Mount Joy tp. mort.to Mary Black & John Black, Sr., both of same
110a Mount Joy tp.: HISTORY: Part of a larger tract pat. 15 Dec 1762 to said John Black, Sr. On 15 Mar 1785, John Black, Sr., granted 110a to John Black. [Subject to certain privileges reserved to said John Black, Sr., & his wife Maria—who is not the Mary Black, party hereto—see W338].
9 Apr 1785: Jacob Cook & Abraham Black
--[Advisement: Only the first page of this indenture is copied. A side notation states that this deed has been errantly placed on this page. The full text of the deed begins on page 342; however, I have placed all relevant information here.]

W323: Christley Eater (or Etter) & his wife Mary Ann of Mount Joy tp. mort.to Simon Karbaugh (or Carbaugh) of same
155a Mount Joy tp.: HISTORY: Same tract war. 30 Apr 1765 to said Simon Karbaugh. On equal date herewith, Simon Karbaugh granted the same to Christley Etter.
22 June 1785: Conrad Gross & Leonard Negle

--Ulrich Tanner & Jacob _______ [obscured], the executors of Simon Karbaugh, ack.sat. 24 Mar 1792.

W324: James McElvane, yeoman, of Drumore tp. mort.to Nathaniel Kelly of same
143 ¾ a. Drumore tp.: HISTORY: Not given.
--30 Apr 1785: Hannah Irwin, Moses Irwin, & James Buckhannon, Jr.
--Nathaniel Kelly ack.sat. 25 Mar 1792.

W326: Christian Kagey, yeoman, & his wife Mary of Conestoga tp. mort.to Abraham Kagey & Christian Shenk [the executors of Abraham Kagey, late of Martic tp.]
--The residue of 268a, 40p Conestoga tp.: HISTORY: On 6 Aug 1785, the said executors granted 268a, 40p Conestoga tp. to Christian Kagey. On 6 Aug 1785, Christian Kagey & his wife Mary granted 80a to Michael Hess.
12 Aug 1785: Christian Whisler & Michael Hess
--Abraham Kagey & Christian Shenk ack.sat. 17 June 1788.

W329: Charles Drum, innkeeper, & his wife Elizabeth of Germantown in Philadelphia County mort.to Manuel Josephson, merchant, of Philadelphia
191a Bart tp.: HISTORY: Same tract pat. 11 June 1784 to Charles Drum (Ref. PB #2, page 474).
--8 Jul 1785: LW & Frederick Bates
--By a Power of Attorney (Ref. Deed HH-581, or is it HH-381?—obscured), Alexander __________ [too dark to read] ack.sat. 20 Sep 1791.

W332: Andrew Foltz, taylor, & his wife Margaret of Lancaster Borough mort.to Andrew Wissler, yeoman, of Warwick tp.
14a Manheim tp.: HISTORY: Same tract that Martin Weybrecht granted 10 Jul 1779 to Andrew Foltz.
--3 Sep 1785: Henry Bugh & PG
--Andrew Wissler ack.sat. 9 Mar 1789.

W334: Peter Ecker (or Acker, or Eacker, or Eaker), tanor (?), of Earl tp. mort.to James Martin (or Marten), yeoman, of same
--House & lot in the Village of New Holland in Earl tp.: HISTORY: Not given. Both parties are bound to Abraham Barr of Earl tp.; however, it is the only proper debt of Peter Ecker.
30 June 1785: Sarah Kuhn & FK
--James Martin ack.sat. 7 Nov 1787.

W336: George Weiss of Philadelphia mort.to Samuel Garrigues, merchant, of same
--His undivided fifth part of the Lancaster County real estate of John Dehuff, Esq., late of Lancaster Borough: HISTORY: Same right that Christopher Baker, conveyancer, & his wife Catharine of Philadelphia granted 7 May 1784 to George Weiss.
10 Aug 1785: Matthew Walker & R. Whitehead

W338: Edward Hand, Esq., & his wife Catharine of Lancaster Borough mort.to Samuel Boyd & Alexander Kinkead, yeomen, both of same [the executors of James Davis, yeoman, late of same]
160a, 20p near Lancaster Borough on the east side of the Conestoga Creek: HISTORY: Not given.
--14 Sep 1785: JY & Galb. Paterson
--Samuel Boyd ack.sat. 1 Aug 1791.

W340: Abraham Black, (or Swartz) yeoman, & his wife Ann of Mount Joy tp. mort.to John Black, Sr., & Mary Black, spinster, both of same
80a Mount Joy tp.: HISTORY: Part of a larger tract pat. 14 Dec 1762 to John Black, Sr. On 15 Mar 1785, John Black, Sr., granted 80a to Abraham Black [subject to certain privileges reserved to said John Black, Sr., & his wife Mary—who is <u>not</u> that same Mary as in these presents.]

9 Apr 1785: Jacob Cook & John Swartz
--John Black, Sr., ack.sat. 10 Mar 1794.

W342: See Deed W321.

W344: John Stouffer, yeoman, & his wife Elizabeth of Rapho tp. mort.to Isaac Hershy (or Harshy), yeoman, of Hempfield tp.
--Two tracts: (1.) 53a, 15p Rapho tp. and (2.) 70a Rapho tp.: HISTORY: Not given.
21 Sep 1785: FK & Peter Musser
--Isaac Hershy ack.sat. 7 Feb 1787.

W346: John Gehr (or Ger) of Eln tp., Cumberland County, mort.to Christian Weist of Cocalico tp.
140a Cocalico tp.: HISTORY: Late the estate of Paul Gehr, the father of John Gehr, the party hereto.
--19 Sep 1785: Lewis Lauman, Jr., & Thomas Jones

W348: Charles Hamilton, merchant, of Lancaster Borough mort.to Joseph Tidball, John Ferguson, & Alexander Scott, merchants, of Philadelphia
299a, 103p in Rapho tp. & Hempfield tp.: HISTORY: Same tract that Andrew Smith & his wife granted 26 Aug ____ [omitted] to Charles Hamilton.
15 Oct 1785: Stephen Chambers & Maxwell Bines
--Joseph Tidball ack.sat. 9 June 1787; John Ferguson ack.sat. 10 June 1787; Alexander Scott ack.sat. 5 Jul 1787.

W350: Philip Shower of the town of Manheim mort.to Sickmond Shower & Steven Shower, both of same
--Two lots in the town of Manheim, numbered 331 and 332 in the town plan: HISTORY: Not given.
21 May 1785: William Smith & George Werner
--Steven Shower ack.sat. 25 Feb 1795.

W351: Solomon Myer, bookbinder, of the town of Ephrata in Cocalico tp. mort.to Michael Defiderfer & John Hubley, both of Lancaster Borough
--Two properties: (1.) all his right title, interest, & claim to assorted lots in the town of Middletown in Paxton tp. [excepting lots previously sold to the following persons: Abner Wickersham, Conrad Bombaugh, William Crab, and Mark Sneider] and (2.) 2a, 3p Cocalico tp.

1. HISTORY: Same lots that John Myer, by his last will & testament, granted to his son Solomon (the party hereto).
2. HISTORY: Same tract that said Michael Diffenderfer & John Hubley granted on equal date herewith to Solomon Myer.

--29 Oct 1785: Philip Deifenderfer & Lewis Lauman, Jr.
--John Hubley ack.sat. 27 Nov 1788.

W353: James Douglass, the elder, yeoman, of Salisbury tp. mort.to John Wilson of Leacock tp. & Samuel John Atlee of Salisbury tp.
43a Salisbury tp.: HISTORY: Not given; however, it is noted that James Douglass has agreed to satisfy a debt that Benjamin Miller, late of Salisbury tp., owed to one Thomas White, Esq., late of Philadelphia, deceased.
22 Oct 1785: William Boyd & Herman Skiles, Jr.

W355: John Fowler & his wife Salome (late Hains) of Lampeter tp. mort.to James Gibbons, scrivener, of the Borough of Wilmington in Newcastle County, Delaware
17a, 70p Lampeter tp. [it being the total acreage of three lots in a town called Hains Town, numbered 2, 9, and 15 in the town plan]: HISTORY: Part of 68a, 42p Lampeter tp. that Francis Smith granted 1 Apr 1783 to Salome Hains. The property was then divided into lots and given the name "Hains Town". Salome Hains is now the wife of John Fowler.
25 Jul 1785: Abraham Gibbons & William Gibbons

--By a Power of Attorney (Ref. Deed W438), Michael Wither ack.sat. 19 Sep 1786.

W357: Samuel Miles & William Wister, merchants, both of Philadelphia appoint Adam Reigart, Esq., of Lancaster Borough as their lawful attorney to ack.sat. for the following mortgage: on 16 Jan 1783, Andrew Ream of Cocalico tp. mortgaged 62 ½ a. Cocalico tp. to Samuel Miles & William Wister (Ref. Deed W45).

31 May 1785: James Miles & George Douglass, Jr.

W358: Adam Weaver (or Weber), innholder, & his wife Rosina of Lancaster Borough mort.to Christian Baughman, yeoman, of Manor tp.

--Lot on Queen St. in Lancaster Borough: HISTORY: Same lot that Frederick Frick & his wife Sophia granted 23 Mar 1779 to Adam Weaver.

5 Nov 1785: JJACK & Bernard Hubley

--Peter Bachman, the executor of Christian Bachman, ack.sat. 21 Dec 1811.

W360: Christian Wentzly, blue dyer, of Rapho tp. mort.to William Bousman & John Bousman, yeoman, of Lancaster Borough, and Gabriel Hiester, yeoman, of Bern tp., Berks County

--Two lots in the town of Manheim on High St., numbered 5 and 6 in the town plan: HISTORY: Not given.

7 Nov 1785: Mathias Young & PG

--William Bousman & John Bousman ack.sat. 10 Sep 1788.

W362: Jacob Bear, yeoman, of Cocalico tp. mort.to Jacob Hershey, yeoman, of same

101a, 124p Cocalico tp.: HISTORY: Part of 362 ½ a. Cocalico tp. that Peter Carpenter & his wife Anna granted 5 Feb 1784 (?-year smudged) to Jacob Bear (Ref. Deed BB-389). On 18 Oct 1785, Jacob Bear & his wife Catharine granted 357 ½ a., 124p to Jacob Hershey (the party hereto). On 19 Oct 1785, Jacob Hershey & his wife Catharine re-conveyed 101a, 124p to Jacob Bear.

___ [obscured] Oct 1785: AN & Michael Bear

W364: Margaret Graham of Chanceford tp., York County [the widow of John Graham, late of Martic tp.] appoints John W. Kittera as her lawful attorney to ack.sat. for the following mortgage: Samuel Ankrim mortgage certain property in Martic tp. the said the John Graham (Ref. Deed H148-149).

29 Aug 1785: James Long & ________ [omitted]

W366: John Offner, hatter, & his wife Salome of Lancaster Borough mort.to John Hambright, shoemaker, of same

--Lot on Queen St. in Lancaster Borough: HISTORY: Not given.

4 Nov 1785: Daniel Witmer & CS

W367: John Brubaker, yeoman, of Earl tp. mort.to Jacob Barge, gentleman, of Philadelphia

108a, 26p Earl tp.: HISTORY: Same tract that said Jacob Barge & his wife Elizabeth granted on the day before the date of these presents to John Brubaker, subject to certain considerations owing to Catharine Rein by virtue of the last will & testament of Michael Rein.

1 Oct 1785: William Gaskill & Peter Thompson, Jr.

--By a Power of Attorney, David Witwer ack.sat. 5 May 1804.

W370: Joseph Paschall appoints Henry Rhode, potter, of Earl tp. as his lawful attorney to ack.sat. for the within mentioned mortgage [no further information].

10 Dec 1785: PMR & William Magill

W371: Frederick Hoffman, yeoman, of Manor tp. mort.to James Jacks, Esq., of Lancaster Borough

106 ¾ a. Manor tp.: HISTORY: Same tract that Andrew Kauffman & Jacob Neff [the executors of Isaac Kauffman, late of Manor tp.] granted 13 Jan 1784 (or 1781?—hard to read) to Frederick Hoffman.

24 Dec 1785: PG & Johannes Steman

--James Jacks ack.sat. 6 June 1801.

W372: Archibald Steel, Esq., & his wife Jane of Lancaster Borough mort.to Alexander Scott, Jr., merchant, of Philadelphia

--Lot on Orange St. in Lancaster Borough: HISTORY: Same lot that William Cross & his wife Elizabeth granted 7 May 1779 to Archibald Steel.

9 Dec 1785: JJACK & Michael Mosser

--Alexander Scott ack.sat. 8 Sep 1786.

W373: Adam Kimmel assigns the "within mortgage" over to Jacob Neagly & Jacob Ecker [no further information].

3 Aug 1772: JJ & Jacob Kimmel

W373: Zacharias Bard, yeoman, & his wife Catharine of Lampeter tp. mort.to Bernhard Hubley, yeoman, of Lancaster Borough

120a Lampeter tp.: HISTORY: Same tract that George Bard granted 27 May 1762 to Zacharias Bard (Ref. Deed N535).

7 Jan 1786: PG & _______ [obscured]

--Bernhard Hubley ack.sat. 19 Jan 1789.

W375: Archibald McDowell, yeoman, of Bart tp. mort.to Samuel McDowell of same

150a Bart tp.: HISTORY: Not given.

--10 Nov 1785: James Miller & Samuel Wilson

--Samuel McDowell ack.sat. 21 Apr 1786.

W376: John David Frank assigns the "within mortgage" over to James Jacks of Lancaster Borough [no further information].

28 Jan 1786: Jacob Stall & PG

W377: George Lesh (or Lash) appoints Christopher Demuth, tobacconist, of Lancaster Borough as his lawful attorney to ack.sat. for the following mortgage: Stephen Curtz & his wife Feronica mortgaged 110 ½ a. Heidelberg tp. to said George Lesh (Ref. Deed N173).

8 Dec 1785: John Lash & David Wineland

--On 16 Dec 1785, said John Lash affirmed his signature as a witness before the Northampton County Court of Common Pleas.

W377: John Booth of Lancaster Borough mort.to Moses Edwards of Leacock tp.

--Lot #390 on Mulberry St. in Lancaster Borough: HISTORY: Same lot that said Moses Edwards & his wife Sarah granted on equal date herewith to John Booth.

13 Aug 1785: CS & CS Jr.

W379: Henry Hasslebach, yeoman, of Lancaster Borough mort.to Moses Edwards of Leacock tp.

--Lot #391 on Mulberry St. in Lancaster Borough: HISTORY: Same lot that John Booth granted 13 Aug 1785 to Henry Hasslebach.

13 Aug 1785: CS & CS Jr.

W380: Michael Shank, Nicholas Becker [or Pecker], & Abraham Hare, all of Lancaster County, appoint Jacob Stall, taylor, of Lancaster Borough as their lawful attorney to ack.sat. for the following mortgage: On 21 Oct 1768 [date hard to read], Christian Kauffman & his wife Rachel mortgaged 170 ½ a. Manor tp. to the said Shank, Becker, & Hare (Ref. Deed O43).

1 Feb 1786: John Burg & Henrich Funck

W381: John Fowler & his wife Salome of Lampeter tp. mort.to James Gibbons, scrivener, of the Borough of Wilmington in Delaware

403a in Lampeter tp. & Leacock tp.: HISTORY: Same tract that said James Gibbons & his wife granted on the first day of the fourth month last to John Fowler.

6 Aug 1785: JMR & PH

W383: John Schaffer & George Schaffer, merchants, both of Philadelphia mort.to Charles de Grafey, merchant, of same

191a Bart tp.: HISTORY: Same tract that Charles Drum & his wife Elizabeth granted 10 Sep last to John Schaffer & George Schaffer.

2 Jan 1786: ESH & Thomas Ross

W385: John Kendig, yeoman, & his wife Anne of Conestoga tp. mort.to Henry Witmer & Benjamin Witmer (or Whitmer), yeomen, both of Lampeter tp.

160a Conestoga tp.: HISTORY: Martin Kendig died intestate seized in possession of 160a Conestoga tp. On 1 May 1785, his eldest son John [the party hereto] petitioned the Orphans Court, offering to hold the property and pay the other heirs [a widow and three minor children] their legal share. The said court subsequently confirmed the property to him. The said Henry Witmer & Benjamin Witmer are John Kendig's sureties—this indenture serves to indemnify them from the debts owed to the other heirs.

2 Sep 1785: David Witmer & Henrich Witmer

--Henry Witmer & Benjamin Witmer ack.sat. 3 Apr 1810.

W388: Robert Strettle Jones assigns to Adam Musser (or Mocer), tanner, of Cocalico tp. the "within mortgage" [no further information, but a notation in the margin refers to Deed T188].

19 Jan 1786: Sarah Johnston & Nicholas Wilt [who is further identified as Nicholas Wilt, cordwainer, of Cocalico tp.]

W389: George Cummins (or Commins), yeoman, & his wife Susanna of Manheim tp. mort.to Christian Bamberger of same

6a, 29p Manheim tp.: HISTORY: Not given.

--10 Feb 1786: CS & CS Jr.

--Christian Bamberger ack.sat. 10 Feb 1791.

W390: Peter Kurtz, yeoman, & his wife Mary of Earl tp. mort.to Christian Kurtz of Caernarvon tp. & Jacob Kurtz of Cumru tp., Berks County [the executors of Abraham Kurtz, yeoman, late of Earl tp.]

--Two tracts: (1.) 180a Earl tp. and (2.) 53a, 57p Salisbury tp.: HISTORY: Same tracts that Abraham Kurtz deceased, by his last will & testament, devised to his son Peter Kurtz (party hereto). On equal date herewith, the said executors made a deed good for the same.

1 Mar 1786: IK & PG

--Christian Kurtz ack.sat. 11 Mar 1799.

--Jacob Kurtz ack.sat. 22 Apr 1799.

W395: William Davis, fuller, of Manheim tp. mort.to Daniel Rudy, Jr., yeoman, of same

50a Manheim tp.: HISTORY: Same tract that John Davis granted 18 Feb 1751 to William Davis.

--9 Mar 1786: CS & CS Jr.

--Daniel Rudy ack.sat. 10 Aug 1790.

W397: Christophel Ort (or Ord), yeoman, & his wife Margaret of Conestoga tp. mort.to Jacob Boyer & John Bare, both of Lancaster County [the executors of Samuel Boyer]

97a on the Pequea Creek: HISTORY: Same tract that the said executors granted 2 Mar 1786 to Christophel Ort.

2 Mar 1786: JJACK & James Webb

--Jacob Boyer & John Bare ack.sat. 23 Aug 1790.

W399: Jacob Getz, Jr., & his wife Barbara [but signed Catharine] of Hempfield tp. mort.to Jacob Getz, yeoman, of same

178 ¾ a. Hempfield tp.: HISTORY: Not given.

--29 Oct 1785: CS & CS Jr.

--John Getz, one of the executors of Jacob Getz, ack.sat. 14 Nov 1804.

W402: John Frederick, yeoman, & his wife Juliana of Rapho tp. mort.to Abraham Frederick, yeoman, of Warwick tp.

113a, 7p Rapho tp.: HISTORY: Not given.

--29 Mar 1786: John Shaffner & CS Jr.

--Satisfaction acknowledged 11 May 1803, but the film is too dark to read the signer—see the following indenture for a possible clue.

W404: Peter Frederick, yeoman, & his wife Eve of Rapho tp. mort.to Abraham Frederick, yeoman, of Warwick tp.

55 ½ a. Rapho tp.: HISTORY: Not given.

--29 Mar 1786: John Shaffner & CS Jr.

--Philip Frederick & John Ricksecker, the executors of Abraham Frederick, ack.sat. 30 Mar 1799.

W406: William McCausland, yeoman, of Leacock tp. mort.to James Crawford, merchant, of Philadelphia

--Sundry items and one Negro named Dina.

31 Mar 1786: James Mercer & Samuel Turbett

W407: John Geib, yeoman, & his wife Feronica of Warwick tp. mort.to Daniel Longenecker, yeoman, of Rapho tp.

--Two tracts: (1.) 178 ½ a. Warwick tp. and (2.) 35a Warwick tp.: HISTORY: Same tracts that George Meyer & his wife Ann of Warwick tp. granted on equal date herewith to John Geib.

29 Apr 1786: CS & CS Jr.

--Daniel Longenecker ack.sat. 1 Feb 1798.

W410: Abraham Gisch of Donegal tp. mort.to John Mease, merchant, of Philadelphia

--Two tracts: (1.) 428a Donegal tp. and (2.) 137a Donegal tp., called Mease's Addition: HISTORY: Not given.

17 Nov 1785: CS & CS Jr.

--Satisfaction acknowledged, but the names and date are obscured on the microfilmed record. Clear reference is made to an assignment recorded in Book HH on page 19.

W412: John Churchman of Susquehanna Hundred in Cecil County, Maryland, mort.to John Field & Richard Adams, merchants, of Philadelphia

--Four properties:

1. 170a Little Britain tp.: HISTORY: Same tract pat. 8 Mar instant to John Churchman [Ref. PB #6, page 96].
2. 321a Little Britain tp.: HISTORY: Same tract pat. 8 Mar instant to John Churchman [Ref. PB #6, page 97].
3. 400a partly in West Nottingham tp., Chester County and partly in Cecil County, Maryland: HISTORY: Same tract that John Dixon & his wife Agnes granted 19 Apr 1781 to John Churchman.
4. 260a West Nottingham tp., Chester County: HISTORY: Same tract that Robert Marquis & his wife Hannah granted 12 Mar 1781 to John Churchman.

--18 Mar 1786: William Hillwells & John Hallawill

W414: Philipp Lenherr, yeoman, of Warwick tp. mort.to Christian Stouffer, miller, of same

113a, 156p Warwick tp.: HISTORY: Same tract that Christian Lambach granted 4 Apr 1785 to Philipp Lenherr (Ref. Deed CC-573).

3 May 1786: John Cunkle & PG
--Christian Stouffer ack.sat. 26 May 1790.

W415: James Johnston of Salisbury tp. [the son of Samuel Johnston, deceased, late of same] mort.to John Hopkins of same

168a Salisbury tp.: HISTORY: By his last will & testament dated 30 Mar 1757, Thomas Johnston devised 168a Salisbury tp. to his son Samuel Johnston. By his last will & testament dated 15 Jan 1781, Samuel Johnston devised the same to his son Samuel Johnston, Jr., with the condition that if his said son Samuel died without issue, then the property was to descend to James Johnston, son of Samuel Johnston, the elder. On 12 Sep 1783, Samuel Johnston, the younger, died without issue.

8 Feb 1786: George Thompson & William Boyd

W417: Andrew Moore, weaver, & his wife Rebecca of Conestoga tp. mort.to James Moore of Sadsbury tp.
--Two adjoining tracts: (1.) 57a, 60p Sadsbury tp. and (2.) 5a Sadsbury tp.: HISTORY: Not given.
_____ (obscured) 1786: JJH & WH
--By a Power of Attorney (Ref. Deed F-3-246), Will Webb ack.sat. 19 Aug 1800.

W420: Jacob Brubaker, distiller, & his wife Christina of Lancaster Borough mort.to Henry Gross, innkeeper, of same
--Lot on Water St. in Lancaster Borough: HISTORY: Not given.
16 May 1786: CS & CS Jr.
--Henry Gross ack.sat. 12 Dec ____ [obscured]

W421: Jacob Huber, yeoman, of Manheim tp. mort.to Abraham Leib, yeoman, of same

82 ½ a. Manheim tp. (excepting six acres that Frederick Kissel & his wife Fronica granted 3 Aug 1768 to Michael Bender): HISTORY: Part of a larger tract patented to Nicholas Kissel. Said Nicholas Kissel & his wife Barbara granted 82 ½ a. to Frederick Kissel. Said Frederick Kissel & his wife Fronica granted the same [excepting the aforesaid parcel] to Jacob Huber.

20 May 1786: JJACK & Christian Blickensderffer

W423: Peter Beck, yeoman, of Earl tp. mort.to John Nees, George Swickert, & Mary Harlacher [the executors of Benjamin Harlacher, late of same]

--Two tracts: (1.) 113a Earl tp. and (2.) 139a Earl tp. [excepting one acre previously granted to Christian Gunkle]: HISTORY: Not given.

____ [obscured] Apr 1786: Daniel Braft (?) & AN
--George Swickert ack.sat. 12 Mar (or May?) 1803

W425: Henry Hubley, yeoman, of Rapho tp. mort.to Jacob Beidler, yeoman, of the State of Virginia

166a Rapho tp.: HISTORY: Part of 366a (or 306?) pat. 9 Apr 1760 to Christian Beidler. By his last will & testament, Christian Beidler devised 166a to his son Jacob (party hereto). On 10 June 1785, Jacob Beidler & his wife Barbara granted the same to Henry Hubley.

9 June 1786: JJACK & Michael Reinhart

--Satisfaction acknowledged, but the microfilmed record is too dark to read. The date *appears* to be 16 Apr 1827.

W426: Samuel Miles & William Wister, merchants, both of Philadelphia appoint Jacob Hubley, Esq., as their lawful attorney to ack.sat. for a mortgage given to them by Philip Marsteller, yeoman, of Lebanon on 2 Jul 1784 (Ref. Deed W244). Philip Marsteller has since sold the lot to Samuel Moore, merchant, of Lebanon.. [Note: Philip Marsteller stills owes them money; however, the property is formerly released to Samuel Moore.]

____ May 1786: Daniel Wister & Philip Zeller

W428: Catharine Wister of Philadelphia appoints Josiah Haines, merchant, of same as her lawful attorney to ack.sat. for a mortgage given to her on 6 May 1776 by Philip Sheffer & his wife Elizabeth for 140a Earl tp.

22 May 1786: Casper Wister & B. Wister

W428: Roger Hartly, yeoman, of Martic tp. mort.to James Hartly, merchant, of Philadelphia
160 ¼ a. Martic tp.: HISTORY: Same tract purchased from Patrick Campbell. Said Robert Hartly procured a patent on 27 May 1786.
20 June 1786: Joseph Ash & Patrick Campbell
--By a Power of Attorney (Ref. Deed O-3-299), Benjamin Hartly ack.sat. 26 Mar 1805.

W430: John Roesler, hosier, of Lancaster Borough mort.to Jonas Metzger
--Two stocking weaver looms & frames.
13 May 1786: John Grossel & Anthony Seyfert

W431: John Armor, yeoman, & his wife Susanna of Salisbury tp. mort.to Richard Dutton, yeoman, of Upper Chichester tp., Chester County
187a Salisbury tp.: HISTORY: Not given.
--22 Mar 1786: John Willson & William Boyd

W432: William McCausland, yeoman, of Leacock tp. mort.to James Crawford, merchant, of Philadelphia
54 ¾ a., 20p Leacock tp.: HISTORY: Not given.
--5 Apr 1786: DW & James Moore

W434: Henry Wolf, yeoman & shoemaker, of Brecknock tp. mort.to Catharine Petre, widow, of Cocalico tp.
150a Brecknock tp.: HISTORY: Same tract apparently taken up by one Jacob ____ler [obscured], who granted the same to Charles Cochran, who had the tract surveyed. On 21 ______ [obscured], Adam Petry granted the same to Henry Wolf. [Incomplete history]
11 Apr ___ [obscured]: John Shaffner & CS
--Philip Jacob Messner [the executor of Catharine Petre] ack.sat. 28 Feb 1793.

W435: John Detweiler, yeoman, & his wife Eve of Conestoga tp. mort.to James Reed & Samuel Reed of Drumore tp.
200a Drumore tp.: HISTORY: Same tract that said James Reed & Samuel Reed granted 3 Aug 1786 to John Detweiler.
5 Aug 1786: JJACK & John Hoober
--By a Power of Attorney given by said James Reed & Samuel Reed [the latter the administrator of Samuel Reed, deceased], Joseph Read ack.sat. 9 Jan 1793.

W438: Philip Eberman, yeoman, of Lancaster Borough mort.to Peter Denig, yeoman, of same
--Lot on King St. in Lancaster Borough: HISTORY: Same lot that said Peter Denig & his wife Elizabeth granted on equal date herewith to Philip Eberman.
5 Aug 1786: John Eberman & Peter Bugh
--By a Power of Attorney (Ref. Deed OO-7), Philip Gloninger ack.sat. 17 Oct 1791.

W440: Christian Stoner of Manor tp. mort.to Jacob Maynard & Henry Shop, both of same
244a Manor tp.: HISTORY: All three men are bound to the following [however, it is the only proper debt of said Christian Stoner: (1.) Daniel Musser & his wife Catharine; (2.) Henry Brenneman, the guardian of Frederick Stoner; (3.) Jacob Maynard, the guardian of Anna Stoner; (4.) Christian Herr, the guardian of John Stoner; (5.) Michael Shenck, the guardian of Veronica Stoner; and (6.) Henry Shop, the guardian of Jacob Stoner, Henry Stoner, Abraham Stoner, Isaac Stoner, & Joseph Stoner. The said Catharine (wife of Daniel Musser), Frederick, Anna, John, Veronica, Jacob, Henry, Abraham, Isaac, & Joseph are the children of Christian Stoner, deceased, late of Manor tp., yeoman. Reference is made to Orphans Court proceedings dated 2 Mar 1785. [Note: It appears that Christian Stoner, party hereto, is the eldest son to whom his father's real estate was confirmed.]
12 Aug 1786: Christian Herr & JH

W443: William Allison & Samuel Caldwell, merchants, both of Philadelphia [the executors of David Caldwell, merchant, late of same] appoint John W. Kittera, Esq., of Lancaster Borough, as their lawful attorney to ack.sat. for a mortgage dated 4 May 1768, given to the said executors by James Old, yeoman, & his wife Margaret, concerning 771a Warwick tp. (Ref. Deed H380).

20 Jul 1786: Margaret Caldwell & Andrew Doz

W444: Christian Mellinger, yeoman, of Manor tp. mort.to John Musser, gentleman, of Lancaster Borough

116a, 66p Manor tp.: HISTORY: Not given.

--4 Mar 1786: WH & CS

--John Musser ack.sat. 15 Aug 1791.

W445: John Salter, merchant & biscuit maker, of Philadelphia appoints John Hubley as his lawful attorney to ack.sat. for a mortgage dated 17 Oct 1774, given to him by Peter Weiland, concerning 265a Manheim tp. (Ref. Deed O621). [Court of Common Pleas proceedings dated 5 Apr 1782 are also referenced.]

18 Aug 1786: Peter Thompson & Peter Thompson, Jr.

W446: Philip Hottenstein & Henry Hottenstein, yeoman, both of Hempfield tp. mort.to (1.) John Fisher, yeoman, of Hempfield tp.; (2.) Barbara Hottenstein, widow, of same [the guardian of Margaret Hottenstein, a daughter of Jacob Hottenstein, deceased]; and (3.) Jacob Voneada [the guardian of Jacob Hottenstein & John Hottenstein, two children of said Jacob Hottenstein, deceased]

--Two adjoining tracts: (1.) 74a, 45p Hempfield tp., now in the possession of said Philip Hottenstein, and (2.) 77a, 126p Hempfield tp., now in the possession of said Henry Hottenstein: HISTORY: Not given. However, each must separately pay the aforementioned mortgagees a particular sum. [Note: While not stated as such, it appears that the mortgagers have acquired parcels of their late father's real estate and are required to pay the other heirs their equal share.]

5 Sep 1786: John Gloninger & Casper Fordney

--John Fisher, Barbara Hottenstein, & Jacob Voneada ack.sat. 6 Nov 1802.

W456: Nicholas Yount, yeoman, of Earl tp. mort.to John Yount, yeoman, of same

3a, 3p Earl tp.: HISTORY: Not given.

--26 Aug 1786: John Luther & Michael Hober

W458: James Gibbons, scrivener, of the Borough of Wilmington in New Castle County, Delaware, appoints Michael Wither of Strasburg tp. as his lawful attorney to recover debts owed to him by John Fowler, who has defaulted on a mortgage dated 1 Feb last and also a previous mortgage, concerning a plantation, merchant mill, and 170 acres of meadow ground. [No further information.]

13 6mo. 1786: Jane Kirk & Hannah Commons

--Added notation: This Power of Attorney has been revoked (Ref. Deed HH-64).

W458: Jacob Smith, yeoman, of Cocalico tp. mort.to Daniel Levan, yeoman, of Oley tp., Berks County

150a Cocalico tp.: HISTORY: Same tract that Jacob Hershy & his wife Catharine granted 16 May last to Jacob Smith.

30 June 1786: John Christ & Henry Christ

--By a Power of Attorney (Ref. Book 33, page 144), Marcus Montelius ack.sat. 19 May 1797.

W460: George Ferdig (or Fertieth), yeoman, & his wife Magdalena of Warwick tp. mort.to Peter Huber & John Grosh [the executors of Christopher Frey, late of Warwick tp.]

104a Warwick tp.: HISTORY: Not given.

--22 Sep 1786: Christian Blickensderfer & Christian Reist

W462: Jacob Young, yeoman, & his wife Elizabeth of Warwick tp. mort.to Peter Godshall, yeoman, of Hempfield tp.

92a Warwick tp.: HISTORY: Not given. Both parties are bound to Joseph Long of Rapho tp.; however, it is the only proper debt of Jacob Young.

19 Oct 1786: Peter Schoenberger & MH
--Jacob Kaufman & Martin Pyfer [the executors of Peter Godshall] ack.sat. 31 Dec 1792.

W464: James Pratt, yeoman, of Manor tp. mort.to John Musser of Lancaster Borough
414 ¾ a. Manor tp. [called the Indian Town tract]: HISTORY: Same tract that said John Musser & his wife Sarah granted 24 Apr 1786 to James Pratt.
24 Apr 1786: Maria Ross & CS
--By a Power of Attorney (Ref. Deed OO-459), Johannes Schmit [?-hard to read] ack.sat. 28 May 1794.

W466: Benedict Eshleman ack.sat. for the following two mortgages given to Christian Herr and him by John Brackbill, the executor of Abraham Borkotter [no further information].
31 May 1777: Christian Burkholder

W466: John Huber, miller, of Hempfield tp. mort.to John Salter, gentleman, of Philadelphia
--Two tracts: (1.) 87a Manheim tp. and (2.) 16 ¾ a. Manheim tp.: HISTORY: Same two tracts that John Hoober & his wife Susanna granted 9 Jan 1779 to John Huber (Ref. Deed R618).
28 Oct 1786: JJACK & JH
--By a Power of Attorney (Ref. Deed HH-178), Joseph Hubley ack.sat. 19 Jan 1789.

W468: Christian Musselman & his wife Magdalena of Manor tp. mort.to Andrew Bausman, yeoman, of Lancaster tp.
76a, 15p Manor tp.: HISTORY: Same tract that said Andrew Bausman & his wife Elizabeth granted on equal date herewith to Christian Musselman.
19 May 1786: CS & CS Jr.
--John Reitzel [executor of Andrew Bausman] ack.sat. 6 Jan 1816.

W470: Frederick Druckenmiller, potter, of Rapho tp. mort.to Peter Eby of Warwick tp.
--Sundry items.
25 Jul 1786: John Becker & Philip Becker

W471: John Robinson & his wife Margaret of Drumore tp. mort.to James Morrison, Jr., of same
126a Drumore tp.: HISTORY: Not given; however, both are bound to George Hess of Martic tp. [but it is the only proper debt of John Robinson].
25 Jul 1786: Agnes Irwin, Rosanna Irwin, & Moses Irwin

W473: Nicholas Yunt, yeoman, of Earl tp. mort.to JohnYunt, yeoman, of same
--Two Tracts: (1.) 5a Earl tp. and (2.) 1a Earl tp. [excepting a one-third part reserved to a certain "Joseph"]: HISTORY: Same two tracts that Sebastian Bower & his wife Magdalena granted 30 May 1785 to Nicholas Yount.
4 Nov 1786: John Luther & Jo. Hetzel
--John Yunt ack.sat. 2 Nov 1791.

W474: David Miller, yeoman, of Hempfield tp. mort.to Henry Huttenstein, practitioner of physic, of Lancaster Borough
122a, 11p Hempfield tp.: HISTORY: Same tract that Christian Miller & his wife Barbara granted 24 May 1770 to David Miller (Ref. Deed N537).
13 Nov 1786: IK & PG
--Henry Huttenstein ack.sat. 28 Nov 1794.

W476: Benjamin Bender of Rapho tp. mort.to Stephen Wenger of same
--Sundry items.
28 June 1786: Elizabeth Hubley & MH

W477: Michael Koehler (or Kochler?), joiner, of Manor tp. mort.to John Musser, yeoman, of Lancaster Borough

5a Manor tp.: HISTORY: Same tract that said John Musser & his wife Sarah granted 28 June 1786 to Michael Koehler.

28 June 1786: Joseph Shippen, Jr., & Conrad Raever

W478: John Craemer, yeoman, of Lampeter tp. mort.to Joseph Bowman, yeoman, of same

--Lot #13 in Haines Town in Lampeter tp., containing 4a: HISTORY: Not given.

10 Oct 1786: Philip Diefenderfer & EG

--Joseph Bowman ack.sat. 5 Mar 1791.

W480: Isaac Ferree, yeoman, of Strasburg tp. mort.to (1.) Susanna Ferree [the widow of Isaac Ferree, deceased, late of same]; (2.) Benjamin Bowman & his wife Elizabeth, Isaac Ferree & his wife Mary, Thomas Ferree, Joel Ferree, and Mathias Slaymaker & his wife Susanna [the said Elizabeth, Mary, Thomas, Joel, & Susanna being children of the said Isaac Ferree, deceased] and (3.) John Carpenter & Isaac Ferree, the guardians of Elisha Ferree, John Ferree, Ephraim Ferree, Lydia Ferree, Catharine Ferree, Sarah Ferree, & Rebecca Ferree [the minor children of said Isaac Ferree, deceased]

--Two tracts: (1.) 150a Strasburg tp. and (2.) 154a Bart tp.: HISTORY: Not given.

20 Jul 1786: John Ferree & EG

--Isaac Ferree, one of the mortgagees, ack.sat. 8 Apr 1817.

W483: Elizabeth Klick, widow, of Warwick tp. appoints John Bower, yeoman, of same as her lawful attorney to ack.sat. for a mortgage dated 7 Feb 1785, given to her by Christian Lambach, yeoman, of Warwick tp., concerning 64a Warwick tp. (Ref. Deed W276).

23 Dec 1786: Elizabeth Bower & Lorentz Dietrich

W485: Charles Philips, yeoman, of the Village of Strasburg mort.to Jacob Eshleman, yeoman, of same

1a, 65r lot in the Village of Strasburg: HISTORY: Not given.

--1 Jan 1787: EG & Conrad Schaffer

--Jacob Eshleman ack.sat. 21 Jul 1791.

W487: Charles Boyd assigns to Andrew Bausman, distiller, of Lancaster tp. the "within mortgage" for a lot on Orange St. given by Nathaniel Hauntch.

27 Jan 1787: JJACK & PG

W488: John Thomas, yeoman, & his wife Eva of Warwick tp. mort.to Andrew Hoog, Sr., of same

150a Warwick tp.: HISTORY: Not given.

--___ Jan 1787: MH & Andras Zok(?)

W489: John Musser, yeoman, of Lancaster Borough mort.to James Jacks, Esq., of same

--One moiety of 144a Lancaster tp.: HISTORY: 144a Lancaster tp. patented to John Musser (Ref. PB A-8-314). After his death, the tract descended to his sons Henry Musser & Peter Musser as tenants in common. The moiety of said Peter Musser has come into the possession of his [Peter's] son John Musser (the party hereto).

1 Nov 1786: Andrew Weaver & Adam Weber

--James Jacks ack.sat. 3 Dec 1788

W491: John Gibbony, yeoman, of Lampeter tp. mort.to Samuel Boyd & Alexander Kinkead [the executors of James Davis, late of Lancaster Borough

92 ½ a. Lampeter tp. [excepting nine acres previously sold by the said James Davis, deceased]: HISTORY: Not given.

6 Feb 1787: CS & CS Jr.

W493: John Zeller & George Zeller, yeomen, both of Tulpehocken tp., Berks County, appoint Jacob Swoope of Lebanon tp., Dauphin County, as their lawful attorney to ack.sat. for a mortgage date 19 Oct 1762, given to them by Daniel Herbster & Godfried Stemple, then both of Lebanon tp. (Ref. Deed H86).
27 Sep 1786: Peter Spycker, Jr., & John Spycker

W493: Charles Boyd, cooper, & his wife Sarah of Lancaster Borough mort.to John Jefferies of Hempfield tp.
--Lot on Orange St. in Lancaster Borough & also sundry items: HISTORY: Not given.
____ 1787: JJACK & PG
--John Jefferies ack.sat. 30 Nov 1787.

W496: Samuel Walker of Drumore tp. mort.to Dunkin Keynon of Colerain tp.
96a Colerain tp.: HISTORY: Purchased from John Forsyth. Said Dunkin Keynon now resides on the property. [Note: I find the history a bit vague—not clear which party purchased the property from John Forsyth. Furthermore, both parties signed this indenture—normally only the mortgagee signs the document.]
23 Sep 1786: William Miller & William Martin

W497: Henry Keppele, merchant, of Philadelphia appoints Adam Reigart of Lancaster Borough as his lawful attorney to ack.sat. for a mortgage dated 16 June 1777, given to him by John George Urey, yeoman, of Cocalico tp., concerning 200a Cocalico tp. (Ref. Deed T300).
7 Mar 1787: Richard Wister & Benjamin Brooke

W498: Jacob Frey, yeoman, & his wife Catharine of Brecknock tp. mort.to Adam Texter of Cumru tp., Berks County
198a Brecknock tp.: HISTORY: Not given.
--2 Feb 1787: Adam Brua & AN
--Adam Texter ack.sat. ___ Oct 1793.

W500: Matthew Henderson, miller, & his wife Rachel of Salisbury tp. mort.to James Clemson, Thomas Douglass, & John Anderson, all of Salisbury tp. [the trustees of the Protestant Episcopal Church of St. John's on Pequea]
--Three tracts: (1.) 4 ¼ a., 35p Salisbury tp., (2.) 3 ¼ a., 15p Salisbury tp., and (3.) 113 ½ a. Salisbury tp.

1. HISTORY: Same tract that John Douglass & his wife Rebecca granted 6 May 1765 to Matthew Henderson.
2. HISTORY: Same tract that John Douglass & his wife Rebecca granted 6 May 1765 to Matthew Henderson.
3. HISTORY: Same tract that the said trustees granted on equal date herewith to the said Matthew Henderson.

--3 Feb 1787: James Armor & James Henderson
--John Anderson, the surviving trustee, ack.sat. 19 June 1800.

W501: David Longenecker, yeoman, of Lampeter tp. mort.to Peter Miller, John Longenecker, Elizabeth Longenecker, Mary Longenecker, & Benjamin Longenecker, all of Lancaster County
75a Lampeter tp.: HISTORY: Not given.
--27 Mar 1787: EG & PH
--Side notation: For petition and decree dated 12 June 1939, see Mortgage Book 426, page 88.

W503: Valentine Rummel, Peter Rummel, & Joseph Hinkle, yeomen, of Manor tp., mort.to John Musser, gentleman, of Lancaster Borough
45a Manor tp.: HISTORY: Same tract that said John Musser & his wife Sarah granted 7 Feb 1787 to Valentine Rummel, Peter Rummel, & Joseph Hinkle.
7 Feb 1787: Fanny Musser & James Webb
--John Musser ack.sat. 3 Mar 1793.

W505: John Eshleman, yeoman, of Manor tp. mort.to John Musser, gentleman, of Lancaster Borough
14a, 15p Manor tp.: HISTORY: Same tract that said John Musser & his wife Sarah granted 8 Feb 1787 to John Eshleman.
8 Feb 1787: Fanny Musser & James Webb
--John Musser ack.sat. 13 Feb 1792.

W506: John Longenecker, yeoman, of Lampeter tp. mort.to Peter Miller, David Longenecker, Elizabeth Longenecker, Mary Longenecker, & Benjamin Longenecker, all of Lancaster County
--75a Lampeter tp.: HISTORY: Not given.
10 Apr 1787: CS & CS Jr.
--Side notation: For petition and decree dated 12 June 1939, see Mortgage Book 426, page 91.

W509: Conrad Shitz, yeoman, of Lampeter tp. mort.to Frederick Dorsh, yeoman, of Lancaster Borough
--Sundry items.
13 Apr 1787: George Hoff & Jacob Krug

W509: John Unger, yeoman, of Warwick tp. mort.to Joseph Gingrich, Esq., of same
133 ½ a. Warwick tp. [being the total of two adjoining tracts]: HISTORY: Same tract that Christian Hershey, late of Warwick tp., died seized in possession thereof. On 15 Mar last, his executors, Jacob Hershey & Isaac Hernly, granted the same to John Unger. [Note: Both parties above are bound to the said executors; however, it is the only proper debt of said John Unger.]
30 Apr 1787: JJACK & PG
--Joseph Gingrich ack.sat. 8 Aug 1796.

W512: Philip Kessler, yeoman, of the Village of Strasburg mort.to Frederick Weiss, yeoman, of same
--1a in the Village of Strasburg: HISTORY: Not given.
2 Apr 1787: Paul Trout & EG
--Susanna Weiss & Adam Draugher [the executors of Frederick Weiss] ack.sat. 28 Aug 1798.

W513: Jacob Krug, tanner, & his wife Rebecca of Lancaster Borough mort.to William Branson Hockley, gentleman, of Philadelphia
--Two tracts: (1.) 215a Hempfield tp. and (2.) 61 ½ a. Manor tp.: HISTORY: Late the estate of James Patton. Seized by the sheriff due to unpaid debts and granted 26 Mar 1787 to Jacob Krug.
14 May 1787: CS & J. Reiger
--By a Power of Attorney [place of recording unreadable], Isaac Kagey ack.sat. 14 June 1787 (?—date hard to read).

W515: John Zuck, yeoman, of Brecknock tp. mort.to Daniel Hahn, yeoman, of Earl tp.
47a, 71p Brecknock & Earl tps.: HISTORY: Not given.
--19 May 1787: John Mohler & Mary Binkle (or Brindle?—hard to read)
--Daniel Hahn ack.sat. 14 Apr 1802.

W517: Jacob Krug, tanner, & his wife Rebecca of Lancaster Borough mort.to William Branson Hockley, gentleman, of Philadelphia
--Two tracts: (1.) 215a Hempfield tp. and (2.) 61 ½ a. Manor tp.: HISTORY: Late the estate of James Patton. Seized by the sheriff due to unpaid debts and granted 26 Mar 1787 to Jacob Krug.
14 May 1787: CS & J. Reiger
--By a Power of Attorney [Ref. Deed OO-___], Casper Shaffner ack.sat. 30 May 1793.

W518: Henry Pletcher, yeoman, of Martic tp. mort.to Christian Eightenach, taylor, of Strasburg tp.
--48 ¼ a. Martic tp.: HISTORY: Not given.
14 May 1787: Johannes Schaffer & EG
--Christian Eightenach ack.sat. 18 Sep 1790.

W520: Christian Hostetter, yeoman, of Warwick tp. mort.to John Reist, yeoman, of same

--Two tracts: (1.) 194a Warwick tp. and (2.) 6a, 60p Warwick tp.: HISTORY: Same tracts that Abraham Hostetter & his wife Catharine granted 28 Apr last to Christian Hostetter.

31 May 1787: PG & IK

--John Reist ack.sat. 25 Jul 1794.

W522: David Morgan, yeoman, of Earl tp. mort.to Moses Brinton, yeoman, of Leacock tp.

284 ½ a. Earl tp.: HISTORY: Same tract that Sarah Keimer, Thomas May, Thomas Keimer, & James Keimer [the executors of James Keimer] granted 14 Apr 1785 to David Morgan.

4 June 1787: JJACK & Michael Lind

W523: James Farquher, yeoman, of Drumore tp. mort.to Margaret Farquher of same [the widow of Hugh Farquher]

100a Drumore tp.: HISTORY: Not given.

--Robert Miller & Joseph Ward

W525: William Branson Hockley, gentleman, of Philadelphia appoints Isaac Kagey as his lawful attorney to ack.sat. for the following two mortgages: On 16 Feb 1776, James Patton, yeoman, late of Hempfield tp., mortgaged 215a Hempfield tp. and 61 ½ a. Manor tp. (Ref. Deed T91). Said James Patton defaulted and the county sheriff seized the property. On 25 Mar last, the sheriff sold the same to Jacob Krug, tanner, of Lancaster Borough. Said Jacob Krug took out two additional mortgaged on the property (Ref. Deeds W513 and W517). William Branson Hockley know acknowledges that all mortgages, save for the last one (W517), have been satisfied.

31 May 1787: Abraham Singer & John Singer

W527: Henry Wittmer & Benjamin Wittmer, yeomen, both of Lampeter tp., acknowledge having received satisfaction from John Kendig, yeoman, for a mortgage dated 2 Sep 1785 (Ref. Deed W385).

6 June 1787: Solomon Etting & Andrew Lee

W529: Jacob Ratfang, yeoman, & his wife Elizabeth of Lampeter tp. mort.to Daniel Kibortz (or Kinportz), yeoman, of Conestoga tp.

66a Lampeter tp.: HISTORY: Not given; however, both parties are bound to Mathias Slough, merchant, of Lancaster, but it is the only proper debt of Jacob Ratfang.

16 June 1787: CS & CS Jr.

--Daniel Kinports (or Keenbort) Jr. & Michael Greider [the administrators of Daniel Kibortz] ack.sat. 8 Mar 1802.

W531: Melchior Laudermilch, miller, of Earl tp. mort.to James Crawford of Lampeter tp.

150a Earl tp.: HISTORY: Same tract that James Crawford & his wife Ann granted to said Melchior Laudermilch.

22 June 1787: JJACK & James Webb

--By a Power of Attorney (Ref. Deed HH-145), J. Hubley ack.sat. 30 Aug 1788.

W533: Martin Carpenter, yeoman, of Lampeter tp. mort.to John Hare, Sr., & John Carpenter, both of Strasburg tp. [the executors of Jacob Carpenter, yeoman, late of Lancaster County, the father of the said Martin Carpenter]

--Two undivided third parts of three plantations [no description]: HISTORY: By his last will & testament dated 2 Dec 1773, Jacob Carpenter devised his three plantations to his sons Henry Carpenter, Martin Carpenter, & Jacob Carpenter. On 17 Jan 1786, Henry Carpenter granted his undivided third part to said Martin Carpenter. [Subject to a mortgage dated 1 Nov 1783 (Ref. Deed EE-407)].

14 Feb 1787: John Funck & EG

--John Carpenter ack.sat. 6 Aug 1788.

W535: Jacob Strickler, Jr., of Hallam tp., York County, mort.to Joseph Sherck, Jr., yeoman, of Hempfield tp.
--40a Hempfield tp.: HISTORY: Not given.
30 June 1787: CS & CS Jr.
--By a Power of Attorney (Ref. Deed HH-524), ______ [unreadable] ack.sat. 17 May 1791.

W536: John Cromwell, yeoman, of Conestoga tp. mort.to Conrad Haas (or Hass), merchant, of Lancaster Borough
--5a Conestoga tp.: HISTORY: Not given.
6 Jul 1787: Samuel Myers & CS
--[Reference is made to an assignment recorded in Book HH-75 to Philip Wager & George Habacker.]

W538: William Smith, doctor of divinity, of Newtown Chester in Maryland, appoints Stephen Chambers, Esq., of Lancaster Borough as his lawful attorney to recover debts owed to him by Martin Weaver & Francis Lerone (or Leroue?), late of Lancaster but now of Dauphin County [said William Smith had sold land to them].
24 May 1786: Thomas Smith & JY

W539: Jacob Wittmer, yeoman, & his wife Catharine of Manor tp. mort.to John Hopson, merchant, of Lancaster Borough
--150a Donegal tp.: HISTORY: Not given.
30 June 1787: CS & CS Jr.
--John Hopson ack.sat. 15 May 1792.

W540: George Bressler, innkeeper, of Lampeter tp. mort.to John Fromberger, merchant, of Philadelphia
--60a Lampeter tp.: HISTORY: Not given.
19 Jul 1787: JJACK & JH
--By a Power of Attorney (Ref. Deed HH-315), Joseph Hubley ack.sat. 2 Jan 1790.

W542: Martin Weybreght, yeoman, & his wife Elizabeth of Manheim tp. mort.to Andrew Foltz of Lancaster Borough & Abraham Heestand, house carpenter, of Cocalico tp.
60a Manheim tp.: HISTORY: Not given.
--20 Jul 1787: PG & IK
--Andrew Foltz & Abraham Heestand ack.sat. 12 May 1789.

W544: Zacharias Bart, yeoman, of Lampeter tp. mort.to Samuel Miles & William Wister, merchants, of Philadelphia
120a Lampeter tp.: HISTORY: Not given.
19 Jul 1787: MH & JH
--By a Power of Attorney (Ref. Deed HH-328), Jacob Greider ack.sat. 23 Feb 1790.

W546: John Fowler, yeoman, & his wife Salome of Lampeter tp. mort.to Michael Wither, yeoman, of Strasburg tp.
403a Lampeter tp., including a merchant mill: HISTORY: Same tract that James Gibbons & his wife Deborah granted 1 4mo. 17__ to John Fowler (Ref. Deed EE-153).
27 Mar 1787: Elizabeth Hains & George Withers

W548: John Neip, blacksmith, & his wife Anna Maria of Heidelberg tp. mort.to Henry Meyer & David Lebenstein, yeoman, both of same
--Lot #5 in the town of Heidelberg: HISTORY: Not given.
21 Feb 1789: George Tissinger & Henry Sheffer

W550: Joseph Gerber (or Gerver) of Salisbury tp. mort.to Jacob Shibley of Earl tp.
--Sundry items [Reference to grain in the ground on Curtz's plantation].

30 Jan 1789: Nathaniel Ellmaker & Elizabeth Ellmaker

W551: Andrew Hoog, Sr., assigns the "within mortgage" to his daughter Elizabeth.
7 Jul 1794: John Albert & Abraham Tucts(?)
--[Notation in the margin says to see page 488]

Abstracts of Lancaster County Deed Book X

X1: Ann Pinckle (or Pinckli), spinster, of Lampeter tp. gr.to her brother Felix Pinckle

--Her undivided share of 200a Lampeter tp.: HISTORY: Late the estate of her father John Pinckle.

16 June 1764: David Jenkins & GR

X2: Jacob Mayer of Manheim tp. & Martin Bare of Conestoga tp. [the surviving executors of John Bare, late of Conestoga tp.] enf-rel.to Abraham Miller, yeoman, of Conestoga tp.

100a Conestoga tp.: HISTORY: Part of 350a Conestoga tp. that Jeremiah Langhorn granted 16 Sep 1720 to Henry Paxson. By his last will & testament, Henry Paxson devised the property to his nephew James Kirkham. Said James Kirkham died intestate leaving issue five children, William Kirkham (his eldest son), James Kirkham, Rebecca Kirkham [now wife of Thomas Curtis], Mary Kirkham [now wife of Timothy Lane], and Sarah Kirkham. On 1 & 2 Jan 1738, James Kirkham & Sarah Kirkham granted their undivided sixth parts to Patrick Carrigan. On 23 & 24 May 1739, Timothy Lane granted his sixth part to said Patrick Carrigan. On 28 & 29 Jan 1741, Patrick Carrigan & his wife Susanna one sixth part to the said John Bare. On 1 & 2 Jan 1738, William Kirkham & his wife Mary and Thomas Curtis & his wife Rebecca granted one moiety (or three sixths part) to Thomas Lindee [or Lindey]. On _______ [date omitted], Thomas Lindee & his wife Hannah granted the same to said John Bare—giving him a four-sixths part of the 350a tract.

After a partition agreement, Patrick Carrigan & his wife Susanna granted 233 1/3 a. Conestoga tp. to said John Bare on 30 Jan 1741—it being his four-sixths right to the larger property. By his last will & testament, John Bare ordered his executors [to wit, Benedict Eshelman, Jacob Mayer, & Martin Bare] to sell a 100a parcel. // It is further noted that, at the time of John Bare's death, one Jacob Eshelman was entitled to a 77a parcel. On 13 May 1782, Jacob Eshelman & his wife Barbara granted their right to the same to the said executors.

13 May 1782: Samuel Mayer & CS

X5: Sheriff Joseph Work enf-rel.to James Hamilton of Salisbury tp.

200a Salisbury tp.: HISTORY: Same tract that Elizabeth Cookson granted 13 May 1753 to John Douglass (Ref. Deed L28). On 11 Aug 1781, the Court of Common Pleas ordered the sheriff to seized the real estate of the said John Douglass, yeoman, late of Lancaster County, for debts owed to one Gabriel Davis. The sheriff duly seized said 200a tract in Salisbury tp. from John Willson, the administrator of the said John Douglass, who had died intestate.

9 Mar 1782: PH & Matthew McAllister

X7: John Taylor, Godlip Hartman & his wife Mary, Elizabeth Taylor, Sarah Taylor, and William Taylor, all of Lancaster County [the children & heirs of John Taylor, yeoman, late of Strasburg tp.] quitclaim to Peter Taylor, yeoman, of Strasburg tp.

196 ½ a. Strasburg tp.: HISTORY: Part of two contiguous tracts: (1.) 173-¼ a. Strasburg tp. pat. 17 Mar 1760 to John Taylor [Ref. PB A-19-150], and (2.) 196a Strasburg tp. pat. 18 Mar 1760 to the said John Taylor in TRUST for both himself & the widow and heirs of Aaron Taylor—the father of the said Peter Taylor (the party hereto) [Ref. PB A-19-154]. // This indenture fulfills an agreement towards the settlement of the estate of Peter Snider, alias Peter Taylor—the father of the said Aaron Taylor. Aaron Taylor died leaving a widow named Eve and issue several children, including eldest son Peter Taylor [the party hereto]--all minors at the time of his death. By an agreement dated prior to 13 Apr 1753, John Taylor and the said widow Eve Taylor agreed to the following: (1.) John Taylor should hold the tract that he lived on and (2.) Eve Taylor should have a 12a parcel [part of the larger tract], and (3.) said Peter Taylor should hold 196 ½ a. when he comes of age as his father's due portion of the estate. This agreement went into effect; however, they never executed deeds for the same. John Taylor has since died intestate leaving issue the following children: John Taylor, Mary the wife of Godlieb Hartman, Elizabeth Taylor, Anna the wife of the said Peter Taylor, Sarah Taylor, & William Taylor [the parties hereto]. Now, by this indenture, the heirs of John Taylor release their claim to the property allotted to Peter Taylor by the aforesaid agreement.

6 Oct 1781: John Graft & EG

X10: Daniel Byrnes of New Castle County on the Delaware & Rumford Dawes of Philadelphia [the acting executors of Isaac Whitelock, late of New Castle County] enf-rel.to William Parr & Henry Dering, gentleman, both of Lancaster County

--Two adjoining tracts: (1.) 102a Manheim tp. and (2.) 86a Manheim tp.

HISTORY: On 13 Sep 1762, Samuel Bethel granted 102a Manheim tp. to Isaac Whitelock & Francis Sanderson. In 1763, Francis Sanderson granted his moiety to Isaac Whitelock.

HISTORY: On 15 Feb 1769, Joseph Galloway of Anne Arundel County, Maryland, granted 86a Manheim tp. to Isaac Whitelock.

--By his last will & testament dated 1 May 1779, Isaac Whitelock ordered his brewhouse, dwelling, and two lots in Lancaster Borough purchased from Caleb Sheward and his plantation in Manheim tp. purchased from Joseph Galloway & others to be sold by his executors [to wit, Sarah Whitelock, Abraham Gibbons, & Joseph West—who all renounced--in addition to the above-named acting executors].

8 Jul 1782: Jonathan Dawes & Edward Dawes

--[A draught of the properties is attached and copied on the record.]

X13: Simon Sneyder (or Shneider, or Snyder), innkeeper, & his wife Catharine of Hempfield tp. enf-rel.to Henry Dering of Lancaster Borough

--Half lot on Prince St. in Lancaster Borough: HISTORY: Part of a larger lot that Sheriff John Ferree granted 1 Mar 1774 to Peter Albright. On 25 Mar 1777, Peter Albright & his wife Mary granted half of the lot to William Flick (Ref. Deed R443). On 29 Jan 1779, William Flick & his wife Catharine granted the same to Charles Liederson. On 4 May 1779, Charles Liederson & his wife Elizabeth granted the same to Simon Sneyder.

17 May 1782: ES & CS

X16: Peter Albright, yeoman, & his wife Mary of Lancaster Borough rel.to John Wagoner, yeoman, of Hempfield tp.

100a Derry tp.: HISTORY: On 8 June 1775, Sheriff John Ferree granted the same to Peter Albright.

--28 Mar 1778: Frederick Romele & John Eberman

X17: Catharine Knup (or Knop) [the widow of John Knup, yeoman, late of Paxton tp.] & Jacob Knup [the eldest son of the said John Knup, deceased] quitclaim to Jacob Erisman

--Any further right or claim to the estate of John Knup: HISTORY: By his last will & testament—which has been unfortunately canceled and destroyed since his death—John Knup made certain provisions. By the sworn testimony of those present at the time of writing, the will has lately been rewritten and the intended provisions executed. By an order of the Orphans Court, the said Jacob Erisman is the guardian of Anna Knup, Elizabeth Knup, Mary Knup, and Catharine Knup—the minor children of the John Knup, deceased. Now, by this agreement, Catharine Knup and Jacob Knup pledge to make no further claim on the estate apart from those provisions given in the reconstituted last will & testament [Note: Under intestate law, they would each be entitled to more.]

7 Oct 1782: No witnesses—all parties appear personally at the courthouse.

X18: Peter Hess, yeoman, & his wife Susanna of Manheim tp. enf-rel.to Jacob Shively (or Schiveley), yeoman, of same

42 ¼ a. Manheim tp.: HISTORY: Same tract that Michael Hess & his wife Dorothea granted on equal date herewith to Peter Hess.

27 May 1782: Jacob Sharer & Martin Mayer

X21: Nicholas Waln & Mordecai Lewis, both of Philadelphia, rel.to George Fagler, yeoman, of Paxton tp.

375a Paxton tp.: HISTORY: Same tract pat. 31 Jan 1733 to Jacob Littlemore in right of Thomas Williamson. By divers conveyances, the property is now in the possession of said Waln & Lewis.

10 Oct 1782: Isaac Milnor & John Todd, Jr.

X22: Tripartite agreement between the following parties:

1. John Torbet, yeoman, & his wife Margaret of Leacock tp.

2. John McCoy, yeoman, of same
3. William Porter, yeoman, of same

--The party of the first part releases 200a Leacock tp. to the party of the second part; however, the party of the third part reserves the right to bring a lawsuit concerning the property to the Court of Common Pleas by the end of the next November Term.

3 Nov 1782: JE & Matthew McAllister

X25: Sheriff Thomas Edwards rel.to Thomas Neil of Drumore tp.

140a Drumore tp.: HISTORY: The Court of Common Pleas ordered the sheriff to seize the real estate of Jacob Baker of Martic tp. & Adam Fakler of Heidelberg tp. for debts owed to one Thomas Neil [the executor of Adam Neil]. The sheriff duly seized 140a Drumore tp., late the property of said Jacob Baker. At public sale, the sheriff sold the property to Thomas Neil.

4 Dec 1782: JY & Stephen Chambers

X28: Sheriff Thomas Edwards enf-rel.to John Moore of Leacock tp.

--Lot on King St. in Lancaster Borough, numbered two in the town plan: HISTORY: On 11 May 1782, the Court of Common Pleas ordered the sheriff to seize the real estate of Anne Kennedy, widow, of Lampeter tp. for debts owed to one Peter Miller. The sheriff duly seized the said lot in Lancaster Borough and later sold it at public vendue to John Moore.

5 Dec 1782: JY & JH

X30: Sheriff Thomas Edwards enf-rel.to Michael Spade of Derry tp.

--Three lots in Hummelstown in Derry tp., numbered 18, 19, and 20 in the town plan: HISTORY: On 10 Feb 1782, the Court of Common Pleas ordered the sheriff to seize the real estate of Frederick Hoffman, yeoman, of Lancaster County for debts owed to one Anthony Terr. The sheriff duly seized the said three lots in Hummelstown and later sold them at public vendue to Michael Spade.

5 Dec 1782: JY & JH

X33: Sheriff Thomas Edwards enf-rel.to David Krause of Lebanon tp.

--Lot on Cumberland St. in the town of Lebanon, being the total of three contiguous lots numbered 40, 50, and 51 in the town plan: HISTORY: On 9 Feb 1782, the Court of Common Pleas ordered the sheriff to seize the real estate of John McElrath of the town of Lebanon for debts owed to one William Paine. The sheriff duly seized the said three lots in the town of Lebanon and later sold them at public vendue to David Krause.

5 Dec 1782: JH & JY

X36: Sheriff Thomas Edwards enf-rel.to Christian Musselman of Manor tp.

--7a Manor tp.: HISTORY: On 11 May 1782, the Court of Common Pleas ordered the sheriff to seize the real estate of Henry Eberly, blacksmith, of Manor tp. for debts owed to one George Moore. The sheriff duly seized the said tract in Manor tp. and later sold it at public vendue to Christian Musselman.

5 Dec 1782: JY & JH

X39: James Allison, cooper, of Donegal tp. enf-rel.to William Allison, carpenter, of Mount Joy tp.

75a Donegal tp.: HISTORY: Part of 376 ¼ a. Donegal tp. pat. 1 Jul 1738 to Richard Allison (Ref. PB A-9-72). By his last will & testament dated 31 Oct 1757, Richard Allison devised the same tract to his son James Allison. Said James Allison died intestate leaving issue four children, to wit, Martha Allison, Richard Allison, Elizabeth Allison, & James Allison. On 5 Dec 1770, the Orphans Court ordered the larger tract divided among the heirs, with the said 75a parcel being allotted to son James Allison [the party hereto].

12 Dec 1782: William McKeary & Thomas Bayly

X42: Frederick Hummell, yeoman, & his wife Barbara of Derry tp. rel.to Daniel Stouffer (or Stoupher), yeoman, of same

--Lot #30 in Frederickstown in Derry tp.: HISTORY: Part of 151a Derry tp. pat. 28 Oct 1757 to Valentine Kloninger (Ref. PB A-___-171). The property was later seized by the sheriff due to unpaid debts.

On 2 Aug 1757, Sheriff Joseph Pugh granted the same to Thomas Willing (Ref. Deed D495). On 5 Nov 1761, Thomas Willing granted the same to John Cambel (Ref. Deed C202). On 6 Oct 1762, John Cambel & his wife Margaret granted the same to Frederick Hummel (Ref. Deed H100).

26 May 1779: Andrew Scredly & Nicholas Smyt

X45: Daniel Stouffer, yeoman, & his wife Eve of Lebanon tp. enf-rel.to Andrew Gambell (or Gamble) of Derry tp.

--Lot #30 in Frederickstown: HISTORY: It being the same lot as given in the preceding indenture.

1 Oct 1779: Samuel Jones & JT

X49: Andrew Gamble, yeoman, & his wife Agnes (or Nancy) of Paxton tp. enf-rel.to John Barnett, yeoman, of Hanover tp.

--Lot #30 in Frederickstown: HISTORY: It being the same lot as given in the preceding indenture.

20 Feb 1782: Samuel Swan

X52: Frederick Hummel, yeoman, & his wife Barbara of Derry tp. rel.to Daniel Stouffer (or Stoupher), yeoman, of same

--Lot #31 in Frederickstown in Derry tp.: HISTORY: Part of 151a Derry tp. [see deed X42 for the history of Frederickstown, otherwise known as Hummelstown].

26 May 1779: Joshua Elder

X56: Daniel Stouffer, yeoman, & his wife Eve of Lebanon tp. enf-rel.to Andrew Gambell (or Gamble) of Derry tp.

--Lot #31 in Frederickstown: HISTORY: It being the same lot as given in the preceding indenture.

1 Oct 1779: Samuel Jones & JT

X59: Andrew Gamble, yeoman, & his wife Agnes (or Nancy) of Paxton tp. enf-rel.to John Barnett, yeoman, of Hanover tp.

--Lot #31 in Frederickstown: HISTORY: It being the same lot as given in the preceding indenture.

20 Feb 1782: Samuel Swan

X63: John Barnet of Hanover tp. enf-rel.to James Clunle (or Clunie?) of Frederickstown in Derry tp.

--Two lots in Frederickstown in Derry tp., numbered 30 and 31 in the town plan: HISTORY: See deeds X49 and X59.

20 Sep 1782: Joshua Elder & Robert Elder

X65: Peter Lane (or Len), Sr., of Manheim tp. gr.to his son Cornelius Lane

160a Manheim tp.: HISTORY: Part of a larger tract now in the possession of said Peter Lane. As part of this agreement, Cornelius Lane may not sell any portion of this property without first giving his brother Peter Lane the first right to purchase. [Note: As opposed to an indenture, this appears to be an agreement. See the following indenture.]

11 June 1762: Henry Lehn & William Jones

X67: Peter Lane, yeoman, & his wife Margaret of Manheim tp. enf-rel.to Anna Maria Lane, widow, of same

158a Manheim tp.: HISTORY: On ______, Peter Lane & his wife Margaret granted 158a Manheim tp. to his son Cornelius Lane. By his last will & testament dated 2 Sep 1780, Cornelius Lane devised one moiety of his real & personal estate to his wife Anna Maria [the party hereto] *after the death of his parents* for the rest of her natural life—then the full right to the property descended to his brother Peter Lane. By this indenture, the said Peter Lane [the party hereto] releases his right and claim to the property, giving the said widow full ownership.

18 Nov 1782: PH & Johannes Mayser

X69: David Hays & his wife Anna of Rapho tp.; Arthur Hays of Rapho tp.; and Adam Tate & his wife Jane of Hempfield tp. [the children & heirs of Robert Hays, deceased, the eldest son of David Hays, deceased, late of Rapho tp.] enf-rel.to John Haymaker of Hempfield tp.

25a Rapho tp.: HISTORY: Part of 200a Rapho tp. that Patrick Hays & his wife Susanna and John Hays [the said Patrick & John being the two younger sons of said David Hays, deceased] granted 27 May 1782 to the said David Hays, Arthur Hays, & Adam Tate.

23 Aug 1782: John Emranh & George Vance

X72: Abraham Ream (or Reim), Sr., tavernkeeper, & his wife Anna Maria of Cocalico tp. rel.to Abraham Ream, Jr., miller, of same

21 ½ a. Cocalico tp.: HISTORY: Part of a larger tract pat. 12 Feb 1755 to Abraham Ream, Sr.

--14 Mar 1774: JJ

X75: Salomea Hains, widow, of Lampeter tp. enf-rel.to John Creamer of Strasburg tp.

--Lot #12 in Hains Town in Lampeter tp.: HISTORY: On 25 Mar 1774, Christian Forrer granted 18a, 42p Lampeter tp. to Francis Smith. On equal date herewith, Francis Smith granted the same [along with a 50a tract] to Salomea Hains. [Note: Christian Forrer may have granted a larger property on 25 Mar 1774—I found the wording was a bit vague.]

1 Apr 1783: JK & IK

X76: Michael Scharer (or Sharer), yeoman, & his wife Susanna of Leacock tp. enf-rel.to his son Jacob Scharer, yeoman, of same

132a Leacock tp.: HISTORY: Part of 549a Leacock tp. pat. 9 Feb 1769 to Abraham Bare (Ref. PB A-7-443) [sic—perhaps book AA]. On 3 Apr 1769, Abraham Bare & his wife Veronica granted 132a to Michael Scharer. // As part of this agreement, Jacob Scharer is to pay his sister Elizabeth, the wife of John Carpenter, a certain legacy.

10 Oct 1771: WB & Michael Diefenderfer

X79: John Weller, yeoman, & his wife Mary of Hempfield tp. enf-rel.to John Mummer, yeoman, of same

15a Hempfield tp.: HISTORY: Part of 95a Hempfield tp. that Yost Heneinan & his wife Mary, Adam Girdel & his wife Margaret, and Barbara Weller granted 17 Sep 1779 to John Weller.

28 May 1783: J. Weitly & CJ

X81: Christian Swartzwelder, yeoman, of Earl tp. rel.to Peter Swartzwelder, weaver, of same

12a Earl tp.: HISTORY: Part of 152a Earl tp. war. 11 Mar 1744 to Nicholas Frenger. On 6 Feb 1762, Nicholas Frenger granted 12a to Christian Swartzwelder.

26 Oct 1781: Peter Good & ZD

X84: Frederick Zimmerman, yeoman, & his wife Margaret of Lebanon tp. enf-rel.to their son Michael Zimmerman, yeoman, of same

133 ½ a. Lebanon tp.: HISTORY: Same tract [formerly in Heidelberg tp., but now in Lebanon tp.] pat. 20 Apr 1761 to George Reynolds (Ref. PB AA-1-238). On 25 June 1761, George Reynolds & his wife Eleanor granted the same to Adam Bach (Ref. Deed G447). On 29 Apr 1767, Adam Bach & his wife Barbara granted the same to Frederick Zimmerman (Ref. Deed O132).

14 May 1783: Hannes Royble & PG

X89: Ursula Hetherling [the widow of Jacob Hetherling, late of Vincent tp., Chester County] enf-rel.to Conrad Haas, yeoman, of Cocalico tp.

--Her moiety of 166a Cocalico tp.: HISTORY: Abraham Shonower, late of Cocalico tp., died seized of two contiguous tracts, to wit, 152a Cocalico tp. and 14a Cocalico tp. He left issue two children, the said Ursula Hetherling and Veronica, the wife of Conrad Haas (the party hereto). Since Abraham did not make disposition of his property, it descended equally to his children.

6 Feb 1779: Mathias Keeley Jr., Conrad Shunk, & Michael Sypher

--On 3 May 1783, Ursula Hetherling, now wife of Philip Refferd, affirms her signature.

X92: John Eppley, yeoman, & his wife Catharine of Lancaster Borough and Sophia Eppley [the widow of John Eppley, yeoman, late of same] rel.to Michael Guntacker, yeoman, of same

--Lot on King St. in Lancaster Borough: HISTORY: On 27 Nov 1753, Samuel Boude & his wife Mary granted the a lot on King St. to Michael Gross. On 6 Jan 1761, Michael Gross & his wife Elizabeth granted the same to John Eppley. Said John Eppley died intestate seized in possession of part of the larger lot. He left the said widow and issue the said John Eppley (party hereto).

3 Mar 1783: MH & CJ

X95: Salome Hains, widow, of Lampeter tp. enf-rel.to Christian Miller, weaver, of Lampeter tp.

9a Lampeter tp. near Hains Town [woodland]: HISTORY: Part of 50a Lampeter tp. that Francis Smith granted 1 Apr last [with another 18a tract] to Salome Hains.

6 May 1783: JK & John Fowler

X97: Sheriff Thomas Edwards rel.to Daniel Keeports of Conestoga tp.

--House & two lots on Queen St. in Bethels Town in Lancaster Borough: HISTORY: The Court of Common Pleas ordered the sheriff to seize the real estate of John Hamilton, yeoman, of Lancaster Borough for debts owed to the said Daniel Keeports & David Hess. The sheriff duly seized the above-said house and two lots on Queen St. in Bethels Town. At public vendue, he sold the same to the said Daniel Keeports.

26 Mar 1783: JY & Stephen Chambers

X100: Curtis Grubb, ironmaster, of Lebanon tp. enf-rel.to Peter Grubb [the eldest son of the said Curtis Grubb]

--The following properties: (1.) Undivided sixth part of Cornwall Furnace, (2.) Undivided third part of Hopewell Forge, and (3.) Undivided sixth part of all lands of the said Curtis Grubb in Lancaster County [excepting the mills and lands on Swatara Creek lately purchased from Michael Straw]: HISTORY: Not given; however, as a condition of this agreement, said Peter Grubb may not sell any of the lands during the lifetime of his father.

28 June 1783: Samuel Sinclair & JT

X102: Abraham Latcha & his wife Catharine and Daniel Bradley & his wife Mary, all of Hanover tp., enf-rel.to Robert Boal of Mount Joy tp.

242a Hanover tp.: HISTORY: Same tract pat. 22 Jan 1742 to Robert Young (Ref. PB A-1-317). On 5 Oct 1749, Robert Young & his wife Kristian granted the same to his son John Young (Ref. Deed D174). By his last will & testament dated 31 Jan 1775, John Young devised the same to his son William Young. On 27 Feb 1779, William Young assigned the same to Abraham Latcha & Daniel Bradley.

22 Mar 1779: Timothy Green, James Hamel, & Andrew Berryhill

X106: Andrew Robinson, yeoman, & his wife Agnes of Donegal tp. enf-rel.to his son John Robinson

--Two tracts: (1.) 105 ½ a. and (2.) 43 ½ a. [locations not given]: HISTORY: Both part of two larger tracts, one in Donegal tp. and the other in Mount Joy tp. One patented 26 Nov 1745 to Andrew Robinson and the other patented 17 Feb 1764, also to the said Andrew Robinson, totaling 461 ½ a. in Donegal & Mount Joy tps. Said Andrew Robinson has recently partitioned the lands.

2 May 1783: James Bayly & Thomas Robinson

X109: George Geiger, yeoman, & his wife Barbara of Warwick tp. enf-rel.to John Huber, yeoman, of Manheim tp.

119a, 27p Warwick tp.: HISTORY: Same tract pat. 19 June 1761 to Christian Geiger, alias Guyger. On 4 May 1779, Christian Geiger & his wife Christina granted the same to his son George Geiger (the party hereto).

15 Jan 1783: Johannes Bauman & CS

X112: Isaac Kendig, Henry Kendig, & George Kendig (sons of John Kendig, late of Lampeter tp., yeoman, deceased) acknowledge having received their due shares of their late father's 160 ½ a. plantation in

Conestoga & Lampeter townships from Abraham Kendig & Adam Kendig. They also acknowledge having received certain legacies owing to them since the death of Christian Kendig, the son of their deceased brother John Kendig [Reference is made to the last will & testament of John Kendig, the father].

19 Jul 1783: Michael Wither & JY

X113: Martin Bear (or Bar), yeoman, & his wife Barbara of Washington County, Maryland, enf-rel.to Christian Hare, yeoman, of Manor tp.

78a Conestoga tp.: HISTORY: On 28 Oct 1761, Joseph Pugh, Esq., & his wife Mary granted 168a Conestoga tp. to John Bare [excepting a 56p burying ground] (Ref. Deed N304). By his last will & testament dated 18 Mar 1767, John Bare devised the same to his son Martin Bear (the party hereto).

9 Jul 1783: Abraham Newcomer & Jacob Miller

X116: Daniel Miller, yeoman, & his wife Elizabeth of Strasburg tp. enf-rel.to Jacob Fritz, yeoman, of same

83 ¼ a. Strasburg tp.: HISTORY: Part of 200a Strasburg tp. that Henry Weaver & his wife Fronica granted 30 Dec 1771 to John Miller, who died seized in possession thereof. On 26 Jul 1780, his children & heirs quitclaimed the same to Jacob Kindich in trust for the said Daniel Miller [son of the deceased John Miller]. On equal date herewith, Jacob Kindich assigned the same to Daniel Miller, who is now of full age.

13 Jan 1783: JMR & EG

X119: Jacob Fritz, yeoman, & his wife Ann of Strasburg tp. gr.to Daniel Miller, yeoman, of same

--Water rights & privileges: HISTORY: Both own adjoining tracts in Strasburg tp. On 26 Jul 1780, the heirs of John Miller quitclaimed 22a Strasburg tp. to Jacob Fritz [see also the preceding indenture].

9 Apr 1783: Thomas Heemer & EG

X121: Jacob Fritz, yeoman, & his wife Ann of Strasburg tp. gr.to Daniel Miller, yeoman, of same

--One moiety of 162a Bart tp.: HISTORY: On 1 Apr 1761, George Murray granted 162a Bart tp. to John Miller, yeoman, late of Lancaster County. Said John Miller died intestate leaving issue the following children: John Miller (the eldest son), Anna the wife of Jacob Fritz [the parties hereto], Mary the wife of Henry Witmer, Daniel Miller [the other party hereto], and Simon Miller. By agreement, the heirs allotted the 162a tract in Bart tp. to Jacob Fritz & his wife Anna on 26 Jul 1780.

13 Jan 1783: JMR & EG

X124: Moses Vance & his wife Ann of Hanover tp. enf-rel.to James Long of Lebanon tp.

180a Hanover tp.: HISTORY: Not given.

--13 Oct 1779: Christian Montgomery & William Vance

--William Vance, the eldest son of Moses Vance, deceased, affirms his father's signature on 28 May 1783.

X125: David Mitchell, yeoman, & his wife Mary of Londonderry tp. enf-rel.to Thomas Mitchell, yeoman, of same [the son of the said David Mitchell]

300a Londonderry tp. (but formerly Derry tp.): HISTORY: Same tract war. 14 June 1750 to David Mitchell.

--2 June 1781: Christopher Uhler & JT

X128: James Todd, Sr., of Hanover tp. enf-rel.to his son James Todd, Jr., of same

--Two adjoining tracts: (1.) 150a Hanover tp. and (2.) 100a Hanover tp.

1. HISTORY: Same tract pat. 15 Aug 1765 to James Todd, Sr.
2. HISTORY: Same tract warranted to John Strain by virtue of application #527 dated 16 Aug 1765. On 3 June 1768, John Strain granted the same to James Todd, Sr.

--29 Oct 1778: John Todd, William Strain, & James McCreight

X130: George Schneider (or Snider) & his wife Margaret of Hempfield tp. and Philip Schneider & his wife Jean of the same [the heirs of Philip Schneider, deceased, late of same] enf-rel.to John Bayley, yeoman, of Donegal tp.

187a Donegal tp.: HISTORY: Same tract pat. 26 Aug 1772 to Philip Schneider (Ref. PB AA-13-___). By his last will & testament dated 27 Aug 1774, Philip Schneider devised the same to his sons George & Philip.

1 Aug 1777: James Bayley & Christian Martin

X133: John Bayly & his wife Hannah of Donegal tp. enf-rel.to Matthew Swan of same

--One moiety of 187a Donegal tp.: HISTORY: It being the same tract as given in the preceding deed.

11 Jan 1782: James Bayly & Thomas Bayly

X137: Samuel Jones of Bethel tp. [the surviving executor of William Jones, yeoman, late of same] rel.to John Jones, surveyor, of Cocalico tp.

--The residue of two contiguous tracts in Bethel tp. and all yearly rent charges for the town of Williamsburgh: HISTORY: (1.) 139 ¼ a. Bethel tp. pat. 20 Dec 1759 to William Jones [Ref. PB A-19-345]. (2.) 114a Bethel tp. pat. 3 Sep 1761 to William Jones [Ref. PB AA-2d-371]. // On these tracts, William Jones laid out the town of Williamsburgh, granting divers outlots and lots to sundry persons. By his last will & testament dated 12 Mar 1768, William Jones appointed his wife Catharine and his son Samuel Jones as his executors, ordering them to dispose of his estate after his youngest child turned 14 years of age.

26 June 1781: Henrich Shaub (or Snaub?) & Abraham Wider

X140: Griffith Evans & his wife Ann enf-rel.to James Old, yeoman, of Caernarvon tp.

23 ½ a. Caernarvon tp.: HISTORY: Same tract pat. 12 Aug 1760 to Evan Evans (Ref. PB AA-5-45). Said Evan Evans died intestate. By law, his lands came into possession of his son David Evans. On 11 Mar 1760 [sic], the other heirs released their claim to the real estate to the said David Evans. On 11 Mar 1768, David Evans & his wife Elizabeth granted the same to Frederick Wallick. On 30 Jan 1769, Frederick Wallick & his wife Mary granted the same to Peter Livengood. On 29 Apr 1775, Peter Livengood & his wife Barbara granted the same to Henry Weaver. On 1 May 1775, Henry Weaver, miller, & his wife Fronica granted the same to Griffith Evans [who is noted as another son of the said Evan Evans, deceased].

4 Oct 1782: Henry Weaver & John Morgan

X143: George Hacker & his wife Margaretha of Philadelphia County enf-rel.to George Wachter of Cocalico tp.

132a, 51p Cocalico tp.: HISTORY: Part of 301a pat. 26 Apr instant to George Hacker (Ref. PB AA-5-530).

--30 Apr 1764: ASK & PMR

X146: George Hacker & his wife Margaretha of Philadelphia County enf-rel.to George Wachter of Cocalico tp.

49 ½ a. Cocalico tp.: HISTORY: Being one moiety of 90a Cocalico tp. pat. 26 May 1762 to George Hacker (Ref. PB AA-3-305).

30 Apr 1764: ASK & PMR

X148: Jacob Shoff, yeoman, & his wife Fronica of Conestoga tp. enf-rel.to Peter Gramer

50a Conestoga tp.: HISTORY: Same tract war. 23 Aug 1749 to Samuel Swallow. On 1 Mar 1764, Samuel Swallow granted the same to James Malston. On 25 Jul 1768, James Malston assigned the same to the said Peter Gramer. On 7 Apr 1781, Peter Gramer granted the same to Jacob Shoff.

16 Aug 1783: ES & CS

X150: Rebecca Steel, widow, of Philadelphia appoints her friend William Parr, Esq., of Lancaster Borough as her lawful attorney to ack.sat. for the following mortgage: On 20 May 1768, James Wallace mortgaged certain property to Rebecca Steel (Ref. Deed M483 and also a judgment by the Court of Common Pleas in the November Term 1768).

5 Apr 1783: Mary Bartram & John Steel

X151: Christian Brandt of Lebanon tp. appoints Jacob Karch as his lawful attorney to ack.sat. for the following mortgage: On 4 Dec 1781, George Folck mortgaged certain property to Christian Brandt (Ref. Deed T450).

5 Apr 1783: Henry Herchelroth & JT

X151: Peter Lane, yeoman, & his wife Margaret of Manheim tp. enf-rel.to Anna Maria Lane, widow, of same

148a, 58p Manheim tp.: HISTORY: Part of 312a Manheim tp. pat. 29 Dec 1749 to Peter Lane (Ref. PB A-15-333). On 11 June 1762, Peter Lane granted 160a to his son Cornelius Lane (Ref. Deed X65). On ______ [omitted], the said Peter Lane & his wife Margaret granted 158a Manheim tp. to his son Cornelius Lane (see Deed X67). By his last will & testament dated 2 Sep 1780, Christian Lane devised his estate to his widow Anna Maria for the rest of her natural life—then the property reverted to his eldest brother Peter Lane (the party hereto). By this indenture, the said Peter Lane [the brother] grants his right to the widow.

7 Aug 1783: PH & James Webb

X156: Benjamin Mishey, yeoman, of Rapho tp. gr.to John Mishey, yeoman, of same

--Sundry items [no land].

1 Mar 1783: Sebastian Keller & Christian Erhart

X157: John Gensemer, weaver, & his wife Eve of Millersburg enf-rel.to John Gennet, yeoman, of same

--Five-acre lot on Frederick St. in Millersburg in Manor tp.: HISTORY: Same lot that John Miller & his wife Elizabeth granted 1 May 1765 to Mathias Miller. By his last will & testament, Mathias Miller ordered his executors, Benjamin Barr & Jacob Miller, to sell the property. On 20 May 1772, they granted the same to John Miller, the younger. On 8 Feb 1773, John Miller & his wife Esther granted the same to Gabriel Behm. On 25 Jul 1781, Gabriel Behm & his wife Catharine Elizabeth granted the same to John Gensemer.

20 Mar 1783: ES & CS

X160: Tobias Ream, yeoman, & his wife Juliana of Cocalico tp. rel.to Andrew Ream & Jacob Rupp in TRUST for the use of a free school house & Presbyterian church with a burying ground

--Lot #54 in the town of Zohar in Cocalico tp.: HISTORY: Part of 389a Cocalico tp. pat. 28 June 1734 to Eberhard Ream (Ref. PB A-8-96). On 15 Feb 1759, Eberhard Ream & his wife Elizabeth granted 54a to Tobias Ream.

28 June 1773: Martin Crause & ZD

X162: John Stoner & his wife Fanny of Little Britain tp. enf-rel.to Hugh Cunningham of Manor tp.

88a Little Britain tp.: HISTORY: Same tract war. 29 Aug 1753 and later surveyed to Robert Morgan [no further information].

3 Apr 1783: Francis Armstrong, John Penell, & William Gibson

X164: Jacob Alter, yeoman, & his wife Margaret of Warwick tp. enf-rel.to Peter Hull, yeoman, of Earl tp.

17 ¼ a. Warwick tp.: HISTORY: Part of 91 ¾ a., 5p Warwick tp. pat. 24 Jul 1741 to Henry Landis (Ref. PB A-9-410). By his last will & testament dated 17 May 1760, Henry Landis devised the property to his children, to wit, Mary [wife of Michael Shank], Frena [wife of John Shrantz], Anna [wife of John Downer], Christina [wife of Peter Good], Barbara [wife of Arnold Becker], Susanna [wife of John Hess], Elizabeth [wife of Abraham Hershey], Magdalena [wife of Abraham Downer], Margaret [wife of Jacob Alter], Catharine [wife of Benjamin Hershey], and Henry Landis.

--Daughter Frena Shrantz died without issue; thus, her share reverted to her brother Henry Landis. Said Henry Landis, with sisters Mary, Anna, Susanna, Christina, Elizabeth, and Magdalena, with their respective husbands, each granted their 1/11 part to the said John Shrantz, giving him a 7/11's part. // Benjamin Hershey & his wife Catharine granted their 1/11 part to Jacob Stiess. // Henry Landis granted his other 1/11 part [in right of his sister Frena] to Jacob Alter. // Thus, out of eleven parts, John Shrantz had seven, Jacob Stiess one, Jacob Alter two, and Arnold Becker one.

--By agreement, the heirs partitioned the property. As their two-eleventh's part, Jacob Alter & his wife Margaret were allotted 17 ¼ a. Warwick tp. On 1 Jul 1772, Arnold Becker & his wife Barbara, John Shrantz, & Jacob Stiess released the same to the said Jacob Alter.

4 Dec 1779: CJ, Samuel Grebill, & Johannes Weist

X171: Jacob Musselman, the younger, yeoman, & his wife Anna Maria of Warwick tp. enf-rel.to Christian Stouffer of same

13 ½ a. Warwick tp.: HISTORY: On 11 Jul 1748, Jacob Stouffer & his wife Magdalena granted 188a Warwick tp. to Jacob Musselman, the elder (Ref. Deed M347). On 11 Oct 1782, Jacob Musselman & his wife Barbara granted the same to Jacob Musselman, the younger.

2 Apr 1783: Frederick Kehler & Jacob Stiegel

X174: Abraham Fulton & his wife Margaret and their son James Fulton of Paxton tp. rel.to George Shoop of same

103 ½ a. Paxton tp.: HISTORY: Same tract pat. 11 Apr 1775 to Abraham Fulton (Ref. PB AA-15-583).

--27 Oct 1775: Timothy Green & William Wright

X177: Michael Ranck, yeoman, & his wife Barbara of Lancaster Borough enf-rel.to to his son Samuel Ranck, yeoman, of Earl tp.

57 ¾ a. Earl tp.: HISTORY: Part of 272a Earl tp. pat. 29 Oct 1747 to Michael Ranck (Ref. PB A-13-280).

--11 Nov 1769: JJ & Samuel Miles

X180: John Sollenberger, yeoman, & his wife Elizabeth of Earl tp. enf-rel.to Samuel Ranck, yeoman, of same

26 ¼ a. Earl tp.: HISTORY: Part of 225a pat. 15 June 1732 to Amos Lewis (Ref. PB A-6-180). On 28 Feb 1733, Amos Lewis granted the same to Rees David. On 9 Mar 1730 [sic], Rees David granted 50a to his son David (Ref. Deed M218). On 27 Apr 1770, David David & his wife Margaret granted the same to Peter Baker. On 16 Oct 1771, Peter Baker & his wife Christina granted the same to John Sollenberger.

9 June 1783: Valentine Ranck & ZD

X184: Samuel Boyd, tavernkeeper, & his wife Sidney of Hempfield tp. rel.to James Byers, yeoman, of the State of North Carolina

--Part of a lot on Prince St. in Lancaster Borough: HISTORY: On 14 Jan 1740, James Hamilton granted a lot on Prince St. to Richard Lowdon. On 8 Aug 1744, Richard Lowdon & his wife Patience granted the same to Henry Hayns. On 10 Nov 1745, Henry Hayns & his wife Christina granted the same to Thomas Poultney. On 13 Feb 1760, Thomas Poultney & his wife Elizabeth granted part thereof to Samuel Boyd.

30 June 1779: JJACK & Samuel Wright

X186: James Byers, yeoman, of Roan County, North Carolina, enf-rel.to Robert Maxwell, yeoman, of Drumore tp.

--Lot on Prince St. in Lancaster Borough: HISTORY: It being the same lot as given in the preceding deed.

2 Oct 1783: CJ & Ignatius Wheeler, Jr.

X188: George Churchman, yeoman, & his wife Hannah of East Nottingham tp., Chester County, formerly in Pennsylvania but now in Maryland, rel.to John MacPherson, mariner, of Philadelphia

212a Little Britain tp.: HISTORY: Same tract pat. ___ Dec 1774 to George Churchman (Ref. PB AA-15-372) and later mortgaged to the General Loan Office on 28 Dec 1774.

9 Jan 1777: Stephen White Jr., David Brown, & John Churchman

X191: John MacPherson, mariner, & his wife Mary Ann of Philadelphia enf-rel.to Peter Le Maigre, merchant, of same

212a Little Britain tp.: HISTORY: It being the same tract as given in the preceding deed.

--18 May 1781: Charles Biddle & Ashton Humphreys

X194: Peter Le Maigre, merchant, of Philadelphia enf-rel.to Stephen Siccord & Peter Van Noemer, merchants, of Philadelphia

212a Little Britain tp.: HISTORY: It being the same tract as given in the preceding deed.

--12 Mar 1783: Ashton Humphreys & William Cavernough

X197: Peter Van Noemer, merchant, & his wife Dina Van Sint Tryen of Philadelphia assign to Stephen Sicard, merchant, of same

--Their moiety of 212a Little Britain tp.: HISTORY: See the preceding indenture.

25 Apr 1783: Francis Redmond & William Sonntag

X199: Alexander Lowrey, Esq., & his wife Ann (or Nancy) of Donegal tp. enf-rel.to Walter Bell, taylor, of Maytown in Donegal tp.

50a, 57p Donegal tp.: HISTORY: Part of 333a pat. _____ [omitted] to Lazarus Lowrey. Said Lazarus Lowrey died seized in possession thereof in debt to one Richard Hockley. The sheriff duly seized the property and sold it at public vendue to the highest bidder. On 3 Sep 1757, the sheriff granted the same to Alexander Lowrey (Ref. Deed D440).

21 Apr 1779: James Bayly & David Cook

X202: Alexander Lowrey, Esq., & his wife Ann (or Nancy) of Donegal tp. enf-rel.to Frederick Kilbaugh, tavernkeeper, of Maytown in Donegal tp.

49a, 114p Donegal tp.: HISTORY: Part of the same 333a tract as given in the previous indenture.

--12 Apr 1779: James Bayly & Ann Alricks

X204: Alexander Stockslager & his wife Esther of Manor tp. enf-rel.to Ulrich Stouffer of same

6a Manor tp.: HISTORY: Part of 100a Manor tp .that Michael Kauffman & his wife Gertrude granted 29 Oct 1765 to Alexander Stockslager.

29 Oct 1765: John Feree & James Webb Jr.

X207: Ulrich Stouffer, yeoman, & his wife Feronica of Manor tp. enf-rel.to Michael Koenig, yeoman, of Windsor tp., York County

6a Manor tp.: HISTORY: It being the same tract as given in the previous indenture.

--1 Sep 1769: Daniel Frank & CS

X210: Michael Kauffman, yeoman, & his wife Gertraut of Manor tp. enf-rel.to Michael Kenigh, yeoman, of same

14a, 46p Manor tp.: HISTORY: Part of 134a, 50p Manor tp. pat. 7 Apr 1762 to Michael Kauffman (Ref. PB AA-3d-170).

18 May 1771: WH & WH Jr.

X212: Christian Hare (or Harr), yeoman, & his wife Mary of Manor tp. enf-rel.to John David Frank, doctor of physick, of same

10a Manor tp.: HISTORY: Part of 134a, 50p Manor tp. pat. 7 Apr 1762 to Michael Kauffman (Ref. PB AA-3d-170). On 1 Jul 1778, Michael Kauffman granted 20a to Christian Hare.

11 Jul 1782: JK & CJ

X215: Mary Scott of Mount Joy tp. [the widow of Abraham Scott, late of same] quitclaims to William Scott & Abraham Scott

--Her dower in and of the lands of the late Abraham Scott, deceased: HISTORY: By his last will & testament, Abraham Scott ordered his sons William & Abraham [the parties hereto] to pay certain legacies to his wife Mary for the rest of her natural life. [Abraham the father had previously conveyed his real estate to his said sons.[

26 Aug 1783: Jacob Cook & William Kelly

X216: Peter Frankhouser, yeoman, & his wife Eva of Brecknock tp. enf-rel.to Christian Frankhouser, yeoman, of Lebanon tp.

254a Brecknock tp.: HISTORY: Same tract pat. 18 May 1767 to Peter Frankhouser (Ref. PB AA-8-296).

--1 Sep 1783: HR & AN

X219: Tobias Ream, yeoman, & his wife Juliana gr.to Andreas Ream, yeoman, of same

--Lot #10 in the town of Zohar in Cocalico tp.: HISTORY: Part of 389a Cocalico tp. pat. 28 June 1734 to Everhard Ream (Ref. PB A-8-96). On 15 Feb 1759, Everhard Ream & his wife Elizabeth granted 54a to Tobias Ream.

29 Oct 1765: John Fierstone & David Davis

X223: Tobias Ream, yeoman, & his wife Juliana gr.to Andreas Ream, tavernkeeper, of same

--Lot #9 in the town of Zohar in Cocalico tp.: HISTORY: Part of 389a Cocalico tp. pat. 28 June 1734 to Everhard Ream (Ref. PB A-8-96). On 15 Feb 1759, Everhard Ream & his wife Elizabeth granted 54a to Tobias Ream.

9 Jul 1774: Martin Masler & JJ

X227: Agreement between Curtis Grubb, ironmaster, of Lebanon tp. and Peter Grubb, the elder, ironmaster, of Lancaster County

--The said parties have entered into a partnership, taking joint possession of their later father's estate, including Cornwall Furnace and the forges and lands belonging thereto. Now, concerning lands lately purchased by each party separately, they agree to the following: (1.) Curtis Grubb will hold a two-thirds undivided part of all lands purchased by Peter Grubb. (2.) Peter Grubb will hold a one-third part of all lands purchased by Curtis Grubb. –This agreement excepts Peter Grubb's own plantation in Warwick tp. that he purchased from Jacob Hager. Further, the mills and land purchased of Michael Straw & Jacob Kettle on the Swatara Creek, on which they intend to erect "Union Forge", are to be held equally between them.

27 June 1783: Samuel Sinclair & JT

X229: Jonas Miles, joiner, & his wife Anna of Little Britain tp. gr.to Isaiah Brown, blacksmith, of same

45a Little Britain tp.: HISTORY: Part of a larger tract that Jonas Miles purchased 4 Aug 1760 from Elizabeth White [the widow of Andrew White] and her son Joseph White. Originally, the property had been in the possession of one James Rowland, but the right thereto came into the hands of said Andrew White.

9 6mo. 1783: A. Mitchel & Patrick Ewing

X233: Thomas McDowell [the eldest son of James McDowell, late of Little Britain tp.] & Elizabeth McDowell [the widow of the said James McDowell] enf-rel.to John Webster of same

96a Little Britain tp.: HISTORY: Same tract pat. 19 Sep 1743 to Thomas Jacobs (Ref. PB A-11-222). Said Thomas Jacobs devised the same to his son Joseph; however, the land was "entailed". At the September 1763 Term of the Provincial Court at the City of Annapolis, Joseph Jacobs (then of Cecil County, Maryland) broke the entailment. On 25 June 1764, Joseph Jacobs & his wife Eleanor granted the 96a tract to James McDowell. Said James McDowell died intestate leaving issue several children. The Orphans Court confirmed his real estate to his eldest son Thomas—subject to the widow's dower.

13 Oct 1783: Patrick Ewing, Thomas Plummer, & Thomas Carmichael

X235: Stewart Herbert, yeoman, & his wife Sidney of Leacock tp. enf-rel.to James Hamilton, weaver, of same

70a, 149p Leacock tp.: HISTORY: Part of 300a Leacock tp. patented to William McCasland. Said William McCasland died intestate. By law, the Orphans Court allotted a parcel of the larger tract, or 70a, 149p, to his son Alexander McCasland, practitioner of physick. Due to unpaid debts, the county sheriff seized the property and sold the same to Stewart Herbert at public vendue (Ref. Deed S433).

27 Feb 1776: Baltzer Boshor, Daniel Boshor, & Jacob Herbert

X238: John Nisli (or Nissly), yeoman, & his wife Mary of Donegal tp. enf-rel.to his son John Nisli, yeoman, of same

112a Donegal tp.: HISTORY: Part of two larger tracts: (1.) 209 ¼ a. pat. 18 Nov 1771 to John Nisli [Ref. PB AA-11-579] and (2.) 173a pat. 23 May 1754 to John Nisli [Ref. PB A-17-483].

17 Oct 1774: Michael Nisli & Abraham Rihm

X241: John Nissly, yeoman, & his wife Barbara of Donegal tp. enf-rel.to Benjamin Whisler, yeoman, of same

112a Donegal tp.: HISTORY: It being the same tract as given in the preceding indenture.

--15 Nov 1783: Peter Shaffner & CS

X244: Joseph Latta, yeoman, of Mecklenburg County in North Carolina enf-rel.to Adam Tate, yeoman, of Donegal tp.

--Two adjoining tracts: (1.) 170a Hempfield tp. and (2.) 51a Hempfield tp.

HISTORY: Same tract pat. 14 Aug 1744 to John Latta (Ref. PB A-12-144).

HISTORY: Same tract that Hugh Padden granted 8 May 1754 to John Latta (Ref. Deed D124).

--By his last will & testament dated 16 Apr 1758, John Latta devised all his real estate to his son Joseph Latta [party hereto].

3 Dec 1779: Ruth Bayly & Alexander Lowrey

X248: Adam Tate, yeoman, & his wife Jane of Hempfield tp. enf-rel.to Peter Musser, yeoman, of same

170a Hempfield tp.: HISTORY: It being the same 170a tract as given in the preceding indenture.

--10 Nov 1783: CJ & John Hays

X251: David Musselman, yeoman, & his wife Barbara of Hempfield tp. enf-rel.to Christian Swar & Andrew Hirshy of same

51a Hempfield tp.: HISTORY: It being the same tract that Adam Tate granted 1 Aug 1780 to David Musselman (Ref. Deed U132). –Also see Deed X244.

--13 June 1783: ES & CS

X254: Alexander Lowrey of Donegal tp. rel.to David Musselman

51a Hempfield tp.: HISTORY: On 3 Dec 1779, Adam Tate mortgaged the said tract to Alexander Lowrey (Ref. Deed T394). On 1 Aug 1780, Adam Tate granted the said tract to David Musselman (Ref. Deed U132). Now, with this indenture, Alexander Lowrey releases the property from the said mortgage. [See also the preceding indenture.]

8 Aug 1783: ES & CS

X256: John Christopher Hayne, yeoman, & his wife Anna Regina of Lancaster Borough enf-rel.to Michael Bowsman, yeoman, of same

--Lot on King St. in Lancaster Borough: HISTORY: On 15 Aug 1740, James Hamilton granted a lot on King St. to John Henneberger. On 2 Jan 1751, John Henneberger & his wife Magdalena granted part thereof to Jacob Fetter. On 29 Feb 1752, Jacob Fetter & his wife Magdalena granted the same to John Christopher Hayne (Ref. Deed D350).

27 Jan 1768: John Hopson & WA

X260: Michael Bausman & his wife Margaretha assign to Baltzer Stertzer, yeoman, of Lancaster Borough

--"the within mentioned lot": HISTORY: No further mention, but probably the same as given in the preceding indenture.

9 Dec 1778: Charles Hall & CJ

X261: John Witmer, yeoman, & his wife Frena of Lampeter tp. enf-rel.to Baltzer Stertzer, yeoman, of Lancaster Borough

110a Lampeter tp.: HISTORY: Part of 150a Lampeter tp. that Benjamin Witmer & his wife Ann granted 11 Oct 1771 to John Witmer, the younger (Ref. Deed O497). On 22 Sep 1779, John Witmer & his wife Mary granted the same to John Witmer, the elder & party hereto.

2 Mar 1782: JK & CJ

X264: George Bressler, innkeeper, & his wife Fronica of Lampeter tp. enf-rel.to Baltzer Stertzer, yeoman, of Lancaster Borough

40a Lampeter tp.: HISTORY: Same tract that John Witmer, Jr., & his wife Mary granted 10 Jul 1775 to George Bressler (Ref. Deed S395).

20 Apr 1782: Andrew Graff & JK

X267: Mary Seiger (or Seger), widow, of Lampeter tp. enf-rel.to Elizabeth Seiger of same

6a Lampeter tp.: HISTORY: Same tract that the county sheriff, in pursuance to a court order dated 10 Dec 1757, granted to Frederick Seiger (since deceased) & his wife Mary in right of the said Mary. Said Frederick Seiger & his wife Mary had brought a suit against Abraham Haines & William Hains.

20 Oct 1783: Jonas Metzger & JJH

X271: George Reynolds, gentleman, & his wife Eleanor of the town of Lebanon rel.to Christopher Crafford, gentleman, of Lancaster Borough

2 ½ a., 27p lot in the town of Lebanon, numbered ____ [omitted] in the town plan: HISTORY: Part of two tracts pat. 27 May 1753 to George Stites of Lebanon (Ref. PB A-17-304). On 19 Jan 1761, George Stites granted the same to George Reynolds (Ref. Deed G95).

22 Jul 1761: John Cunningham, Thomas Miles, & PM

X275: Christopher Crafford & his wife Mary rel.to Philip Gloninger of the town of Lebanon

2 ½ a., 27p lot in the town of Lebanon: HISTORY: It being the same lot as given in the preceding indenture.

29 Aug 1764: John Feltman & WA

X276: Philip Gloninger, the elder, yeoman, & his wife Barbara of Lebanon tp. rel.to their son Philip Gloninger

2 ½ a., 27p lot in the town of Lebanon: HISTORY: It being the same lot as given in the preceding indenture.

1 May 1781: Adam Rice & P. Marsteller

X280: Thomas Poultney, merchant, & his wife Elizabeth of Philadelphia enf-rel.to Jasper Yeates, Esq., of Lancaster Borough

--Eastern part of a lot on Prince St. in Lancaster Borough: HISTORY: See Deed X174—it being part of the same lot.

15 Oct 1783: John Poultney & Edward Burd

X282: Sheriff John Hay enf-rel.to George Ross, Esq.

222a Donegal tp.: HISTORY: The Court of Common Pleas ordered the sheriff to seize the real estate of Thomas Mitchel, Jr., for debts owing to one David Frank—the surviving partner of Nathan Levy & David Frank. The sheriff duly seized a 222a tract in Donegal tp., which he sold at public vendue to the said George Ross [the said tract being part of a larger tract patented to James Mitchel, which he later devised to his son Thomas Mitchel].

7 Mar 1764: David Jenkins & Stephan Porter

X285: Charles Hamilton, merchant, of Lancaster Borough enf-rel.to John Heistand, yeoman, of Manor tp.

222a Donegal tp.: HISTORY: It being the same tract as given in the preceding indenture. On 4 Dec 1777, George Ross granted 222a Donegal tp. to Charles Hamilton (Ref. Deed R478).

18 Nov 1783: JJH & Arthur Greer, Jr.

X288: Charles Stedman & his wife Ann and Alexander Stedman & his wife Elizabeth, merchants, of Philadelphia, quitclaim to Henry William Stiegel, ironmaster, of Elizabeth tp.

--Five lots in the town of Manheim, numbered 9, 23, 26, 34, and 35 in the town plan: HISTORY: By a partition agreement, the said five lots have been allotted to Henry William Stiegel.
14 Mar 1765: Clemt Humphreys & Mary Brooks

X292: Henry William Stiegel, glass manufacturer, & his wife Elizabeth of the town of Manheim rel.to Henry Etter, yeoman, of same
--Out lot #5 in the town of Manheim, containing ten acres: HISTORY: Not given.
1 Feb 1774: EW & WCA

X294: Henry Etter & his wife Eva of the town of Manheim assign to John Noaker
--"the within mentioned lot": HISTORY: Not given but see the preceding indenture.
19 May 1777: Jacob Schertzer, Jr., & Jacob Erhart

X295: John Noecker, yeoman, & his wife Catharine of Warwick tp. enf-rel.to William Bausman of Lancaster Borough
--Out lot #5 near the town of Manheim: HISTORY: See the two preceding indentures.
6 Apr 1782: Hannes Gibbel & CS

X297: Frederick Nauman & his wife Elizabeth gr.to William Bowsman of Lancaster Borough
--"the within mentioned three lots of ground": HISTORY: No further information.
28 May 1783: JHZ & C. Pritz

X298: William Bausman, innkeeper, & his wife Catharine enf-rel.to Frederick Nauman of the town of Manheim
--Large out lot #22 in the town of Manheim, containing 10 acres: HISTORY: Same lot that Henry William Stiegel & his wife Elizabeth granted 4 Feb 1774 to Henry Etter (Ref. Deed R460). On 22 Mar 1777, Henry Etter & his wife Eva granted the same to William Bausman.
10 June 1778: WB, Jr., & Nicholas Bausman

X301: Frederick Nauman & his wife Anna Elizabeth assign to Jacob Haller, weaver, of Warwick tp.
--"the within mentioned lot," numbered 22 in the town plan: HISTORY: Not given but see the preceding indenture.
2 Apr 1783: David Nieckey & C. Pritz

X302: Jacob Haller & his wife Elizabeth enf-rel.to William Bausman
--Large out lot #22 in the town of Manheim, containing 10 acres: HISTORY: See the two preceding indentures.
16 Apr 1783: JHZ & George Burckher

X304: Elizabeth Stedman, spinster, of Philadelphia enf-rel.to William Bausman, Esq., of Lancaster Borough
--Out lot #6 near the town of Manheim, containing 10 acres: HISTORY: Not given.
13 June 1782: Charles Stedman, Gabriel Hiester, & WB, Jr.

X306: Curtis Grubb [the eldest son of Peter Grubb, deceased, ironmaster, late of Newcastle County, Delaware] quitclaims to Peter Grubb [the younger son of the said Peter Grubb, deceased]
--Between 1752 and 29 June 1764, Peter Grubb the younger received certain monies on behalf of the estate of his father, Peter Grubb, deceased. Of these monies, two-thirds rightly belong to the said Curtis Grubb. Now, by this indenture, Curtis Grubb acknowledges having received satisfaction for the time period indicated—but not for the time period beyond.
8 Mar 1775: Thomas Edwards & William Paine

X308: Curtis Grubb, ironmaster, of Lebanon tp. rel. to Peter Grubb
--For some years, pig and bar iron have been produced at Cornwall Furnace and Hopewell Forge in Lancaster County under the partnership of said Curtis Grubb & Peter Grubb, ironmasters, of Warwick tp.

During this time, Curtis Grubb purchased certain lands from Jacob Giles, merchant, of Maryland and others in his own name; however, they are intended to be part of the partnership. Thus, by this indenture, Curtis Grubb releases a one-third part of said Peter Grubb [it being his due share as outlined in their partnership agreement].

____ Mar 1775: T.B. Bowen & William Paine

X310: Isaac Haines, gunsmith, & his wife Catharine of Lampeter tp. enf-rel.to Christian Miller, weaver, of same

2a, 14p Lampeter tp., near Hains Town: HISTORY: By his last will & testament dated 3 7mo. 1762, Jacob Haines, late of Lampeter tp., devised his plantation in Lampeter tp to his son Isaac Haines (the party hereto)—subject to certain legacies to be paid to the other heirs. On 27 Apr 1774, Daniel Haines, Samuel Haines, & Jacob Hains released the same to their said brother Isaac Hains.

14 Nov 1783: WH & CS

X313: Michael Fordine & Casper Shaffner [two executors of Melchior Fordinee, butcher, late of Lancaster Borough] gr.to Rudolph Gamper [or Gamber]

--Lot on Prince St. in Lancaster Borough: HISTORY: Same lot that James Hamilton granted 23 Mar 1749 to Melchior Fordine. By his last will & testament dated 3 Dec 1754, Melchior Fordine ordered his executors to sell the same.

7 Aug 1770: CW & Casper Fordiney

X315: Rudolph Gamber & his wife Elizabeth assign to Henry Rung of Lancaster Borough

--"the within mentioned lot": HISTORY: Not given but see the preceding indenture.

18 Aug 1783: Philip Dietrich & CS

X317: Martin Spickler, Michael Spickler & his wife Barbara, Christian Spickler, Nicholas Spickler, Margaret Spickler, Joseph Huber & his wife Catharine, and John Sumy [the guardian of Frederick Spickler, Simon Spickler, Jacob Spickler, Peter Spickler, & Justina Spickler] (the children and heirs of Martin Spickler, late of Warwick tp.) enf-rel.to John Spickler of Warwick tp. [another son of the said Martin Spickler, deceased]

--Three tracts: (1.) 107a Warwick tp., (2.) 2a, 120p Warwick tp., and (3.) 27a Warwick tp.

1. HISTORY: Same tract that Jacob Burghard, Jr., & his wife Maria granted 7 Apr 1772 to Martin Spickler (Ref. Deed S94).
2. HISTORY: Part of a larger tract pat. 25 Feb 1760 to Martin Spickler (Ref. PB A-20-489).
3. HISTORY: Part of the same larger tract above.

--By his last will & testament, Martin Spickler devised 137a Warwick tp. to his son John.

17 Jul 1783: Martin Gross & CS

X321: John Spickler & his wife Mary, Michael Spickler & his wife Barbara, Christian Spickler, Nicholas Spickler, Margaret Spickler, Joseph Huber & his wife Catharine, and John Sumy [the guardian of Frederick Spickler, Simon Spickler, Jacob Spickler, Peter Spickler, & Justina Spickler] (the children and heirs of Martin Spickler, late of Warwick tp.) enf-rel.to Martin Spickler of Warwick tp. [another son of the said Martin Spickler, deceased]

--153a, 30p Warwick tp.: HISTORY: Part of a larger tract pat. 25 Feb 1760 to Martin Spickler (Ref. PB A-20-489). By his last will & testament, Martin Spickler devised 153a Warwick tp. to his son Martin.

17 Jul 1783: Martin Gross & CS

X325: John Duncan, yeoman, & his wife Mary of Upper Paxton tp. rel.to John Gross, yeoman, of Skippach & Perkoeming tp., Philadelphia County

265 ½ a. Upper Paxton tp.: HISTORY: Same tract pat. 28 Feb 1769 to John Montgomery (Ref. PB AA-10-508). On 30 Mar 1774, John Montgomery granted the same to William Patterson. On 17 Mar 1779, William Patterson & his wife Esther granted the same to John Duncan.

11 Nov 1783: Anthony McCreight & JT

X328: Peter Kramer (or Gramer), yeoman, of Conestoga tp. rel.to Jacob Mehnert, yeoman, of same

50a Conestoga tp.: HISTORY: Same tract war. 23 Aug 1749 to Samuel Swallow. On 1 Mar 1764, Samuel Swallow granted the same to James Malston. On 25 Jul 1768, James Malston granted the same to said Peter Kramer. On 7 Apr 1781, Peter Kramer granted the same to Jacob Shoff. On 16 Aug 1783, Jacob Shoff & his wife Fronica re-conveyed the same to Peter Kramer.

5 Nov 1783: Charles Brandon & CS

X330: Samuel Miller, yeoman, of New Garden tp., Chester County [the surviving executor of Joseph Hains, yeoman, late of Chester County] enf-rel.to Michael Wither, yeoman, of Strasburg tp.

10a Lampeter tp.: HISTORY: On 28 Sep 1767, Rudolph Hains granted 10a Lampeter tp. to Joseph Hains. By his last will & testament dated 5 Apr 1779, Joseph Hains ordered his executors to sell the property.

4 Aug 1783: CJ & EG

X333: John Meyer, yeoman, & his wife Barbara of Shrewsbury tp., York County [she late being Barbara Weaver, the widow of Samuel Weaver, late of Earl tp.] quitclaim to Henry Weaver & Christian Weaver [the executors of the said Samuel Weaver and also the testamentary guardians of his minor children]

--Their right, claim, and interest in and of Samuel Weaver's plantation in Earl tp.: HISTORY: Not given.

16 Jul 1783: Michael Garber & William Kersey

X335: Sheriff Thomas Edwards rel.to Patrick Campbell of Martic tp.

130a Martic tp.: HISTORY: On 11 May 1782, the Court of Common Pleas ordered the sheriff to seize the real estate of Jacob Baker & Adam Fackler for unpaid debts owed to Thomas Neil [the executor of Adam Neil]. The sheriff duly seized 140a Drumore tp.; however, after making sale of the same, it was found that debts were still outstanding. The sheriff then further seized 130a Martic tp., which he sold to the Patrick Campbell at public vendue [it being the same tract that Andrew McCleary granted to Samuel Rogers, who granted the same to Robert Caldwell, who granted the same to Adam Fackler].

4 Dec 1783: John Jago & JH

X340: Adam Oberlin, yeoman, of Warwick tp. enf-rel.to Philip Hoffman, yeoman, of same

97a, 50p Warwick tp.: HISTORY: Same tract war. 19 May 1749 to Adam Oberlin.

--30 Nov 1772: Peter Gottshall & Valentin Brassler

X342: Philip Hoffman, yeoman, of Warwick tp. enf-rel.to Philip Lambach, yeoman, of same

97a, 50p Warwick tp.: HISTORY: It being the same tract as given in the preceding indenture.

--30 Nov 1772: Christian Langrunder & Johannes Geib

X344: Elizabeth Lambach & Christian Lambach [the administrators of Philip Lambach, yeoman, late of Warwick tp.] gr.to John Resht (or Rescht)

97a, 50p Warwick tp.: HISTORY: It being the same tract as given in the preceding indenture. Said Philip Lambach died intestate seized in possession thereof. The Orphans Court ordered the property to be sold in order to pay debts and to maintain & educate his minor children.

29 Mar 1774: Frederick Kehler & WA

X346: John Rescht, yeoman, of Warwick tp. gr.to Christian Lambach, yeoman, of same

97a, 50p Warwick tp.: HISTORY: It being the same tract as given in the preceding indenture.

--29 Mar 1774: Frederick Kehler & WA

X349: Andrew Hershey & his wife Mary and Jacob Neff & his wife Elizabeth, all of Hempfield tp. [the said Mary & Elizabeth being daughters of Jacob Acker, deceased, late of same] enf-rel.to Henry Acker of Rapho tp. [the son of the said Jacob Acker, deceased]

--Two tracts: (1.) 187a Rapho tp. and (2.) 15 ¾ a. Rapho tp.

1. HISTORY: Part of a larger tract that Casper Acker granted 6 Aug 1748 to Jacob Acker.

2. HISTORY: Same tract that Jacob Rohrer & his wife Ann granted 2 Nov 1750 to Jacob Acker (Ref. Deed C260).

--Said Jacob Acker died intestate leaving a widow Catharine and issue three children [the said Mary, Elizabeth, and Henry] to whom the properties descended. [Note: The wording suggests that the widow is still alive.]

23 Aug 1783: Jacob Erisman & CS

X352: Alexander McClure & his wife Martha of Paxton tp. enf-rel.to John Neesly of Donegal tp.

202a, 1p Paxton tp.: HISTORY: Part of 516a Paxton tp. war. 30 Jan 1737 and later surveyed to Richard McClure. By his last will & testament dated 29 Jan 1774, Richard McClure devised 202a, 1p to his son Alexander McClure [the party hereto].

28 Oct 1783: James Burd & John Steel

X356: James Rinkin, merchant, of Detroit appoints Alexander Lowrey of Donegal tp. as his lawful attorney to sue for, recover, and receive of and from any persons whatsoever in and concerning a piece of land laying in or near Franks Town.

12 Mar 1773: WH & L. Andrew Levy

X357: Peter Baker, Sr., yeoman, of Earl tp. enf-rel.to his son Peter Baker, yeoman, of same

158a Earl tp. & Leacock tp. [partly in both]: HISTORY: Same tract pat. 4 June 1735 to Thomas Small (Ref. PB A-7-207). On 12 Apr 1748, Thomas Small & his wife Mary Ann granted the same to Peter Summy. On 26 Dec 1748, Peter Summy & his wife Margaret granted the same to Peter Baker.

28 Oct 1765: Jenkin Davis & ZD

X361: Christian Herman, yeoman, of Earl tp. rel.to his son Christian Herman, Jr., of same and his son-in-law Valentine Breneisen of Lancaster Borough

45a, 86p Earl tp.: HISTORY: Part of 617a Earl tp. pat. 13 Mar 1733 to Daniel Herman (Ref. PB A-6-288). On 16 Dec 1739, Daniel Herman granted one moiety to Christian Herman.

10 Dec 1783: CS Jr. & CS

X364: Peter Ferree & John Shertz, both of Lancaster County [the executors of Daniel Leman, yeoman, late of Lampeter tp.], enf-rel.to Jacob Brubaker, weaver, of Lampeter tp.

1a, 6 ½ p. Lampeter tp.: HISTORY: In his lifetime, Daniel Leman agreed to sell the said lot to Jacob Brubaker by an agreement dated 8 Jan 1783 (Ref. Deed U468). By his last will & testament dated 9 Jan 1783, Daniel Leman ordered his executors to make a deed good for the same.

_____ 1783: HD & Melchior Moellinger

X366: Jacob Brubaker & his wife Magdalena assign to Melchior Moellinger, weaver, of Lampeter tp.

--"the within described lot": HISTORY: Not given but see the preceding indenture.

____ Dec 1783: HD & Peter Feree

X368: Benjamin Graff, Jacob Ashleman & his wife Barbara, Christian Herr & his wife Frances, and John Herr & his wife Mary, all of Lancaster County [the heirs & devisees of Jacob Graft, yeoman, late of same, deceased] enf-rel.to Jacob Bare, yeoman, & his wife Ann of same

25a [location not given]: HISTORY: On 10 Nov 1735, John Kyle & his wife Ann granted 100a to Jacob Graft. By his last will & testament dated 15 Mar 1760, Jacob Graft devised 25a of this land [amongst other land] to his daughter Ann, wife of Jacob Bare [he further mentions that Jacob Bare owns a gristmill].

13 Sep 1770: EG & GR

X371: Daniel Miller, yeoman, & his wife Elizabeth of Strasburg tp. enf-rel.to Jacob Bare, Sr., yeoman, of Bart tp.

10a Strasburg tp.: HISTORY: Part of 200a Strasburg tp. that the heirs of John Miller quitclaim 26 Jul 1780 to Jacob Kindich [the guardian of Daniel Miller, party hereto and son of said John Miller]. On equal date herewith, Jacob Kindich assigned the same to said Daniel Miller, who has now reached full age.

13 Jan 1783: JMR & EG

X374: George Richmond, yeoman, & his wife Jane of Sadsbury tp., Chester County enf-rel.to Nathaniel Sample, minister, of the Village of Strasburg

80p lot in the Village of Strasburg: HISTORY: Same lot that John Feree & his wife Catharine granted 12 Sep 1765 to Everard Gruber. On 24 May 1775, Everard Gruber & his wife Christina granted the same to George Richmond (Ref. Deed S242).

29 Oct 1783: James Hamilton, Peggy Cowan, & Jean Scott

X378: William Allen, Sr., & his wife Elizabeth of Hanover tp. enf-rel.to William Allen, Jr., of same

275a Hanover tp.: HISTORY: Same tract war. ____ [date omitted] to John Knox. On 12 Sep 1755, John Knox granted the same to William Allen.

26 Nov 1778: Timothy Green & John McNaughton

X379: John Schweigart & Adam Schweigart, both of Upper Paxton tp., assign to Lodwick Shelman of same

200a Paxton tp.: HISTORY: Not given.

--22 Dec 1783: George Johnston & William Foulk

X381: John Gisch, yeoman, & his wife Elizabeth of Mount Joy tp. enf-rel.to Frederick Stolar, Sr., of same

43a, 111p Mount Joy tp.: HISTORY: Part of a larger tract pat. 21 Jan 1775 to John Gisch (Ref. PB AA-15-345).

26 Jul 1783: James Bayly & William Miller

X384: Daniel McCasland, yeoman, of Leacock tp. enf-rel.to David Crawford, yeoman, of same

240a Leacock tp.: HISTORY: On 19 June 1769, William McCasland granted 240a Leacock tp. to his son Daniel McCasland (the party hereto) [Ref. Deed O212].

8 Dec 1772: Robert Anderson, Michael Lightner, & Peter Feree

X387: Archibald Murray (or Murrow) & his wife Jane of Upper Paxton tp. gr.to Lecky Murray, physition (physician?), of Lancaster Borough

--Two tracts: (1.) 179a Upper Paxton tp. and (2.) 300 ¾ a. Upper Paxton tp.

1. HISTORY: Same tract war. 14 Oct 1774 to Thomas Alexander. On 15 Aug 1777, Thomas Alexander granted the same to Archibald Murray.
2. HISTORY: Same tract war. 14 Oct 1774 to Archibald Murray.

--8 June 1782: WH & James Turbett

X390: Robert Buck, yeoman, & his wife Deborah of Londonderry tp. enf-rel.to Conrad Wishan of Lancaster County

84a Londonderry tp.: HISTORY: Part of a larger tract war. 2 Nov 1753 to John Espey. On 25 June 1767, John Espey granted the same to Jacob Foulk. On 8 May 1771, Jacob Foulk & his wife Margaret granted the same to William Farmer. On 7 Mar 1777, William Farmer & his wife Susanna granted 84a to Robert Buck.

7 Oct 1778: Martin Frank & JT

X393: Conrad Wishan, yeoman, & his wife Elizabeth of Londonderry tp. enf-rel.to James Sullivan of Lancaster County

84a Londonderry tp.: HISTORY: It being the same tract as given in the preceding indenture.

--6 Nov 1778: Anna Maria Thome & JT

X396: James Sullivan, yeoman, & his wife Esther of Londonderry tp. enf-rel.to Charles Johnston of Lancaster County

84a Londonderry tp.: HISTORY: It being the same tract as given in the preceding indenture.

--8 Dec 1778: JT & John Agnes (Agnew?)

X398: Charles Johnston, taylor, & his wife Catharine of Londonderry tp. enf-rel.to John Hostetter, yeoman, of same

84a Londonderry tp.: HISTORY: It being the same tract as given in the preceding indenture.
--30 Dec 1783: Anna Maria Thome & JT

X401: James Kerr (or Karr) gr.to Andrew Kerr, William Wilson, & William Kerr, all of Donegal tp.

--Plantation in Donegal tp.: HISTORY: Part of a larger tract that James Cunningham granted 18 Mar 1729/30 to John Gass. By his last will & testament, John Gass ordered his executors to sell the property. On 3 Mar 1735/36, Margaret Gass (his wife) & Samuel Smith, Esq., [the said executors] granted the larger tract to William McClelland & Michael McCleery. On 1 Dec 1739, they assigned the same to James Kerr.

27 May 1766: Andrew Kelly, James Work, & John Midelton

X403: William Kerr, yeoman, of Donegal tp. gr.to William Wilson, yeoman, of same

--His undivided third part of 181 ½ a. Donegal tp.: HISTORY: It being the same tract as given in the preceding indenture. A recent survey found the tract to contain 181-½ acres.

22 Feb 1769: JR & GR

X405: Andrew Karr, shoemaker, of Hanover tp. gr.to William Wilson, yeoman, of Donegal tp.

--His undivided third part of 181 ½ a. Donegal tp.: HISTORY: It being the same tract as given in the preceding indenture.

5 Aug 1771: John Bayly & James Wilson

X407: William Wilson, yeoman, & his wife Mary of Donegal tp. enf-rel.to Daniel Stauffer of Codorus tp., York County

181 ½ a. Donegal tp.: HISTORY: It being the same tract as given in the preceding indentures. Patented 13 Apr 1774 to William Wilson.

23 Oct 1783: James Bayly & James Wilson

X410: Joseph Groff (or Grove, or Groft), yeoman, & his wife Barbara of Cocalico tp. enf-rel.to John Mohler, yeoman, of same

43a Cocalico tp.: HISTORY: Part of 50a pat. 28 Sep 1736 to Henry Mohler (Ref. PB A-8-98). On 2 Feb 1749, Henry Mohler granted the same to Jacob Grove, Sr. On 2 Feb 1749, Jacob Grove, Sr., & his wife Mary granted the same to Joseph Grove (Ref. Deed D399).

2 Jan 1784: Conard Hand (Hass?) & AN

X413: Dorothea Klein (or Kline) [the widow & administratrix of Michael Klein, late of Warwick tp.], George Klein & his wife Christina, Leonard Klein & his wife Barbara, Michael Quiggell & his wife Frenia, George Wilt & his wife Catharine, Adam Reisht & his wife Magdalena, George Bauman & his wife Margaret, John Bauman & his wife Dorothea, George Giger & his wife Barbara, and John Brown & his wife Susanna [the children & heirs of said Michael Klein, deceased] quitclaim to Nicholas Klein [another son of said Michael Klein, deceased]

--Two tracts: (1.) 106a Warwick tp. and (2.) 35a Warwick tp.

1. HISTORY: Part of 137a pat. 26 Jan 1749 to Michael Klein (Ref. PB A-17-386).
2. HISTORY: Part of a larger tract of warranted land [no further information].

--Said Michael Klein died intestate leaving a widow and issue six sons and eight daughters [the 10 children above, plus Daniel Klein, Michael Klein, Jacob Klein, & Gertraut Klein, who are yet in their minority].

16 Nov 1781: Jacob Lindy, J. Bickham, Andrew Backenstoes, & Jacob Schindel

X417: Jacob Musselman, the elder, yeoman, & his wife Barbara enf-rel.to Jacob Musselman, the younger, of Lancaster County

188a Warwick tp. [excepting 10a previously granted to Jacob Musselman & Jacob Stouffer]: HISTORY: Same tract pat. 5 June 1746 to Jacob Stouffer (Ref. PB A-13-53). On 11 Jul 1748, Jacob Stouffer & his wife Magdalena granted the same to Jacob Musselman (Ref. Deed M347).

11 Oct 1782: Frederick Kehler & Jacob Stiegel

X420: William Carson, yeoman, of Paxton tp. enf-rel.to John Carson, yeoman, of same
228 ½ a. Paxton tp.: HISTORY: Not given.
--9 Jul 1783: William Foulk & Alexander Berryhill

X423: George Cummins, yeoman, & his wife Susanna of Manheim tp. gr.to John Musser, yeoman, of Lancaster Borough and Abraham Witmer, yeoman, of Lancaster tp.

--Water rights: HISTORY: On equal date herewith, John Musser & his wife Sarah and Abraham Witmer & his wife Mary granted 6a, 29p Manheim tp. to George Cummins. Said Musser & Witmer own adjoining property. This indenture confirms water rights & privileges.

10 Feb 1783: Christian Brubacher & William Parr

X427: Thomas Poultney, merchant, & his wife Elizabeth of Lancaster Borough rel.to William Ross, merchant, of same

--Part of a larger lot on King St.: HISTORY: On 14 Aug 1743, James Hamilton granted a lot on King St. to Peter Worrel. On 3 Aug 1759, Peter Worrel & his wife Susanna granted part thereof to Robert Fulton. On 4 Feb 1767, Robert Fulton & his wife Mary granted the same to Thomas Poultney. Now, Thomas Poultney & his wife grant a smaller portion thereof to William Ross.

28 Aug 1779: HD & Samuel Turbitt

X432: Rebecca Wallace (late Rebecca Anderson) of Salisbury tp. enf-rel.to Alexander Willson, yeoman, of Earl tp.

125a Salisbury tp.: HISTORY: Same tract pat. 18 Jul 1744 to Margaret Anderson (Ref. PB A-11-363). By her last will & testament, Margaret Anderson devised the same to her sons James Anderson & George Anderson equally. On 27 Sep 1762, James Anderson & his wife Ann granted their right to George Anderson. By his last will & testament dated 24 Sep 1770, George Anderson ordered his executors [to wit, his wife Rebecca Anderson (now Wallace, the party hereto) and John Martin] to sell the property if his wife should remarry—and she did.

3 June 1780: Mary Watson, Jane Watson, & William Watson

--John Wallace signs the indenture although he is not named in the text of the deed. Presumably, he is Rebecca Wallace's next husband.

X435: Henry Weaver, yeoman, & his wife Feronica of Caernarvon tp. enf-rel.to Jacob Weaver, the younger, yeoman, of Earl tp.

37a, 50p Caernarvon tp., including a gristmill & sawmill: HISTORY: Not given.

--24 Jan 1784: Johann Schmidt & Angelhard Brown

X440: Christian Brubacher, yeoman, & his wife Elizabeth of Manheim tp. enf-rel.to John Miller, yeoman, of Manor tp.

--Two tracts: (1.) 14 ½ a. Hempfield tp. and (2.) 222a Hempfield tp.

1. HISTORY: Same tract [amongst others] patented to Isaac Norris (Ref. PB A-6-327). By his last will & testament, Isaac Norris ordered his executors (to wit, Mary Norris, Isaac Norris, Charles Norris, & Samuel Norris) to sell the property. On 17 Nov 1740, they sold the same to Martin Cryder. On 10 Mar 1757, Martin Cryder & his wife Elizabeth granted the same to Peter Cryder. On 15 Aug 1766, Peter Cryder & his wife Mary granted the same to Christian Brubacher.
2. HISTORY: Same tract pat. 12 Dec 1748 to Peter Cryder (Ref. PB A-14-167). On 15 Aug 1766, Peter Cryder & his wife Mary granted the same to Christian Brubacher, reserving certain privileges to Christian Swahr for building a road.

--14 June 1773: Abraham Kagey & Johannes Burkholder

X444: Joseph Musser (or Mosser) & Christian Stouffer, both of Manor tp. [the executors of Jon Miller, yeoman, late of same] enf-rel.to John Steman (or Staiman), yeoman, of Hempfield tp.

--Two tracts: (1.) 14 ½ a. Hempfield tp. and (2.) 222a Hempfield tp.: HISTORY: Being the same tracts as given in the preceding indenture. By his last will & testament dated 22 Feb 1777, John Miller ordered his said executors to deed the properties to John Steman.

14 Oct 1782: Christian Schwahr, Johannes Burkholder, & CJ

X447: Robert Young, yeoman, & his wife Susanna of Leacock tp. rel.to William Brisben, yeoman, of Salisbury tp.

18a, 106p Leacock tp.: HISTORY: Part of 68a Leacock tp. pat. 25 Apr 1774 to Robert Young (Ref. PB AA-14-308).

28 May 1777: James Lauther & Samuel Young

X449: Robert Wallace, shopkeeper, & his wife Martha of Earl tp. enf-rel.to Peter Grim, yeoman, of same

12a Earl tp.: HISTORY: Part of 238a pat. 24 June 1760 to David Davies (Ref. PB A-19-621). On 16 Apr 1762, David Davies & his wife Jane granted the same to William Douglass. On 19 Mar 1763, William Douglass & his wife Sarah granted 12a to Jacob Weaver. On 27 Aug 1766, Jacob Weaver & his wife Catharine granted the same to Robert Wallace.

9 Nov 1778: Philip Schnider & William Grof

X452: James Rea & his wife Elizabeth of Lampeter tp. enf-rel.to John Brisbin (or Brizby) of same

153a Lampeter tp.: HISTORY: Part of 200a Lampeter tp. pat. 5 Mar 1735 to William McNabb (Ref. PB A-7-458). By his last will & testament dated 11 May 1748, William McNabb devised the same to his son John. By his last will & testament dated 11 Feb 1757, John McNabb ordered his executors [to wit, his wife Isabella—now wife of said John Brizby—and Joseph Steer] to sell his real & personal estate. On 12 Jan 1763, they granted 153a to James Rea.

12 Jan 1763: Robert Thompson & Lennert Cilort (?)

X457: Joseph Steer and John Brizby (or Brisben) & his wife Isabella, all of Lampeter tp. [the said Joseph and Isabella being the executors of John McNabb] enf-rel.to James Rea, yeoman, of same

153a Lampeter tp.: HISTORY: It being the same tract as given in the preceding indenture.

--12 Jan 1763: Robert Thompson & Lennert Cilort (?)

X462: Joseph Stoneman, yeoman, of Lancaster County enf-rel.to John Kendrick, yeoman, of same

200a [location not given]: HISTORY: Not given but bordering on the Susquehanna River.

--27 May 1751: Christian Stoneman & DS

X464: Michael Smith (or Smitt) & his wife Elizabeth of Paxton tp. [she late being Elizabeth Fissel, a daughter of Daniel Fissel, deceased, who was a son of John Fissel, deceased, late of Mount Joy tp.] rel.to John Fissel, yeoman, of Mount Joy tp. [a son of the said John Fissel, deceased]

--Their right, claim, & interest in and of 153 ½ a. Mount Joy tp.: HISTORY: On 27 Dec 1755, Leonard May & his wife Christina granted the same to John Fissel. By his last will & testament, John Fissel devised his real estate to his son John (the party hereto).

17 June 1783: Richard Keys & Henry Stauffer

X467: Henry Weaver, yeoman, of Caernarvon tp. enf-rel.to Abraham Witmer, yeoman, of Lancaster County

--211 lots in the town of Port Royal: HISTORY: Part of 87 ½ a. adjoining the Swatara Creek and Susquehanna River patented to William Breden (Ref. PB AA-14-118). On 10 May 1773, William Breden (alias Breaden) granted the same to Henry Weaver, Elijah Wickersheim, & Joseph Leacock. They divided the property into 416 lots and named it the town of Port Royal. On 15 June 1774, Joseph Leacock, gentleman, of Philadelphia, assigned his right, claim, & title to the said Henry Weaver & Elijah Wickersheim, who partitioned the land as follows: 205 lots to the said Elijah Wickersheim and 211 lots to the said Henry Weaver. On 15 June 1774, Elijah Wickersheim granted the 211 lots to Henry Weaver. [Note: This indenture identifies all 211 lots by number.]

7 Feb 1784: Henry Witmer & Michael Rine

X471: Sheriff Thomas Edwards enf-rel.to Bartholomew Wister, brewer, & Richard Wister, merchant, both of Philadelphia

240a Lampeter tp.: HISTORY: On 8 Feb 1783, the Court of Common Pleas ordered the sheriff to seize the real estate of Anne Kennedy, widow, of Lancaster Count for unpaid debts owing to Peter Miller, Charles Hamilton, and Myer Solomon. The sheriff duly seized 240a Lampeter tp., which he sold at public vendue to the above grantees.

4 Feb 1784: Edward Burd & JY

X475: Jacob Newcomer (or Neukomer) & Christian Newcomer, yeoman, of Hempfield tp. and John Summy, yeoman, & his wife Anna of Rapho tp. [the said Jacob, Christian, & Anna being three children of Jacob Newcomer, deceased, late of Hempfield tp., yeoman] quitclaim to John Newcomer, yeoman, of Hempfield tp. [the eldest son of said Jacob Newcomer, deceased]

176a Hempfield tp.: HISTORY: Same tract pat. 11 Oct 1750 to Jacob Newcomer (Ref. PB A-15-525). Said Jacob Newcomer died intestate leaving issue the four above children. On 7 Mar 1775, the Orphans Court confirmed the real estate to John, the eldest son.

7 June 1781: Christian Kauffman & Christian Ish

X479: John Newcomer, yeoman, & his wife Anna [her mark: ANK] of Hempfield tp. gr.to John Shenk, yeoman, of Rapho tp.

176a Hempfield tp.: HISTORY: It being the same tract as given in the preceding indenture.

--1 Aug 1782: George Burckhart & Anthony Seyfert

X483: John Shenk, yeoman, & his wife Anna of Rapho tp. rel.to Michael Baughman, yeoman, of Manor tp.

176a Hempfield tp.: HISTORY: It being the same tract as given in the preceding indenture.

--2 Aug 1782: Chris. Kilhoffer & T. Hoofnagle

X486: Abraham Reist of Warwick tp. [the surviving executor of Jonas Nolt, late of Hempfield tp.] gr.to Jonas Nolt of Hempfield tp. [the son of said Jonas Nolt, deceased]

288 ½ a. Donegal tp.: HISTORY: By his last will & testament, Jonas Nolt devised the said tract, which he had purchased from Andrew Berg, to his son Jonas when he reached age 21. He named his two brothers-in-law, John Kauffman and Abraham Reist, as his executors, ordering them to make a deed good for the same.

9 Feb 1784: PG & IK

X488: Abraham Reist of Warwick tp. [the surviving executor of Jonas Nolt, late of Hempfield tp.] gr.to John Nolt of Hempfield tp. [the eldest son of said Jonas Nolt, deceased]

134a Hempfield tp.: HISTORY: By his last will & testament, Jonas Nolt devised the said tract to his son John when he reached age 21. He named his two brothers-in-law, John Kauffman and Abraham Reist, as his executors, ordering them to make a deed good for the same.

9 Feb 1784: PG & IK

X490: Abraham Reist of Warwick tp. [the surviving executor of Jonas Nolt, late of Hempfield tp.] gr.to Christian Nolt of Hempfield tp. [the son of said Jonas Nolt, deceased]

106a. Hempfield tp.: HISTORY: By his last will & testament, Jonas Nolt devised the said tract, which he had purchased from his brother-in-law Frederick Muma, to his son Christian when he reached age 21. He named his two brothers-in-law, John Kauffman and Abraham Reist, as his executors, ordering them to make a deed good for the same.

9 Feb 1784: PG & IK

X493: George Pfeil, yeoman, & his wife Veronica of Warwick tp. enf-rel.to John Eyer (or Eier), yeoman, of Earl tp.

86a, 9p Warwick tp.: HISTORY: Part of 136 ½ a. pat. 23 May 1763 to George Pfeil (Ref. PB AA-5-53).

--27 June 1768: John Eastwood & Henrich Eberle

X496: Abraham Huber & Samuel Huber, yeoman, both of Warwick tp. [the executors of John Eyer, yeoman, late of same] enf-rel.to Christian Eyer of same [the son of the said John Eyer, deceased]

--86a, 9p Warwick tp.: HISTORY: It being the same tract as given in the preceding indenture.

28 Apr 1782: CJ & Benjamin Johnson

X498: Christian Eyer & his wife Magdalena assign to Andrew Betz (or Patz) of Rapho tp.

--86a, 9p Warwick tp.: HISTORY: It being the same tract as given in the preceding indenture.

28 Apr 1782: CJ & Abraham Huber

X500: Nicholas Miller, tinman, & his wife Margaret and Christian Wirtz, shopkeeper, & his wife Margaret, all of Lancaster Borough, enf-rel.to George Moore, bricklayer, of same

--Part of a lot on Queen St. in Lancaster Borough: HISTORY: On 9 Nov 1749, James Hamilton granted a lot on Queen St. to Thomas Cookson. On 7 June 1750, Thomas Cookson granted the same to Robert Thompson. By his last will & testament, Robert Thompson devised the same to his wife Ann, who later married Walter Shee. On 20 Oct 1773, Walter Shee & his wife Ann granted the same to Benjamin Flower. On 14 Sep 1774, Benjamin Flower & his wife Sarah granted the same to Nicholas Miller, Christian Wirtz, & George Moore. [Note: See Deed R540, among others, for additional information.]

4 Jul 1778: PH, CM, & James Ross

X508: Robert Cunningham, yeoman, & his wife Margaret of Mount Joy tp. enf-rel.to David Martin, yeoman, of same

96a, 52p Mount Joy tp.: HISTORY: Part of two tracts: (1.) 174 ½ a. pat. 9 June 1747 to Samuel Cunningham [Ref. PB A-15-265] and (2.) 87 ½ a. pat. 14 May 1760 to Samuel Cunningham [Ref. PB AA-1-3]. // By his last will & testament dated 26 Jul 1774, Samuel Cunningham devised his real estate to his son Robert Cunningham [party hereto].

13 Oct 1783: Joseph Work & Abraham Gisch

X512: William Parr, Esq., & his wife Grace and Henry Dering & his wife Mary, all of Lancaster Borough, enf-rel.to Christian Kurtz, yeoman, of Manheim tp.

104a, 159p Manheim tp.: HISTORY: Part of a larger 188a tract [see Deed X10].

--11 Jan 1784: MH & CS

X515: John Witmer, Jr., & his wife Mary of Lancaster Borough enf-rel.to Adam Weaver of same

3a, 50p Lampeter tp.: HISTORY: Part of 125a Lampeter tp. that Martin Bear & his wife Elizabeth granted 21 Nov 1757 to Jacob Bear. On 3 Apr 1775, Jacob Bear & his wife Elizabeth granted the same to Benjamin Graft (Ref. Deed S164). On 20 Oct 1778, Benjamin Graft granted the same to John Witmer.

16 Feb 1782: William Parr & George Graff

X518: John Witmer, Jr., & his wife Mary of Lancaster Borough enf-rel.to John Christy of Lampeter tp. [joiner or junior?]

5a, 20p Lampeter tp.: HISTORY: Part of 100a Lampeter tp. that Martin Cryder & his wife Elizabeth, John Cryder, Jacob Cryder, and Henry Cryder & his wife Magdalena granted 19 May 1775 to John Witmer (Ref. Deed S284).

13 Feb 1782: WH & CJ

X521: Adam Weaver, innkeeper, & his wife Rosina of Lancaster Borough enf-rel.to John Christy of Lampeter tp. [joiner or junior—says junior where occupation is normally listed]

3a, 50p Lampeter tp.: HISTORY: It being the same lot as given in Deed X515.

--12 Feb 1784: CJ & Christian Drebelt

X524: Arnold Bamberger, breeches maker, & his wife Elizabeth of Lancaster Borough enf-rel.to William Evitt of same

--Half lot on Church St. in Lancaster Borough: HISTORY: It being the eastern moiety of a lot that Adam Simon Kuhn granted 11 Nov 1744 to Joachim Borger. On 19 Oct 1745, Joachim Borger granted the full lot to Andrew Mille. On 23 Feb 1747, Andrew Mille & his wife Margaret granted the same to John Sneyder. On 10 Apr 1751, John Sneyder & his wife Magdalena granted the same to Mathias Boogh, alias Boocke. On 10 May 1769, Mathias Boogh & his wife Catharine granted half of the lot to Stephen Sutton. On 14 Jan 1774, Stephan Sutton & his wife Christina assigned the same to Arnold Bamberger.

3 Feb 1778: ES & CS

X527: William Evitt & his wife Elizabeth assign to John Jordan of Lancaster Borough

--Half lot in Lancaster Borough: HISTORY: No given, but surely the same half lot as given in the preceding indenture.

28 Feb 1781: James Boyd & James Buchanon

X528: Martin Greitter (or Cryter, or Cryder), yeoman, & his wife Elizabeth of Hempfield tp. enf-rel.to Peter Cryder of same

14 ½ a. Hempfield tp.: HISTORY: Part of 500a pat. 1 June 1734 to Isaac Norris, late of Philadelphia (Ref. PB A-6-327). By his last will & testament, Isaac Norris ordered his executors [to wit, his wife Mary Norris, Isaac Norris, Charles Norris, & Samuel Norris] to sell the property. On 17 Nov 1740, they granted 14 ½ a. to Martin Greitter.

10 Mar 1757: Hans Graft & Andreas Kauffman

X530: Peter Kreider (or Cryder), yeoman, & his wife Mary of Hempfield tp. quitclaim to Christian Brubacher, yeoman, of Lancaster County

14 ½ a. Hempfield tp.: HISTORY: It being the same tract as given in the preceding indenture.

--15 Aug 1766: Joseph Boude & Jacob Brubacher

X533: Peter Kreider, yeoman, & his wife Mary of Hempfield tp. enf-rel.to Christian Brubacher, yeoman, of Lancaster County

222a Hempfield tp.: HISTORY: Same tract pat. 12 Dec 1748 to Peter Kreider (Ref. PB A-14-167).

--15 Aug 1766: Joseph Boude & Jacob Brubacher

X536: Daniel Hahn, yeoman, & his wife Barbara of Earl tp. enf-rel.to John Graff of same

15a Brecknock tp.: HISTORY: Part of 112 ¾ a. Brecknock tp. that Philip Epright granted 30 Apr 1759 to David Shark [sic: Sherk] (Ref. Deed H115). Said David Shark died intestate leaving a widow Margaret and issue several children. On 9 Mar 1777, David Shark & his wife, John Gehr & his wife, Henry Coffroth & his wife, and John Diller & his wife granted the same to Jacob Shark [son of said David Shark, deceased]. On 9 May 1777, Jacob Shark granted the same to Christian Eckstein. On 9 May 1777, said John Gehr & Henry Coffroth [the guardians of David Shark's four minor children] agreed to grant the shares of their wards to the said Christian Eckstein. On 19 Mar 1779, Christian Eckstein granted 112a to Philip Fastnacht. On 23 Nov 1782, Philip Fastnacht & his wife Juliana granted the same to Daniel Hahn.

5 Apr 1783: HR & ZD

X539: John Witmer, the younger, gentleman, & his wife Mary of Radnor tp., Chester County enf-rel.to Andrew Graff, gentleman, of Lancaster tp.

29 ½ a. Lampeter tp.: HISTORY: Part of a larger tract that Jacob Graff & his wife Mary granted 1 June 1743 to Theophilus Hartman (Ref. Deed H14). On 28 Nov 1764, Theophilus Hartman & his wife Hannah granted 30a to Godlip Hartman (Ref. Deed K187). On 8 June 1769, Godlip Hartman & his wife Mary granted 29 ½ a. to John Witmer (Ref. Deed S147).

8 Apr 1783: James Woods & _____ ["N.L."—presumably "not listed"]

X543: Henry Shute, yeoman, & his wife Mary of Lampeter tp. enf-rel.to John Parker, yeoman, of same
10a Lampeter tp.: HISTORY: Part of 101a Lampeter tp. that John Funk granted 14 Sep 1739 to Henry Haine, the younger (Ref. Deed D9). Said Henry Haine died intestate leaving issue several children. On 10 Dec 1757, the Court of Common Pleas allotted 96a [part of the 101a tract] to Frederick Seiger in right of his wife Mary, a daughter of the deceased. Said Frederick Seiger has since died and his wife Mary has married the said Henry Shute [party hereto].
17 Dec 1779: Samuel Wilie & CJ

X547: Henry Shute, yeoman, & his wife Mary of Lampeter tp. enf-rel.to Robert Parker, yeoman, of same
2a Lampeter tp.: HISTORY: Part of a larger 101a tract [see the preceding indenture for the complete history].
--13 Apr 1780: Samuel Hains & CJ

X551: Christian Hershy, yeoman, & his wife Ann of Warwick tp.; Jacob Hostetter & his wife Ann; and Benedict Mellinger & his wife Mary [the said Christian, Ann, & Mary being three children of Benjamin Hershy, deceased, late of Lancaster tp.] quitclaim to Benjamin Hershy of Lancaster County [another child of said Benjamin Hershy, deceased]
--Two tracts: (1.) 175a, 75p Lancaster tp. and (2.) 74 ¼ a. Lancaster tp.

1. HISTORY: Part of 1,000a pat. 30 Nov 1717 to Hans Brubacher & Christian Hershy (Ref. PB A-5-271). They partitioned the property, allotting 500a to one another. Said Christian Hershy died intestate leaving a wife named Ode and issue two sons and one daughter; to wit, Benjamin Hershy, Andrew Hershy, and Ann Hershy (wife of Herman Long). On 21 Dec 1733, Herman Long & his wife, Ode Hershy, and Andrew Hershy released the 500a tract to son Benjamin Hershy.
2. HISTORY: Part of the same 1,000a tract—from the portion allotted to Hans Brubacher. On 18 May 1731, the heirs of Christian Hershy granted 74 ½ a. to Hans Brubacher. On 1 Sep 1760, the heirs of Hans Brubacher [not named] granted the same to said Benjamin Hershy.

--Benjamin Hershy died intestate seized in possession of both aforesaid tracts, leaving issue two sons and two sons [the parties hereto].
14 May 1773: Daniel Frank & CS

X555: Benjamin Hershy (or Herschy), Sr., of Lancaster tp. gr.to Benjamin Hershy, Jr.
--[This indenture is written in German, which this compiler cannot read. The date appears to be 20 Feb 1784. Witnesses are Christian Brubacher & Jacob Brubacher. This indenture likely involves a land transfer from father to son—see the preceding indenture.]

X557: Alexander Lowrey & his wife Ann of Donegal tp. gr.to William Peck (or Peack) of Maytown
--Lot #36 on River St. in Maytown and also a small out lot adjoining the said town: HISTORY: Not given.
23 Feb 1784: HD & Nicholas Bond

X561: John David Frank, doctor of physick, & his wife Catharine of Manor tp. enf-rel.to Valentine Kress, shoemaker, of same
10a Manor tp.: HISTORY: Part of 134a, 50p Manor tp. pat. 7 Apr 1762 to Michael Kaufman [Ref. PB AA-3-170]. On 21 Jul 1778, Michael Kaufman & his wife Catharine granted 20a to Christian Hare. On 11 Jul 1782, Christian Hare granted 10a to John David Frank (Ref. Deed X212).
21 Feb 1784: JJACK & PG

X564: Peter Miller, yeoman, & his wife Sybilla of Earl tp. enf-rel.to Christian Burkholder, yeoman, of same
97a, 58p Earl tp.: HISTORY: Same tract pat. 7 Mar 1767 to Henry Sheibley (Ref. PB AA-8-244). On 16 Dec 1769, Henry Sheibley & his wife Elizabeth granted the same to Peter Miller (Ref. Deed Q65).
23 Feb 1784: George Riane & Samuel Carpenter

X568: Peter Miller, yeoman, of Earl tp. enf-rel.to Christian Burkholder, yeoman, of same

30a Earl tp.: HISTORY: Part of 129a Earl tp. war. 4 Dec 1750 to Walter Fishback. On 25 Jul 1752, Walter Fishbach granted the same to Henry Martin. On 27 June 1755, Henry Martin assigned the same to Jacob Ramp. By two separate indentures, one dated 13 June 1766 and the other 9 Aug 1779, Jacob Ramp granted a certain parcel to Charles Miller. On 12 Feb 1783, Charles Miller granted 30a to his son Peter Miller.

____ [omitted] 1784: George Riane & Samuel Carpenter

X570: Jacob Ricksecker (or Rixacker), yeoman, & his wife Elizabeth; Peter Ricksecker, yeoman, & his wife Barbara; Catharine Younging (or Yeungin), John Crush, yeoman, & his wife Barbara; Catharine Cassel (or Kasler); Anna Johanna Ricksecker; Elizabeth Ricksecker; and Cathrough Ricksecker [the children & stepchildren of Peter Ricksecker, deceased, late of Lancaster County, yeoman] rel.to John Ricksecker, yeoman, of Warwick tp. [another child of said Peter Ricksecker, deceased]

177a Warwick tp.: HISTORY: Same tract pat. 20 May 1761 to Peter Ricksecker (Ref. PB AA-1-344). Said Peter Ricksecker died leaving issue the above children plus another son Christian. On 16 Jan 1779, said Christian Ricksecker granted his right to his brother Peter Ricksecker.

10 June 1780: HD & CJ

--[Note: Stepchildren are not distinguished from children. An analysis of the Lititz Moravian records suggests that Catharine Younging (or Jung), Barbara Crush (or Grosch), and Catharine Cassel are stepchildren. Furthermore, Cathrough Ricksecker equates to Gertraut Ricksecker.]

X575: John Ricksecker (or Rixacker), yeoman, & his wife Rachel of Warwick tp. enf-rel.to Jacob Ricksecker, yeoman, of same

29a Warwick tp.: HISTORY: Part of a larger 177-acre tract. See the preceding indenture for the history of this larger tract.

10 June 1780: HD

X578: John Ricksecker (or Rixacker), yeoman, & his wife Rachel of Warwick tp. enf-rel.to Peter Ricksecker, yeoman, of same

50a Warwick tp.: HISTORY: Part of a larger 177-acre tract. See Deed X570 for the history of this larger tract.

10 June 1780: HD & CJ

X582: Jacob Ricksecker, yeoman, & his wife Elizabeth of Manheim tp. enf-rel.to John Longenecker, yeoman, of Strasburg tp.

125a Manheim tp.: HISTORY: Same tract that Henry Kauffman, yeoman, late of Manheim tp., by his last will & testament dated 2 Oct 1771, ordered his executors [to wit, Jacob Meyer & Peter Brubacher] to sell—subject to certain privileges bequeathed to his wife Anna Kauffman. On 19 Dec 1774, the executors granted the property to Jacob Ricksecker (Ref. Deed S179).

27 Feb 1784: Bentz Hirshi & Daniel Franck

X586: John Mosser, Jacob Mosser & his wife Christina, and Ann Mosser, all of Manor tp. [three children of Jacob Mosser, deceased, late of Lancaster County] rel.to Bentz Mosser [son of the said Jacob Mosser, deceased]

83 ½ a. Conestoga Manor: HISTORY: Part of 167a Conestoga Manor pat. 13 Jul 1741 to John Wister (Ref. PB A-10-334). On 24 Apr 1744, John Wister & his wife Catharine granted the same to John Mosser (Ref. Deed B147). On 14 Mar 1752, John Mosser granted the same to his son Jacob. By his last will & testament, Jacob Mosser devised one moiety to his son Bentz Mosser.

6 Feb 1773: CS, ES, & Bentz Hirshi

X590: Henry Weaver, miller, & his wife Veronica of Caernarvon tp. enf-rel.to Joshua Watson & William Sykes, merchants, both of Philadelphia

37a, 50p Caernarvon tp., including a gristmill & sawmill: HISTORY: Part of 244a pat. 2 Sep 1742 to Jacob Light, alias Lloyd (Ref. PB A-11-157). Said Jacob Light died intestate leaving issue five sons [to wit, Jacob Light, John Light, Peter Light, Benjamin Light, and Christian Light] and three daughters [to wit, Elizabeth wife of John Lasha, Barbara wife of Ulrich Grumbacher, and Ann wife of John Stoner]. The Orphans Court confirmed the said property to Peter, the third son [the eldest two refusing to accept]. On 30 Oct 1765, the other heirs [save for Christian, who was yet a minor—his guardian being said John Stoner] quitclaim the property to said Peter Light. // On 20 Jul 1771, Peter Light & his wife Anna granted an undivided moiety of a 6a, 137p parcel, including a gristmill and sawmill, to Henry Weaver (Ref. Deed Q189). // On 1 May 1773, Peter Light & his wife Ann granted the other undivided moiety, plus the residue of the 244-acre tract, to said Henry Weaver (Ref. Deed Q192). // On 17 Feb 1774, Henry Weaver & his wife Veronica granted 230a to his brother George Weaver of Caernarvon tp.

14 Apr 1777: Peter Miller & Benjamin Miller

X599: Henry Weaver, miller, & his wife Veronica of Caernarvon tp. rel.to Joshua Watson & William Sykes, merchants, both of Philadelphia

78a Brecknock tp.: HISTORY: Same tract war. 26 Mar 1776 [no further information—presumably warranted to Henry Weaver.

14 Apr 1777: Peter Miller & Benjamin Miller [Note: This Peter Miller is identified as a scrivener from Philadelphia.]

X602: George Stitz, gentleman, of Lebanon tp. gr.to Martin Zehntbauer of same

--Lot #151 on Market St. in the town of Lebanon: HISTORY: Not given.

10 Jul 1760: George Reynolds, John Nicholas Henicke, & George Whitman

X605: Martin Zeantbauer & his wife Agnes Barbara assign to Jacob Karch [or Kargh]

--"the within mentioned lot": HISTORY: Not given, but probably the same as given in the preceding indenture.

11 Oct 1773: Kasper Schneble & Jacob Tschantz

X606: George Matter (or Maurter), distiller, & his wife Catharine of Earl tp. enf-rel.to Valentine Mendel, distiller, of same

81a, 64p Earl tp.: HISTORY: Part of a larger tract pat. 17 Oct 1776 to George Matter (Ref. PB A-4-172).

--27 Apr 1780: Willis Davis & ZD

X609: Joseph Carpenter (or Zimmerman), yeoman, & his wife Ann of Cocalico tp. [she being late Ann Hershberger, a daughter of John Hershberger, yeoman, deceased, late of same] rel.to Henry Hershberger [the only son of the said John Hershberger, deceased]

--They acknowledge having received Ann's share out of her late father's real estate in Cocalico tp. per the instructions given in the last will & testament.

14 Mar 1783: Henry Martin & Henry Carpenter

X610: William Parry, yeoman, & his wife Mary of Earl tp. enf-rel.to Jacob Weaver, Jr., yeoman, of same

126a Earl tp.: HISTORY: Part of a larger tract pat. 14 Nov 1760 to John Davis. On 2 Mar 1762, John Davis & his wife Elizabeth granted the same to William Parry.

29 Mar 1783: D. Morgan & JJ

X613: William Parry, yeoman, & his wife Mary of Earl tp. enf-rel.to Peter Worst, shoemaker, of same

42 ½ a. Earl tp.: HISTORY: Part of the same larger tract given in the preceding indenture.

--29 Mar 1783: D. Morgan & JJ

X616: George Matter, yeoman, & his wife Catharine of Earl tp. rel.to Christian Ruth, yeoman, of same
161 ½ a. Earl tp., including a gristmill: HISTORY: Same tract pat. 10 Dec 1771 to George Matter (Ref. PB AA-13-1). Since then, George Matter has erected a gristmill on the property. On 22 Apr 1773, George Matter mortgaged the property & mill to Beulah Paschall of Philadelphia (Ref. Deed P279). As part of this agreement, Christian Ruth agrees to pay the remaining principal and interest.
22 Apr 1775: Christian Zimmerman & David Davis

X619: Stewart Herbert, Sr., yeoman, & his wife Sidney of Leacock tp. rel.to Andrew Betree (or Betree—perhaps Petry?), yeoman, of Earl tp.
27a, 20p Earl tp.: HISTORY: Part of 102 ½ a. Earl tp. pat. 7 Nov 1766 to Stewart Herbert (Ref. PB AA-8-113).
4 Apr 1778: Jacob Meyer & Christian Gotz

X621: William Stover, yeoman; Leonard Miller, yeoman, & his wife Margaret; Stophel Miller, mason, & his wife Barbara; the said Stophel Miller in right of his late wife Catharine, deceased [on behalf of their three minor children, to wit, Barbara, Leonard, & John]; Frederick Stover, yeoman; Ludwick Wolfard [the guardian of John Stover]; Adam Brown [the guardian of George Stover], and John Petree (or Peter), shoemaker, & his wife Christina [all being the sons and daughters and heirs of Valentine Stover, deceased, late of Cocalico tp.] quitclaim to Valentine Stover [another son of said Valentine Stover, deceased]
--Two tracts: (1.) 190a Cocalico tp. and (2.) 100a Cocalico tp.: HISTORY: Late the estate of Valentine Stover, deceased. On 5 Sep 1781, the Orphans Court confirmed the said lands to second son Valentine Stover—subject to paying the other heirs their equal shares.
1 Dec 1783: JJ & Christina Mullerin

X623: Valentine Stover, yeoman, of Lancaster County rel.to Christopher Miller, yeoman, of Cocalico tp.
--Three tracts: (1.) 114a Cocalico tp., (2.) 75a Cocalico tp., and (3.) 130a Cocalico tp.

1. HISTORY: Part of 190a pat. 24 June 1774 to Valentine Stover (Ref. PB AA-14-484).
2. HISTORY: Part of 190a pat. 24 June 1774 to Valentine Stover (Ref. PB AA-14-484).
3. HISTORY: Same tract war. 14 Mar 1754 to John Weaver. On 12 June 1766, John Weaver granted the same to Valentine Stover.

--Said Valentine Stover died seized in possession of all three tracts, leaving a wife Eva Elizabeth and issue several children. On 5 Sep 1781, the Orphans Court confirmed the real estate to Valentine Stover, the second son [the eldest son William Stover refusing to accept]. On equal date herewith, the other heirs released the properties to the said Valentine [see the preceding indenture].
1 Dec 1783: JJ & Michael Bear

X627: Daniel Kinportz (or Keenportz), the elder, yeoman, & his wife Anna of Conestoga tp. enf-rel.to Daniel Kinportz, the younger, of same
89 ½ a. Conestoga tp.: HISTORY: It being one moiety of a larger tract pat. 12 May 1748 to Daniel Kinportz (Ref. PB A-13-441). [Note: Transfer made for "love and affection".]
4 Jul 1774: Jacob Shantz & Jacob Kegg [Kagy?]

X629: James Keimer, yeoman, & his wife Sarah of Earl tp. enf-rel.to William Smith, yeoman, of same
10a Bart tp., including yearly rent charges: HISTORY: Part of a town called Smithsburg. It being the same parcel that the sheriff sold to James Keimer at public vendue [the indenture being dated 4 June 1776]. The ten-acre parcel contains sundry lots.
18 Sep 1779: Willis Davis & ZD

X632: Christian Carpenter, yeoman, & his wife Barbara of Earl tp. enf-rel.to Amos Evans, yeoman, of same
15a, 140p Earl & Caernarvon tps.—excluding a milldam: HISTORY: Part of 364a Earl & Caernarvon tps. pat. 13 June 1761 to David Evans and his mother Ann Evans (Ref. PB AA-1-317) [the said mother's moiety for her natural life only, then to her son David]. On 8 Sep 1766, David Evans & his wife Bridget granted 18a, including a milldam, to Henry Weaver. On 30 Aug 1771, Henry Weaver & his wife Fronica granted the same to Christian Carpenter.

16 Oct 1771: SH & Henry Carpenter

X635: John Sensnig (or Sinsinigh), yeoman, & his wife Ann of Paxton tp. enf-rel.to Amos Evans, yeoman, of Caernarvon tp.

18a Caernarvon tp.: HISTORY: Part of the same 364a tract as given in the preceding indenture. On 4 Oct 1765, David Evans & his wife Bridget granted 18a to Abel Griffith. On 5 Oct 1772, Abel Griffith & his wife Barbara granted the same to Henry Weaver. On 6 Jan 1777, Henry Weaver & his wife Veronica granted the same to John Sensnig.

8 Dec 1778: JT & Henry Sheffer

X638: Philip Bushung & his wife Barbara of Lampeter tp. enf-rel.to Henry Witmer, yeoman, of same

--Three tracts, all formerly in Strasburg tp., but now in Lampeter: (1.) 103a Lampeter tp., (2.) 6a Lampeter tp., and (3.) 4a, 6p Lampeter tp.

1. HISTORY: Same tract that the heirs of John Bushung granted 1 Feb 1764 to Philip Bushung (Ref. Deed P519).
2. HISTORY: Same tract that the heirs of John Bushung granted 1 Feb 1764 to Philip Bushung (Ref. Deed P519).
3. HISTORY: Same tract that John Buchwalter & his wife Elizabeth granted 23 June 1773 to Philip Bushung (Ref. Deed P517).

--2 May 1783: Simon Schneider & CS

X642: Jonathan Roland (or Rolland), yeoman, & his wife Catharine of Earl tp. enf-rel.to Andrew Brand & Frederick Seeger, grocers, both of Philadelphia

--Part of Lot #7 in the town of New Design in Earl tp., containing 29p: HISTORY: On 10 Sep 1760, Michael Diffenderfer & his wife Christina granted the full lot to Melchior Kyser. On 31 Aug 1762, Melchior Kyser & his wife Anna Maria granted the same to George Stahly. On 7 Sep 1767, George Stahly & his wife Dorothy granted the same to Jonathan Roland.

5 Mar 1779: William Grof & ZD

X644: Adam Kingmaker, yeoman, & his wife Christina of Cocalico tp. enf-rel.to Andrew Brand & Frederick Seeger, grocers, both of Philadelphia

75a Cocalico tp.: HISTORY: Part of a larger tract patented to Tobias Miller & Jacob Seifert (Ref. PB AA-7-213). On 8 Jul 1768, they granted the same larger tract to Emanuel Carpenter, Jr. On 8 Jul 1768, Emanuel Carpenter, Jr., granted 75a to Jacob Seifert. On 25 Feb 1779, Jacob Seifert granted the same to Adam Kingmaker.

17 May 1779: AN & MN

X648: David Herman, yeoman, of Earl tp. enf-rel.to Valentine Kintzer, yeoman, of same

--Residue of 102 ½ a. Earl tp.: HISTORY: 102 ½ a. Earl tp. pat. 7 Nov 1766 to Stewart Herbert (Ref. PB AA-8-113). In his lifetime, Stewart Herbert granted 42a to George Eaker & Andrew Petre. By his last will & testament, Stewart Herbert ordered his executors [to wit, Daniel Herbert, James Montgomery, & Elizabeth Herbert] to sell the residue. On 17 Mar 1780, they granted the same to James Mercer. On 17 Mar 1780, James Mercer & his wife Margaret granted the same to Daniel Herbert. On 13 Sep 1780, Daniel Herbert granted the same to Jacob Meyer. On 10 Apr 1781, Jacob Meyer & his wife Mary granted the same to David Herman.

14 Mar 1782: Anne Davis & ZD

X651: Henry Witmer, yeoman, & his wife Mary of Lampeter tp. enf-rel.to John Funk, millwright, of same

15a lot in the Village of Strasburg: HISTORY: Part of a larger tract that Mathias Causser & his wife Mary granted 18 Mar 1754 to John Miller (Ref. Deed D501). Said John Miller died intestate leaving issue children John Miller, Anna wife of Jacob Fritz, Mary wife of Henry Witmer [the party hereto], Daniel Miller, & Simon Miller. By agreement among the heirs, the above-described 15a lot was allotted to daughter Mary and her husband. On 26 Jul 1780, the other heirs [with Jacob Kendich representing his wards Daniel Miller & Simon Miller] quitclaimed the same to Henry Witmer.

15 Oct 1781: John Brackbill & EG

X655: Henry Witmer, yeoman, & his wife Mary of Lampeter tp. enf-rel.to John Funk, millwright, of same

51 ½ a. Strasburg tp.: HISTORY: Same tract pat. 30 Nov 1769 to John Miller (Ref. PB AA-11-192). Said John Miller died intestate leaving issue children John Miller, Anna wife of Jacob Fritz, Mary wife of Henry Witmer [the party hereto], Daniel Miller, & Simon Miller. By agreement among the heirs, the above-described 51 ½ a. tract was allotted to daughter Mary and her husband. On 26 Jul 1780, the other heirs [with Jacob Kendich representing his wards Daniel Miller & Simon Miller] quitclaimed the same to Henry Witmer.

4 May 1782: Jacob Stoutsberg & EG

X658: Sheriff Thomas Edwards enf-rel.to William Armstrong of Norrington tp., Philadelphia County

200a Caernarvon tp.: HISTORY: On 11 Nov 1782, the Court of Common Pleas ordered the sheriff to seize the real estate of Benjamin Jacobs, deceased, late of Philadelphia County [the property then in the possession of his executor Israel Jacobs of Lancaster County] for debts owing to one William Armstrong. The sheriff duly seized 200a Caernarvon tp., which he later sold at public sale to said William Armstrong.

5 Feb 1784: Andrew Dunlop & JH

Abstracts of Lancaster County Deed Book Y

Y1: Thomas Penn & Richard Penn, Esquires, the Proprietors & Governors of the Province of Pennsylvania rel.to Ann Steven

147a Manheim tp.: HISTORY: Same property surveyed 21 May 1734 to Jacob Shelley, yeoman. On 26 Mar last, said Jacob Shelley legally acquired the property on a warrant to accept. On 27 Mar last, Jacob Shelley granted the same to his sister Anna Steven, widow, and her children, to wit, Abraham Peidler [by a former husband] and Daniel Steven, Christian Steven, & Elizabeth Steven [by her late husband Frederick Steven].

6 Nov 1751: (Seal)

Y3: Abraham Peidler (or Beidler), Daniel Steven & his wife Mary, and Christian Steven & his wife Sabina, all of Lancaster County, enf-rel.to Jacob Coffman, yeoman, of same

147a Manheim tp.: HISTORY: Same tract pat. 6 Nov 1751 to Anna Steven and her children (Ref. PB A-16-80) [see the preceding indenture]. Said Anna Steven and her daughter Elizabeth Steven have since died intestate.

8 Feb 1760: WJ & DS

Y7: Jacob Kauffman, yeoman, & his wife Barbara of Manheim tp.; Isaac Kauffman, yeoman, & his wife Elizabeth of Hempfield tp.; Peter Baughman, yeoman, & his wife Mary of Manheim tp.; Benedict Eshelman, yeoman, & his wife Elizabeth of Hempfield tp.; Anna Brubaker, widow, of Rapho tp.; and Eve Kauffman, widow, of Hempfield tp. [the said Jacob, Isaac, Mary, Elizabeth, and Anna being children of Jacob Kauffman, deceased, late of Hempfield tp., and the said Eve being his widow] quitclaim to Andrew Kauffman, yeoman, of Hempfield tp. [another son of said Jacob Kauffman, deceased]

165 ¼ a. Lancaster County: HISTORY: It being part of two tracts: (1.) 147a Manheim tp. [the same tract acquired by Jacob Kauffman in the preceding indenture] and (2.) a larger tract pat. 20 Nov 1761 to James Webb [Ref. PB AA-3-17]. On 12 Feb 1762, James Webb & his wife Hannah granted 18 ¼ a. Hempfield tp. to Jacob Kauffman. // By his last will & testament dated 14 May 1767, Jacob Kauffman devised his plantation bought of Christian Stibgen, containing 173 acres, to his son Andrew. However, the heirs have agreed that Andrew's share should be a portion of the two plantations above, in addition to a five-acre tract to be purchased from Peter Brubaker [see the following indenture].

13 Sep 1771: WA, Jacob Neff, & WC

Y13: Peter Brubaker, yeoman, & his wife Anna of Lancaster County enf-rel.to Andrew Kauffman, yeoman, of same

5 ½ a. Hempfield tp.: HISTORY: Part of 90 ½ a. pat. 9 May 1761 to Peter Brubaker (Ref. PB AA-1-282).

--21 Sep 1771: Jacob Brubaker & WA

Y16: John Musser & his wife Sarah of Lancaster Borough and Abraham Witmer & his wife Mary of Lancaster tp. enf-rel.to Adam Reigert, innkeeper, of Lancaster Borough

7a, 95p Manheim tp., "numbered 3 & 4 in the draught": HISTORY: Part of 183a that Henry Landis & his wife Mary granted 28 Feb 1782 to John Musser & Abraham Witmer (Ref. Deed Q668).

12 Aug 1782: William French & J. Funk

Y19: Frederick Nauman & his wife Anna Elizabeth assign to George Britch (or Bridge, or Britz) of the town of Manheim

--Two lots of ground: HISTORY: No further information.

17 Apr 1783: David Nieckey & Christian Hergeroth

Y20: Michael Gerber (or Garver), yeoman, & his wife Ann of Manheim tp. enf-rel.to Felix Binkley (or Pinkley), yeoman, of Lampeter tp.

100a Manheim tp., including a mill: HISTORY: Same tract pat. 4 June 1746 to Michael Gerber, alias Garver.

26 May 1770: MH & A. Hubley

Y22: Bernard Hubley, shopkeeper, & his wife Mary of Lancaster Borough enf-rel.to Gerhard Bubach, butcher, of same

--Half lot on Queen St. in Lancaster Borough: HISTORY: On 14 Jan 1740, James Hamilton granted a lot on Queen St. to George Hortz. On 21 Aug 1744, George Hortz assigned the same to Simon Belsher. On 23 Aug 1752, Simon Belsher & his wife Elizabeth granted the same to John Frederick Handshu and Bernard Hubley—one undivided moiety to each. On 15 Apr 1763, John Frederick Handshu & his wife Susanna Barbara granted their moiety to Bernard Hubley.

13 Jan 1779: HD & CS

Y25: Daniel Kinport, yeoman, & his wife Anna of Conestoga tp. enf-rel.to David Hess, yeoman, of same

--Two tracts: (1.) 110a Conestoga tp. and (2.) 25 ½ a. Conestoga tp.: HISTORY: Same tracts that said Daniel Kinport & his wife Anna granted 10 Jan 1765 to Leonard May. On 23 Aug 1768, Leonard May & his wife Christina re-conveyed the properties to Daniel Kinport.

23 Feb 1771: WA & WC

Y28: Agreement between Adam Tate of Lancaster County and Joseph Latta of Mecklenburg County in North Carolina

--The parties agree to a voluntary exchange of land: Adam Tate gives his 600a tract in Mecklenburg County, North Carolina, to Joseph Latta in exchange for Joseph Latta's 221a tract in Hempfield tp. As Joseph Latta is presently under the age of 21, the actual exchange will not take place until on or about 1 Jan 1780.

1 Dec 1778: James McKown & Robert Poston

Y29: Abraham Buchwalter, miller, of Lancaster County rel.to James Gibbons, miller, of Chester County

403a in Leacock & Lampeter tps., including the mills: HISTORY: Not given.

--29 Mar 1783: John Ferree & George Bressler

Y31: Francis Smith, blacksmith, & his wife Elizabeth of Lampeter tp. enf-rel.to Salome Hains, widow, of same

--Two tracts: (1.) 50a Lampeter tp. and (2.) 18a, 40p Lampeter tp.

1. HISTORY: Part of a larger tract that Henry Carpenter granted 10 Dec 1743 to Daniel Carpenter. On 1 Jul 1759, Daniel Carpenter & his wife Magdalena granted 53a to Jacob Carpenter. On 13 June 1760, Jacob Carpenter granted 50a to Daniel Furrer. On 5 Jul 1762, Daniel Furrer granted the same to Christian Forrer. On 25 Mar 1774, Christian Forrer granted the same to Francis Smith.
2. HISTORY: Same tract that Rudolph Haines granted 18 May 1765 to Christian Forrer (Ref. Deed S385). On 25 Mar 1774, Christian Forrer granted the same to Francis Smith.

--1 Apr 1783: JK & James Smith, Jr.

Y34: John Grouss (or Krouse), taylor, & his wife Mary of the town of New Design in Earl tp. enf-rel.to Henry Marcley (or Martly), saddler, of same

--Lot #10 in the town of New Design, containing two rods and twenty perches: HISTORY: Same lot that Michael Diffenderfer & his wife Christina granted 10 Sep 1760 to Alexander McElvain. On 30 Apr 1764, Alexander McElvain & his wife Rebecca granted the same to John Grouss.

17 Mar 1767: Hannes Diffenderfer & George Rine

Y37: Michael Dieffenderffer, yeoman, of Lancaster Borough rel.to Peter Baker, yeoman, of Earl tp.

--Ground rent charge on Lot #10 in the town of New Design in Earl tp.: HISTORY: It being the same lot as given in the preceding indenture. On 28 May 1777, Henry Marcley & his wife Barbara granted the same lot to Christopher Frederick. On 29 May 1778, Christopher Frederick & his wife Elizabeth granted the same to Peter Baker.

21 Jul 1779: WH & Hannes Dieffenderffer

Y39: Peter Becker (or Baker), yeoman, & his wife Christina of Earl tp. enf-rel.to John Luther, practitioner of physick, of Cocalico tp.

--Lot #10 in the town of New Design in Earl tp.: HISTORY: It being the same lot as given in the preceding indenture.

26 June 1782: Henry Peters & Frederick Seeger

Y42: John Mendenhall, yeoman, of Earl tp. enf-rel.to his son Stephen Mendenhall, carpenter, of same

--Two tracts: (1.) 145a Earl tp. and (2.) 5a, 11p Earl tp.

1. HISTORY: On 3 & 4 May 1682, William Penn, Esq., granted 1,000 to be laid out in the Province of Pennsylvania to James Craven. By his last will & testament dated 4 Feb 1694, James Craven devised the same right to his son Richard Craven, merchant, of the County of Limerick. On 11 & 12 Jul 1728, Richard Craven granted the same right to Benjamin Craven, merchant, of Dublin. On 10 & 11 Mar 1728 [sic], Benjamin Craven granted the same right to James Miller of New Garden tp. in Chester County. On 29 & 30 Oct 1730, James Miller granted a 500a right to John Mendenhall. In pursuance to a warrant dated 16 Apr 1743, John Mendenhall had 500a surveyed in Earl tp., Lancaster County.
2. HISTORY: Part of 100a Earl tp. pat. 17 May 1748 to John Mendenhall (Ref. PB A-13-348).

--2 June 1749: Christian Hildebrand & Aaron Mendenhall

Y46: Stephen Mendenhall, carpenter, & his wife Sarah of Earl tp. rel.to Henry Weaver, yeoman, of same

95a, 14p Earl tp.: HISTORY: Part of a larger 145a tract [see the preceding indenture for the history of this property]. Subject to a mortgage with the General Loan Office dated 10 Apr 1751.

15 May 1754: Jacob Huber & Abraham Kendig

Y48: Henry Weaver, yeoman, & his wife Frena of Lancaster County enf-rel.to George Weaver, yeoman, of same

--Two tracts: (1.) 95a, 14p Earl tp. and (2.) 30a Earl tp.

1. HISTORY: Same tract as given in the preceding indenture.
2. HISTORY: Same tract that Mary Levistone granted 10 Jan 1756 to Henry Weaver.

--13 Feb 1763: WJ & Hannes Witmer

Y51: Sheriff Thomas Smith gr.to Mary Leviston

--Two tracts: (1.) 50a Earl tp. and (2.) 5a, 11p Earl tp.: HISTORY: On 8 Feb in the 28th year of the reign of King George II, the Court of Common Pleas ordered the sheriff to seize the real estate of Archibald McCurdy, blacksmith, late of Earl tp., deceased [now being in the hands of his executors William McCoshry (or McCoskny) and William Miller & his wife Elizabeth (late McCurdy, the widow of said Archibald)] for debts owing to the said Mary Leviston [the administratrix of Henry Leviston]. The sheriff duly seized the above-described tracts in Earl tp., which he later sold at public vendue to the said Mary Leviston. [Note: See Deed Y57 below.]

2 Aug 1755: CM & William Smith

Y54: Mary Leviston, widow, of Earl tp. enf-rel.to Henry Weaver of same

30a Earl tp.: HISTORY: It being part of a larger 50a tract [see the preceding indenture for the larger history of this property].

10 Jan 1756: Frederick Valade [Salade?]& Charles McCarson

Y57: Stephen Mendenhall, yeoman, & his wife Sarah of Earl tp. enf-rel.to Archibald McCurdy, blacksmith, of same

--Two tracts: (1.) 50a Earl tp. and (2.) 5a, 11p Earl tp.

1. HISTORY: It being part of a larger 500a tract [see Deed Y42 for the complete history]. (Note: This indenture adds the note that John Mendenhall is late of Caln tp., Chester County.)
2. HISTORY: Part of 100a Earl tp. pat. 17 May 1748 to John Mendenhall [see Deed Y42 for the complete history].

--17 Apr 1750: John Kittera & Moses Mendenhall

Y61: Sheriff Frederick Stone gr.to James Crawford

17 ¾ a. Earl tp.: HISTORY: On 4 May 1770, the Court of Common Pleas ordered the sheriff to seize the real estate of John White, cooper, of Earl tp. for debts owing to one William McCausland. The sheriff duly seized the above-described tract, which he later sold at public vendue to the said James Crawford.

4 Sep 1771: JH

Y65: James Crawford, yeoman, & his wife Ann of Leacock tp. rel.to Henry Weaver, yeoman, of the Village of Strasburg

17 ¾ a. Earl tp.: HISTORY: On 3 & 4 May 1682, William Penn, Esq., granted 1,000 to be laid out in the Province of Pennsylvania to James Craven. By his last will & testament dated 4 Feb 1694, James Craven devised the same right to his son Richard Craven, merchant, of the County of Limerick. On 11 & 12 Jul 1728, Richard Craven granted the same right to Benjamin Craven, merchant, of Dublin. On 10 & 11 Mar 1728 [sic], Benjamin Craven granted the same right to James Miller of New Garden tp. in Chester County. On 29 & 30 Oct 1730, James Miller granted a 500a right to John Mendenhall. In pursuance to a warrant dated 16 Apr 1743, John Mendenhall had 500a surveyed in Earl tp., Lancaster County. On 2 June 1749, John Mendenhall granted 145a to Stephen Mendenhall. On 17 Apr 1750, Stephen Mendenhall granted 50a to Archibald McCurdy. By court order, the county sheriff seized the property for unpaid debts and sold the same to Mary Leviston. The said Mary Leviston, widow, then married John White. By court order, the county sheriff seized the real estate of John White for unpaid debts. On 4 Sep 1771, the sheriff granted 17 ¾ a. Earl tp. [part of the 50a tract] to James Crawford. [See the preceding indentures for these transactions.]

18 Apr 1772: Thomas McCausland & EG

Y68: George Weaver, yeoman, & his wife Frena of Strasburg tp. enf-rel.to Henry Weaver, yeoman, of the Village of Strasburg

--Two tracts: (1.) 95a, 14p Earl tp. and (2.) 30a Earl tp.

1. HISTORY: Same tract that Stephen Mendenhall & his wife Sarah granted 15 May 1754 to said Henry Weaver.
2. HISTORY: Same tract that Mary Leviston granted 10 Jan 1756 to the said Henry Weaver.

--On 13 Feb 1763, said Henry Weaver & his wife Frena granted both aforesaid tracts to George Weaver.

--8 June 1772: Jacob Kindrick & Emanuel Herr

Y70: John Ludwig, yeoman, & his wife Catharine of Earl tp. enf-rel.to Henry Weaver, yeoman, of the Village of Strasburg

58a, 50p Earl tp.: HISTORY: Part of 88 ½ a. Earl tp. pat. 5 May 1765 to George Brown (Ref. PB AA-1-258). On 9 Nov 1768, George Brown & his wife Susanna granted the same to John Ludwig. Shortly thereafter, John Ludwig conveyed 32 acres to Samuel Stouffer (Ref. Deed O97).

20 Oct 1772: William Jenkins & John Martin

Y73: Henry Weaver, yeoman, & his wife Frena of the Village of Strasburg enf-rel.to Jacob Glasser (or Klauzer), yeoman, of Earl tp.

58a, 50p Earl tp.: HISTORY: It being the same tract as given in the previous indenture.

--30 Apr 1773: Jacob Pfautz & John Stoutesberg

Y75: Henry Weaver, yeoman, & his wife Frena of the Village of Strasburg enf-rel.to Jacob Glasser, yeoman, of Earl tp.

--Three tracts: (1.) 30a Earl tp., (2.) 95a, 14p Earl tp., and (3.) 17 ¾ a. Earl tp.: HISTORY: They being the same three tracts as given in deeds Y65 and Y68.

30 Apr 1773: Jacob Pfautz & John Stoutesberg

Y79: Christian Miller, weaver, & his wife Barbara of Lampeter tp. enf-rel.to Mesha Erb, laborer, of same
--Lot #10 in Hains Town in Lampeter tp., containing four acres: HISTORY: It being the same lot as given in Deed X95.
18 Oct 1783: Elizabeth Hubley & MH

Y81: Casper Diller, Jr., yeoman, & his wife Juliana of Lebanon tp. enf-rel.to Lawrence Siegrist, yeoman, of Lancaster County
253 ¾ a. Lebanon tp.: HISTORY: It being part of two adjoining tracts: (1.) 291 ¾ a. Lebanon tp. pat. 8 Oct 1751 to George Peters [Ref. PB A-17-425]. On 18 June 1755, George Peters & his wife Anna Margaret granted the same to Casper Diller, Sr. On 4 June 1762, Casper Diller, Sr., & his wife Anna Barbara granted 241 ¾ a. to Casper Diller, Jr. (Ref. Deed H34). // (2.) 162a, 134p Lebanon tp. pat. 26 Sep 1770 to Casper Diller, Jr., alias Dealer [Ref. PB AA-11-416].
14 Apr 1774: Adam Orth & JT

Y85: Emanuel Peifer, yeoman, & his wife Barbara of Brecknock tp. enf-rel.to Martin Bowman, yeoman, of Earl tp.
134a Brecknock tp.: HISTORY: Part of 290a pat. 13 June 1764 to Alexander Stedman, Charles Stedman, & Henry William Stiegel (Ref. PB AA-5-581). On 14 Nov 1764, Alexander Stedman & his wife Elizabeth, Charles Stedman & his wife Ann, and Henry William Stiegel & his wife Elizabeth granted the same to Ludwick Mohler. On 14 Nov 1766, Ludwick Mohler & his wife Ann granted 193a to John Rush. On 3 June 1774, John Rush & his wife Elizabeth granted 134a to Bartholomew Alter. On 13 May 1777, Bartholomew Alter & his wife Hannah granted the same to Christian Eckstein (Ref. Deed R412). On 1 Dec 1778, Christian Eckstein granted the same to Griffith Jones. Said Griffith Jones & his wife Hannah later granted the same to Emanuel Peifer.
26 Feb 1782: John Cooper & Adam Oberlin

Y89: John Ream, millwright, & his wife Margaret of Earl tp. enf-rel.to Martin Bowman, Jr., yeoman, of same
45a, 36p Earl tp.: HISTORY: Same tract pat. 15 Apr 1774 to John Ream (Ref. PB AA-14-250).
--22 Apr 1782: Martin Bowman & Christian Shwartzwelder

Y92: Daniel McPherson, yeoman, & his wife Mary of Salisbury tp. enf-rel.to Frederick Baker, yeoman, of Warwick tp.
225 ½ a. Salisbury tp.: HISTORY: Part of 250a pat. 26 May 1714 to Elizabeth Pace (Ref. PB A-5-74). Said Elizabeth Pace later married James Philips. On 8 June 1728, James Philips & his wife Elizabeth granted the same to Robert Hoar. On 20 Aug 1731, Robert Hoar & his wife Sarah granted the same to Daniel McPherson (Ref. Deed N67). Said Daniel McPherson died intestate leaving issue the following children: Daniel McPherson [the party hereto], John McPherson, William McPherson, Stephen McPherson, and Ann the wife of Nathaniel Carter. On 26 Aug 1755, the other heirs released the 250a tract to son Daniel McPherson (Ref. Deed N69).
19 Dec 1769: Samuel J. Atlee & Leonard Ellmaker

Y96: Mary Davis, widow, of Caernarvon tp. rel.to George Ross, attorney, of Lancaster Borough & William Smith, yeoman, of Earl tp. in TRUST
323a Caernarvon tp.: HISTORY: Same tract pat. 3 Mar 1739 to Edward Davis (Ref. PB A-10-55). Said Edward Davis died intestate and the property descended to his only daughter Mary Davis [the party hereto]. Said Mary has had issue the following children: James Davis, Ann Davis, Sarah Davis, and Jane Davis. In consideration of the welfare and advancement of her children, Mary Davis devises the property to the above grantees for a term of eight years, or until her son James arrives at the age of 22. Son James will take partial control of the property and ultimately full control after his mother's death—subject to him paying certain legacies to his siblings as will be directed in his mother's last will & testament. If said James fails to pay these legacies, then the above grantees are authorized to seize and sell the property. [Note: Clearly Mary's husband was also surnamed Davis.]
3 Feb 1768: Henry Weaver & Peter Light

Y101: Thomas Penn & Richard Penn, esquires, the Proprietors & Governors of the Province of Pennsylvania patent to Alexander Brown the following property: 49a, 23p Earl tp.: HISTORY: Same tract warranted & later surveyed to Alexander Brown.
22 Mar 1771: John Penn

Y103: Alexander Brown, distiller, of Salisbury tp. enf-rel.to John Weidler (or Whiteler), yeoman, of Earl tp.
49a, 23p Earl tp.: HISTORY: It being the same tract as given in the preceding indenture (Ref. PB AA-11-523).
25 Nov 1771: Robert McNeill & John Hopkins

Y105: James McAuley (McAvley?), yeoman, of Salisbury tp. rel.to James Smith, surveyor, of Lampeter tp.
20a [location not given, but identified as mountain land]: HISTORY: Part of a larger tract warranted 24 Dec 1740 to John McAuley of Salisbury tp. By his last will & testament, John McAuley devised the larger tract to his two sons, Robert McAuley [lately deceased] and said James McAuley. // As a condition of this indenture, one moiety of the property goes to James Smith and the other moiety to John Smith, Jr. [a minor brother of the said James Smith].
26 5mo. 1783: James Ramsey

Y107: Tobias Stoneman (or Steman), yeoman, & his wife Anna of Conestoga tp. enf-rel.to Andrew Fehl, yeoman, of same
73a Conestoga tp.: HISTORY: In his lifetime, John Postlethwaite, Esq., became seized of four adjoining tracts in Conestoga tp. He mortgaged these properties to the General Loan Office; however, he died before satisfying the mortgage. The General Loan Office seized the properties and granted them to Joseph Pugh, Esq., on 8 June 1760. On 8 Oct 1761, Joseph Pugh & his wife Mary granted 197a to Tobias Stoneman.
26 Apr 1762: JMR & JB

Y110: Tobias Stoneman (or Steman), yeoman, & his wife Anna of Conestoga tp. enf-rel.to Andrew Fehl, yeoman, of same
22a, 102p Conestoga tp.: HISTORY: In his lifetime, John Postlethwaite, Esq., became seized of four adjoining tracts in Conestoga tp. He mortgaged these properties to the General Loan Office; however, he died before satisfying the mortgage. The General Loan Office seized the properties and granted them on 8 June 1760 to Joseph Pugh, Esq. On 8 Oct 1761, Joseph Pugh & his wife Mary granted 197a to Tobias Stoneman. // On 8 Oct 1761, the children of said John Postlethwaite [to wit, John Postlethwaite, Samuel Postlethwaite, & Edmund Postlethwaite] released their right to the said property under the last will & testament of their late father.
2 Apr 1771: Benjamin Poultney & JH

Y114: Jacob Fetterhaff, yeoman, & his wife Barbara of Bethel tp. enf-rel.to George Houk, yeoman, of Cocalico tp.
91a Cocalico tp.: HISTORY: On 4 Sep 1762, John Graff of Warwick tp. & Jacob Erb of the same [the executors of Abraham Shonauer, late of Cocalico tp.] granted two adjoining tracts in Cocalico tp., one containing 114 acres and the other 46-¼ acres to Jacob Shonauer. By his last will & testament dated 13 Dec 1763, Jacob Shonauer devised the same two tracts to his son John Shonauer & his daughter Barbara wife of Jacob Fetterhaff. The heirs divided the property, with a 91-acre tract being allotted to Jacob Fetterhaff & his wife.
21 May 1783: WH & CJ

Y119: Benjamin Hershy, yeoman, & his wife Catharine of Manheim tp. enf-rel.to Benjamin Landis, yeoman, of same
5a, 82p Manheim tp.: HISTORY: Part of 301a Manheim tp. pat. 15 May 1735 to Jacob Funk (Ref. PB A-7-176). On 4 & 5 June 1735, Jacob Funk & his wife Fronica granted the same to John Snabley (Ref. Phil. Deed F-8-249). On 4 & 5 May 1743, John Snabley & wife Anna granted the same to Christian Hershy. Said Christian Hershy died intestate leaving issue three sons and six daughters, to wit: Christian, Abraham,

Benjamin, Elizabeth, Ann, Mary, Barbara, Hester, and Adah. In November 1762, the children and their spouses [to wit, Christian Hershy & his wife Barbara, Abraham Hershy & his wife Elizabeth, Peter Reeshar (in right of his wife Elizabeth), Samuel Heir & his wife Ann, Abraham Neff & his wife Mary, David Heir & his wife Barbara, Henry Heir & his wife Hester, and Jacob Erisman & his wife Adah] granted the property to their brother Benjamin Hershy (the party hereto).

12 May 1783: MH & CJ

Y123: Christian Forrer, clockmaker, & his wife Elizabeth of Lampeter tp. enf-rel.to Francis Smith, blacksmith, of same

--Two tracts: (1.) 50a Lampeter tp. and (2.) 18a, 42p Lampeter tp.: HISTORY: See Deed Y31 for the complete history of both tracts.

25 Mar 1774: Calvin Cooper & John Herr

Y127: Robert Good & James Thompson [the executors of William Good, yeoman, late of Earl tp.] enf-rel.to Jacob Stouffer, yeoman, of same

77a Earl tp.: HISTORY: Same tract pat. 29 Apr last to the said executors under the direction of William Good's last will & testament dated 22 Sep 1779 [Ref. PB #1, page 530]. The will further directed them to sell the property after procuring a patent.

2 June 1783: Martin Bowman & Valentine Werntz

Y130: Henry Wilt, yeoman, & his wife Elizabeth of Lebanon tp. [she late Elizabeth Lenherr, daughter of Jacob Lenherr, deceased, late of Warwick tp., yeoman] rel.to Adam Riess, shopkeeper, of same

--Their share of the real & personal estate of said Jacob Lenherr, deceased.

5 Mar 1784: JT & George Bayler

Y132: Philip Rank, yeoman, & his wife Barbara of Earl tp. enf-rel.to their sons Philip Adam Rank & John Rank, both of same

--Two tracts: (1.) 34a Earl tp., including a gristmill, and (2.) 40 ¾ a., 27p Earl tp.

1. HISTORY: Part of 145a Earl tp. pat. 18 Oct 1753 to Philip Rank (Ref. PB A-17-372).
2. HISTORY: Part of 98a, 50p Earl tp. pat. 4 Oct 1760 to Philip Rank (Ref. PB AA-1-114).

--19 Nov 1770: Alexander Martin & Johannes Weidler

Y135: Philip Rank, yeoman, & his wife Barbara of Earl tp. enf-rel.to their son Ludwick Rank of same

--Two tracts: (1.) 64 ¾ a. Earl tp. and (2.) 31 ¾ a., 27p Earl tp.

1. HISTORY: Part of 145a Earl tp. pat. 18 Oct 1753 to Philip Rank (Ref. PB A-17-372).
2. HISTORY: Part of 98a, 50p Earl tp. pat. 4 Oct 1760 to Philip Rank (Ref. PB AA-1-114).

--19 Nov 1770: Alexander Martin & Johannes Weidler

Y138: Philip Rank, yeoman, & his wife Barbara of Earl tp. enf-rel.to their son Jacob Rank of same

--Two tracts: (1.) 52 ¾ a. Earl tp. and (2.) 31 ¾ a., 27p Earl tp.

1. HISTORY: Part of 145a Earl tp. pat. 18 Oct 1753 to Philip Rank (Ref. PB A-17-372).
2. HISTORY: Part of 98a, 50p Earl tp. pat. 4 Oct 1760 to Philip Rank (Ref. PB AA-1-114).

--19 Nov 1770: Alexander Martin & Johannes Weidler

Y140: Michael Rank (or Ranck), yeoman, & his wife Margaret of Earl tp. [he a son of Philip Rank] rel.to Jacob Rank, yeoman, of same [the brother of said Michael Rank]

8 ¾ a., 8p Earl tp.: HISTORY: Part of 146a Earl tp. pat. 23 Jul 1766 to William Elliot (Ref. PB AA-7-182). Said William Elliot agreed to sell the same to John Roxborough; however, he died before executing a deed. By his last will & testament dated 20 Dec 1768 [recorded in Chester County], William Elliot ordered his executors to make a deed good for the same. On 15 Feb 1770, his executors [not named] granted the property to John Roxborough. Said John Roxborough sold a five-acre parcel to John Weidler; however, he died intestate seized in possession of the residue. On 20 Dec 1771, in pursuance to an order given by the Orphans Court, Isabella Roxborough [the widow & administratrix] granted the residue of the property to Michael Rank.

6 June 1772: Richard Davis & ZD

Y143: James Webb, yeoman, & his wife Hannah of Lancaster tp. rel.to Christian Overholtzer, yeoman, of Hempfield tp.

15 ½ a. Hempfield tp.: HISTORY: It being one of four tracts totaling 200a pat. 20 Nov 1762 to James Webb (Ref. PB AA-3-17).

12 Feb 1762: James Webb, Jr., & Jacob Neff

Y145: Christian Killhoffer, yeoman, & his wife [not named] of Hempfield tp. enf-rel.to Christian Overholtzer, yeoman, of same

--Water race: HISTORY: Christian Killhoffer owns a tract in Hempfield tp.; Christian Overholtzer owns a neighboring tract with sundry mills.

1 Aug 1764: Joseph Boude & Johannes Springer

Y147: Christian Overholtzer, yeoman, & his wife Magdalena of Hempfield tp. quitclaims to Jacob Neff (or Neeve), yeoman, of same

--On 28 Sep 1764, Christian Overholtzer & his wife Magdalena granted (1.) 85a Hempfield tp., (2.) 148a, 128p Hempfield tp., and (3.) 15 ½ a. Hempfield tp., plus a gristmill, sawmill, and shelling mills to said Jacob Neff (Ref. Deed K194). However, it is since been discovered that there was an error in the description of the 85a tract. This indenture corrects that mistake. [It is further noted that Christian Overholtzer & his wife Magdalena granted 30a to Christian Killhoffer, including a certain water race.]

15 May 1773: George Bentz & WA

Y152: Michael Knisely & Christian Knisely, yeomen, both of Cocalico tp. [two sons of John Knisely, yeoman, late of Hempfield tp., deceased] enf-rel.to Jacob Neff, yeoman, of Hempfield tp.

18 ¾ a. Hempfield tp.: HISTORY: 234a Hempfield tp. war. 21 Feb 1734 and later surveyed to John Knisely. By his last will & testament dated 15 June 1757, John Knisely devised his entire estate, including the above tract, to his eleven children, share and share alike. His children are as follows: Michael Knisely (party hereto), Anna the wife of Jacob Folwell, Mary the wife of John Mumma, Anthony Knisely, John Knisely, Abraham Knisely, Maria the wife of Conrad Beaver, Beverly [or Barbara] the wife of John Harnish, Christian Knisely (party hereto), Peter Knisely, and Joseph Knisely.

--By sundry conveyances, one Christian Overholtzer came into the possession of eight undivided eleventh parts of the said 234a tract [i.e., all shares except for Christian, Peter, and Joseph's]. By a writ of partition under the direction of the Court of Common Pleas, the aforesaid three sons were allotted 56 ¼ a. [or 18 ¾ a. to each], with the remainder of the tract being allotted to said Christian Overholtzer. On 16 Aug 1760, the children's guardians (not named) received a patent for the 56 ¼ a. (Ref. PB AA-2-21). Said Joseph Knisely since died in his minority, unmarried and without issue. Now, by this indenture, Christian Knisely grants his share, or 18 ¾ a., to said Jacob Neff. Furthermore, both Christian Knisely & Michael Knisely grant their claim to Joseph Knisely's share, or 18 ¾ a., to said Jacob Neff.

26 June 1773: Jacob Erb, WA, & George Knisely

Y158: John Knisely (or Kneisli, or Knisli), yeoman, of York County; Anthony Knisely, yeoman, of same; Anna Folwell (or Fulweiller), widow, of same; John Harnish, yeoman, & his wife Barbara of same; Peter Knisely, yeoman, of Hempfield tp.; John Mumma, yeoman, & his wife Magdalena of the Province of Maryland; and Conrad Beaver, yeoman, & his wife Mary of the Colony of Virginia [the said John, Anthony, Anna, Barbara, Peter, Magdalena, and Mary being seven children of John Knisely, deceased, late of Hempfield tp.] quitclaim to Jacob Neff, yeoman, of Hempfield tp.

--Their right, claim, interest, & title to 18 ¾ a. Hempfield tp.: HISTORY: It being the portion of John Knisely's real estate allotted to his son Joseph Knisely, who died intestate in his minority, unmarried and without issue [see the preceding indenture for the complete history].

--Furthermore, said Peter Knisely grants his 18 ¾ a. share [again, see the preceding indenture] to said Jacob Neff. Previously, Jacob Neff acquired the shares of the other heirs from Christian Overholtzer [who had purchased same from 23 Mar to 9 Nov 1761]. Said Jacob Neff now has full possession and right to John Knisely's 234a plantation in Hempfield tp.

4 Mar 1775: Numerous witnesses.

Y166: George Smith, yeoman, of Hempfield tp. enf-rel.to Peter Reitzel (or Rautzel), taylor, of Lancaster County

2a Hempfield tp.: HISTORY: Part of 219a pat. 27 Feb 1760 to George Smith (Ref. PB A-20-486).

--18 Dec 1766: ASK & FK

Y169: George Muma & his wife Barbara of Hempfield tp. enf-rel.to Peter Reitzel, yeoman, of same

1a Hempfield tp.: HISTORY: Part of a larger tract that Philip Sneyder & Jacob Stoltz [the executors of George Smith] granted 1 Dec 1767 to George Muma (Ref. Deed O562).

13 Jan 1773: ES & CS Jr.

Y171: Peter Reitzel (or Raitzel), taylor, & his wife Susanna of Mount Joy tp. gr.to Christian Nehrlieh, yeoman, of same

--Two tracts: (1.) 2a Hempfield tp. and (2.) 1a Hempfield tp.: HISTORY: It being the same tracts as given in the two previous indentures.

24 Mar 1784: PG & Jacob Neff

Y174: Michael Downer (or Dauner), yeoman, & his wife Magdalena of Lampeter tp. enf-rel.to John Binkle, miller, of same

--Overflowed lands: HISTORY: Part of 5,553a pat. 25 June 1718 to Tobias Collet, Daniel Quare, & Henry Goldney (Ref. PB A-5-306). By sundry conveyances, Jacob Kindrick acquired 400 acres. He died intestate without issue. By law, his brother George Kindrick took right to the property. On 24 Dec 1731, George Kindrick & his wife Barbara granted 200a, located on both sides of the Pequea Creek, to Michael Downer (Ref. Phil. Deed G-1-18). // Said John Binkle has erected a milldam across the said creek, resulting in part of Michael Downer's lands being flooded.

1 Feb 1755: Hans Guth & JB

Y177: Christian Binckly (or Binkle, or Pinkle) and Henry Binckle & his wife Frena, all of Lampeter tp., enf-rel.to their brother Felix Binckly, yeoman, of same

--Their undivided parts of 200a Lampeter tp.: HISTORY: Late the estate of John Binckly, yeoman, of Lampeter tp., the father of all parties hereto.

12 Jan 1768: JM & CW

Y180: Felix Pinkley, yeoman, & his wife Ann of Lampeter tp. enf-rel.to Henry Pinkley, yeoman, of same

100a Lampeter tp.: HISTORY: On 26 Mar 1737, Felix Landes & his wife Rosina granted 200a Lampeter tp. to John Pinkley. Said John Pinkley died leaving a widow named Barbara and issue four children, to wit, Felix, Henry, Christian, & Ann. On 16 June 1764, said Ann Pinkley granted her undivided share to said Felix Pinkley. On equal date herewith, Christian Pinkley and Henry Pinkley & his wife Frena granted their undivided parts to the said Felix Pinkley. On equal date herewith, the widow, Barbara, released her dower in and of the property.

12 Jan 1768: JM & CW

Y183: Henry Binckly, yeoman, & his wife Frena of Manor tp. enf-rel.to Christian Binckly, yeoman, of Lampeter tp.

100a Lampeter tp.: HISTORY: It being the same tract as given in the preceding indenture.

--17 June 1769: Rosina Hubley & JH

Y186: Christian Binkly, yeoman, of Lampeter tp. enf-rel.to Felix Binkly, miller, of same

100a Lampeter tp.: HISTORY: It being the same tract as given in the preceding indenture.

--23 Mar 1772: James Ross & JR

Y188: Nathan Evans, yeoman, & his wife Mary of Earl tp. enf-rel.to Emanuel Newswanger, yeoman, of Caernarvon tp.

24a Caernarvon tp.: HISTORY: Part of 147a pat. 24 Oct 1771 to Philip Harding (Ref. PB AA-11-572). On 2 Jan 1772, Philip Harding & his wife Catharine granted the same to Nathan Evans.

4 Apr 1783: Evan Evans & ZD

Y191: Nathan Evans, yeoman, of Earl tp. enf-rel.to Emanuel Newswanger, yeoman, of Caernarvon tp.

25a Caernarvon tp.: HISTORY: Part of 48a, 30p war. 3 June 1767 to John Martin (Ref. Application #2656). On 15 Jan last, John Martin granted the same to Nathan Evans.

4 Apr 1783: Evan Evans & ZD

Y193: Tobias Miller, miller, & his wife Barbara of Hempfield tp. enf-rel.to David Bechtel, yeoman, of Manheim tp.

60a Donegal tp.: HISTORY: Part of 333a patented to Lazarus Lowry. The county sheriff later seized the tract due to unpaid debts owing to one Richard Hockly. On 3 Sep 1757, the sheriff granted the entire property to Alexander Lowry (Ref. Deed D440). On 1 Apr 1779, Alexander Lowry & his wife Nancy granted 296a, 8p to James Anderson. On 1 Apr 1779, James Anderson & his wife Margaret granted 100a to Abraham Stouffer. On ____ 1780, Abraham Stouffer & his wife Barbara granted 60a to Martin Horst. On 18 Apr 1781, Martin Horst granted the same to Tobias Miller.

14 Sep 1782: ES & CS

Y196: Adam Nees, yeoman, & his wife Margaret of Cocalico tp. enf-rel.to George Hoe, yeoman, of Cocalico tp.

50a Cocalico tp.: HISTORY: Part of 784a pat. 5 Apr 1753 to Peter Shirk (Ref. PB A-17-276). On 7 Apr 1755, Peter Shirk granted 300a to Ulrick Shirk (Ref. Deed C553). On 1 Jan 1761, Ulrick Shirk & his wife Ann granted the same to Henry Bower. On 24 May 1773, Henry Bower & his wife Margaret granted 100a to Adam Bower. On ___ 177_, Adam Bower granted the same to Adam Nees.

26 Mar 1777: John Butz & JJ

Y200: John Witmer & Valentine Metzler [the executors of Abraham Witmer, late of Lampeter tp.] enf-rel.to Benjamin Witmer of same

150a Lampeter tp.: HISTORY: Same tract that John Musgrave granted 16 Jul 1733 to Abraham Witmer (Ref. Deed A148). On 31 Jul 1747, Thomas Musgrave & his wife Hannah granted their right to 25a, 80p [it being a parcel of the larger tract] to Abraham Witmer (Ref. Deed A139). By his last will & testament, Abraham Witmer devised the 150-acre tract to his son Benjamin Witmer (party hereto), ordering his executors to make a deed good for the same.

24 Apr 1783: WH & CS

Y202: Thomas Harris rel.to William Kelly, Esq.

50a Donegal tp.: HISTORY: Same tract war. 28 Oct 1746 to Thomas Harris.

--30 Apr 1783: John Hay & William Scott

Y204: John Craig (or Creag) & his wife Sables of Hanover tp. enf-rel.to William Wilson of Donegal tp.

166a Hanover tp.: HISTORY: Same tract patented to William Hume. Said William Hume assigned the same to Samuel Blunston, who died intestate seized in possession thereof. His right became vested in Peter Worrell & Thomas Parson, who assigned the same to John Craig. Said John Craig died intestate. In order to pay estate debts, his administrator, David Allen, sold the property to Brice Innis at public sale. On 16 May 1771, Brice Innis & his wife Elizabeth granted the same to John Craig [party hereto].

25 Mar 1784: Timothy Green, George Ward, & Robert McNeall

Y207: George Beshoar (or Bashair), yeoman, & his wife Charlotte of Derry tp. enf-rel.to James Montgomery, shoemaker, of Leacock tp.

126a, 26p Leacock tp.: HISTORY: Same tract pat. 5 Apr 1756 to George Beshoar (Ref. PB A-19-159).

--12 May 1756: Path Allison & William Boyd

Y209: William Montgomery, tavernkeeper, & his wife Rebecca of Lancaster Borough enf-rel.to John Garber, yeoman, of Lancaster County

--Two adjoining tracts: (1.) 126a, 26p Leacock tp. and (2.) 29a Leacock tp.

HISTORY: It being the same tract as given in the preceding indenture.

HISTORY: Part of 229a Leacock tp. pat. 2 Jan 1762 to James Montgomery (Ref. PB AA-3-243).

--By his last will & testament, James Montgomery devised both tracts (126a and 29a) to William Montgomery.

1 May 1762: Robert Thompson & Adam Diffenderfer

Y213: James Montgomery, yeoman, & his wife Agnes of Leacock tp. enf-rel.to Peter Livingood, weaver, of Warwick tp.

12a, 5p Leacock tp.: HISTORY: Part of 229a Leacock tp. pat. 2 Jan last to James Montgomery (Ref. PB AA-3-243). By his last will & testament dated 27 Jan last, James Montgomery devised part thereof to his son James Montgomery (party hereto).

15 Dec 1762: William Hamilton

Y216: John Garber, yeoman, & his wife Elizabeth of Lancaster County enf-rel.to Christian Myer, yeoman, of same

--Two adjoining tracts: (1.) 126a, 26p Leacock tp. and (2.) 29a Leacock tp.: HISTORY: They being the same tracts as given in Deed Y209.

8 Apr 1763: Hans Schantz & Michael Garber

Y218: Peter Livingood (or Lebingood), weaver, & his wife Barbara of Warwick tp. enf-rel.to Christian Myer, yeoman, of Earl tp.

12a, 5p Leacock tp.: HISTORY: It being the same tract as given in Deed Y213.

--19 Apr 1763: AN & Hans Schodt

Y221: John Evans, yeoman, & his wife Hannah of Earl tp. enf-rel.to David Martin, yeoman, of same

156a Earl tp.: HISTORY: Same tract pat. 7 Aug 1740 to Philip Evans (Ref. PB A-9-392). By his last will & testament (recorded in Chester County), Philip Evans devised the same to his son John (party hereto).

26 Sep 1783: Samuel Evans & ZD

Y224: John Evans, yeoman, & his wife Hannah of Earl tp. enf-rel.to David Martin, yeoman, of same

6a, 120p Earl tp.: HISTORY: Same tract pat. 3 Jul 1760 to Philip Evans (Ref. PB AA-2-1). On 22 Nov 1766, Philip Evans & his wife Elizabeth granted the same to their son John (party hereto).

26 Sep 1783: Samuel Evans & ZD

Y227: Agreement between James Bickham and George Moore

--Both own adjoining lots. They agree to share in the cost and maintenance of a brick gable between their lots.

20 Apr 1775: William Hamilton & CJ

Y229: John Hoffman, yeoman, & his wife Elizabeth of Cocalico tp. and Herman Beerbauer, yeoman, & his wife Christina of Chester County [the said John & Christina being the only children of Daniel Hoffman, deceased] enf-rel.to Jacob Huber, yeoman, of Cocalico tp.

50a, 41p Cocalico tp.: HISTORY: Same tract pat. 14 Apr 1764 to Abraham Stone (Ref. PB AA-4-471). On 12 Oct 1767, Abraham Stone & his wife Anna Maria granted the same to Daniel Hoffman, yeoman, late of Cocalico tp.

5 Apr 1777: Philip Breitenstein & JJ

Y232: Jacob Bergman (or Berkman), yeoman, & his wife Elizabeth of Strasburg tp. enf-rel.to Christian Huber, clockmaker, of Cocalico tp.

--Two lots in the town of Zohar in Cocalico tp., numbered 34 and 36 in the town plan: HISTORY: Same lots that Tobias Ream & his wife Juliana granted 18 Apr 1771 to Jacob Kilian. On 1 Apr 1778, Jacob Kilian assigned the same to Jacob Bergman.

30 Mar 1784: Henry Slaymaker & Hannah Slaymaker

Y235: Hugh Moore (or Moor), yeoman, & his wife Ann of Donegal tp. rel.to Daniel Kinsinger, yeoman, of same

38 ½ a. Donegal tp.: HISTORY: Part of 284a Donegal tp. that Zachariah Moore & his wife Mary granted 16 Dec 1783 to Hugh Moore.

16 Dec 1783: William Wilson & Zachariah Moore

Y238: Casper Schrite, yeoman, & his wife Margaret of Cocalico tp. enf-rel.to Margaret Lutz, widow, of same

32a, 126p Cocalico tp.: HISTORY: Part of two tracts, 84a Cocalico tp. and 75a Cocalico tp., both pat. 22 Jan 1762 to Marcus Eckly (Ref. PB AA-2-472). Said Marcus Eckly died seized in possession of the same. On 18 Sep 1767, the Orphans Court ordered his administrators, John Eckly & Philip Kole, to the property in order to pay estate debts. On 10 Apr 1768, they granted both tracts to Charles Miller. Said Charles Miller & his wife Mary granted _____ [not clear, but including the 32a, 126p tract] to Casper Schrite.

8 Apr 1783: George Hoe (or Hos?) & AN

Y241: John Witmer, the younger, gentleman, & his wife Mary of Radnor tp., Chester County enf-rel.to Henry Lougher, tanner, of Lampeter tp.

10a Lampeter tp.: HISTORY: Same tract that the county sheriff granted 8 May 1772 to Christopher Franciscus. On 20 June 1772, Christopher Franciscus & his wife Rosina granted the same to John Witmer (Ref. Deed U51).

8 Apr 1783: N. Lee & James Woods

Y244: Paul Zantzinger, merchant, & his wife Esther of Lancaster Borough enf-rel.to Abraham Witmer, yeoman, of Lampeter tp.

200a Leacock tp.: HISTORY: Part of a larger tract that Hans Good granted 14 May 1748 to Patrick Carrigan (Ref. Deed A128). Said Patrick Carrigan died intestate. On 4 Dec 1766, the Orphans Court confirmed the tract to his son Patrick. On 11 Jan 1779, Patrick Carrigan granted the same to John Burkholder. On 17 Feb 1779, John Burkholder & his wife Barbara granted the same to Paul Zantzinger.

28 Feb 1782: Mary Thornborough & John Musser

Y247: George Adam Lindeberger, yeoman, & his wife Hannah of Lancaster Borough enf-rel.to Peter Albright of same

3 1/3 a. in Lancaster Borough: HISTORY: Part of two tracts: (1.) On 2 Dec 1759, Michael Fortnee, Casper Shaffner, & John Barr [the executors of Melchor Fortine] granted 10 acres in Lancaster Borough to Jacob Icholds. (2.) On 1 May 1760, Samuel Boude & his wife Mary [late Bethel, the daughter of Samuel Bethel, deceased] granted a lot adjoining the above to said Jacob Icholds. // By his last will & testament dated 22 Jul 1760, Jacob Icholds ordered his executors [to wit, Bernard Hoobly & Michael Hoobly] to sell the properties. On 7 Oct 1760, they granted 3 1/3 a. [part of the above lots] to Andrew Eberhart. On 11 Mar 1765, Andrew Eberhart & his wife Catharine granted the same to George Adam Lindeberger.

12 June 1766: WJ & JB

Y250: Henry Eberly, blacksmith, & his wife Barbara of Manor tp. enf-rel.to Jacob Tshantz, yeoman, of Manheim tp.

50a Hempfield tp.: HISTORY: Part of two adjoining tracts, 254a, 114p Manheim tp. and 44 ½ a. Hempfield tp., both pat. 7 June 1753 to John Grebiel (Ref. PB A-17-310). By his last will & testament, John Grebiel devised 180a to his son Peter Grebiel & the residue to his son John Grebiel. On 10 Dec 1768, John Grebiel quitclaimed the 180a to his brother Peter. On 10 Dec 1768, Peter Grebiel granted 50a Hempfield tp. to Henry Eberly.

21 Mar 1778: Christian Diffenderfer & CS

Y254: Joseph Nelson, yeoman, of Manor tp. enf-rel.to Christian Kaufman, yeoman, of same

54 ¾ a., 16p Manor tp.: HISTORY: Part of 109a, 72p Manor tp. pat. 9 Apr 1767 to Joseph Nelson (Ref. PB AA-8-255).

9 Nov 1767: AR & WA

Y257: Peter Grebill, yeoman, of Manheim tp. enf-rel.to Henry Eberly, blacksmith, of Hempfield tp.

50a Hempfield tp.: HISTORY: See Deed Y250 for the larger history.

--10 Dec 1768: ASK & James Gibbons

Y261: William Hamilton, Esq., of Bush Hill in Pennsylvania appoints Jasper Yeates, Esq., as his lawful attorney to collect rents and execute deeds, as well as perform other rights and privileges granted to said William Hamilton under the last will & testament of James Hamilton, late of Bush Hill. By his last will & testament, said James Hamilton devised all land in or near Lancaster Borough, as well as all rent charges, to the said William Hamilton.

3 Apr 1784: James Webb, Jr., & MH

Y266: Thomas Ferree, yeoman, & his wife Martha of Strasburg tp. enf-rel.to John Oxe, yeoman, of Lampeter tp.

2a, 4p Lampeter tp.: HISTORY: Same lot that Daniel Miller & his wife Susanna granted 26 Feb 1781 to Andrew Heges (or Higes). On 5 Oct 1781, Andrew Heges & his wife Elizabeth granted the same to Henry Bushman. On 4 Feb 1782, Henry Bushman & his wife Barbara granted the same to the said Martha, then Martha Carpenter but now the wife of Thomas Ferree.

16 Mar 1784: George Musser & JJH

Y269: Abraham Stone, innkeeper, & his wife Anna Maria of Cocalico tp. enf-rel.to Daniel Hoffman, yeoman, of Nantmeal tp., Chester County

50a, 41p Cocalico tp.: HISTORY: Same tract pat. 14 Apr 1764 to Abraham Stone (Ref. PB AA-4-471).

--12 Oct 1767: EC Jr. & John Smith

Y271: Jacob Root, yeoman, & his wife Barbara of Caernarvon tp. enf-rel.to Abraham Kurtz, yeoman, of Earl tp.

110a, 12p Caernarvon tp.: HISTORY: Part of 400a pat. 7 Jul 1758 to John Davis (Ref. PB A-19-294). On 14 & 15 Jul 1758, John Davis & his wife Elizabeth granted 110a, 12p to Jacob Root (Ref. Phil. Deed H-9-139).

24 May 1766: SH & Peter Light

Y274: Jacob Root, yeoman, & his wife Barbara of Caernarvon tp. enf-rel.to Abraham Kurtz, yeoman, of Earl tp.

114a, 130p Caernarvon tp.: HISTORY: Same tract pat. 17 Feb 1763 to Jacob Root (Ref. PB AA-3-516).

--24 May 1766: SH & Peter Light

Y276: Abraham Kurtz (or Khurtz), yeoman, & his wife Barbara of Earl tp. enf-rel.to their son Christian Kurtz, yeoman, of Caernarvon tp.

--Two tracts: (1.) 110a, 12p Caernarvon tp. and (2.) 114a, 130p Caernarvon tp.: HISTORY: They being the same two tracts as given in the two preceding indentures.

9 June 1767: SH & Hans Frantz

Y279: James Old, ironmaster, & his wife Margaret of Caernarvon tp. enf-rel.to Henry Sherck, potter, of same

--Three tracts in or near Bangor Church Town in Caernarvon tp.: (1.) one-half acre, (2.) three-quarters of an acre, and (3.) three-quarters of an acre: HISTORY: Same three lots that Jacob Hinkle & his wife Elizabeth granted 15 June 1779 to James Old (Ref. Deed Q600).

30 May 1783: ZD & Henrich Folz

Y282: William & Esther Patterson of East Pennsborough tp., Cumberland County, quitclaim to Henry Line of same

250a Leacock tp.: HISTORY: Henry Line has fulfilled a certain obligation set forth in late father's last will & testament.

15 Mar 1782: Robert Cogley & Jeremiah Robison

Y283: George Bumbagh of Derry tp. rel.to James Bickham

--His plantation in Rapho tp.: HISTORY: Same tract warranted in December 1749 & later surveyed [adjoining the lands of Michael Becker & his son Martin Becker]—no further information.

11 June 1759: John Creaig & Christian Kegel

Y284: David Levenstein, the elder, yeoman, & his wife Elizabeth of Heidelberg tp. enf-rel.to his younger son David Levenstein, yeoman, of same

--Four contiguous tracts in Heidelberg tp. totaling 209a, 131p.: HISTORY: (1.) 130a Heidelberg tp. pat. 30 Jul 1741 to David Levenstein [Ref. PB A-9-346]. (2.) 28 ¼ a. Heidelberg tp. pat. 16 Aug 1763 [Ref. PB AA-5-174]. (3.) 30a Heidelberg tp. pat. 16 Aug 1763 [Ref. PB AA-5-174]. (4.) 21a, 91p Heidelberg tp. pat. 16 Aug 1763 [Ref. PB AA-5-174].

16 Mar 1769: Casper Sweytzer & Valentin Viehman

Y287: John Nisley (or Nessly), yeoman, & his wife Mary of Donegal tp. enf-rel.to his son Jacob Nisley, yeoman, of same

137 ¼ a. Donegal tp.: HISTORY: Part of 274 ½ a. pat. 8 June 1774 to John Nisley (Ref. PB AA-13-191). Agreement is subject to certain water privileges previously granted to Michael Nisley.

29 Dec 1783: James Bayly & Benjamin Whisler

Y290: John Gerber (or Garber), yeoman, & his wife Mary of Earl tp. enf-rel.to Michael Gerber, yeoman, of Leacock tp.

--Two tracts: (1.) 256 ½ a. Leacock tp. and (2.) 39 ½ a. Leacock tp.

1. HISTORY: Same tract pat. 12 Apr 1745 to John Garber of Leacock tp. [the father of both parties hereto] (Ref. PB A-11-528).
2. HISTORY: Part of 92a Leacock tp. pat. 16 Aug 1743 to Jacob Thomas (Ref. PB A-11-215). Said Jacob Thomas died intestate leaving issue an only daughter Elizabeth to whom the property descended. Said Elizabeth married Wolrick Shively. On 16 Oct 1745, Wolrick Shively & his wife Elizabeth granted the 92a tract to John Gerber.

--Said John Gerber died intestate. On 25 Mar 1769, the Orphans Court confirmed his real estate to his eldest son John Gerber [the party hereto]. On 13 Nov last, the other children [not named] released their claim to the property to their said brother.

28 Dec 1769: Hans Foltz & Christian Rux

Y295: John Wenger, Christian Wenger, Michael Wenger, & Joseph Wenger [the sons of Christian Wenger, deceased, late of Earl tp., yeoman] and Michael Sensnich & his wife Magdalena, Henry Weaver & his wife Eve, and Henry Sheibly & his wife Elizabeth [the three daughters of said Christian Wenger, deceased] and Joseph Long [the guardian of Anna Long, Mary Long, Eve Long, & Barbara Long, his children by his late wife Mary, deceased, another daughter of said Christian Wenger, deceased] quitclaim to Henry Wenger [another son of said Christian Wenger, deceased]

90 ½ a. Earl tp.: HISTORY: Part of 289a Earl tp. pat. 20 Apr 1741 to Christian Wenger (Ref. PB A-9-311). Said Christian Wenger died seized in possession thereof. By agreement among the heirs, a 90 ½ a. parcel has been allotted to son Henry as his due share.

28 Oct 1774: EC Jr. & Jacob Greiner

Y297: Henry Wenger (or Winger), yeoman, & his wife Anna of Earl tp. rel.to his brother Michael Wenger
57a, 5p Earl tp.: HISTORY: Part of 90 ½ a. Earl tp. See the preceding indenture of the larger history.
--24 Mar 1775: Hannes Wenger & ZD

Y299: John Musser, yeoman, & his wife Sarah of Lancaster Borough and Abraham Witmer, yeoman, & his wife Mary of Lancaster tp. enf-rel.to George Cummins, yeoman, of Manheim tp.

6a, 29p Manheim tp.: HISTORY: Part of 183a Manheim tp. that Henry Landes & his wife Mary granted 28 Feb 1782 to John Musser & Abraham Witmer (Ref. Deed Q668).

10 Feb 1783: J. Funk & William Parr

Y302: Henry Lite & Samuel Stauffer [the executors of Adam Zell, yeoman, late of Caernarvon tp.] enf-rel.to John Zell, yeoman, of same [the son of said Adam Zell, deceased]

--Two tracts: (1.) 100a Caernarvon tp. and (2.) 57 ¼ a. Caernarvon tp.

1. HISTORY: Part of 178a pat. 8 June 1742 to Hugh Davis (Ref. PB A-10-430). On 10 Jul 1744, Hugh Davis & his wife Ann granted the same to Peter Light. On 28 June 1763, Peter Light & his wife Elizabeth granted 100a to Michael Widware. On 28 June 1765, Michael Widware & his wife Mary granted the same to Adam Zell.
2. HISTORY: Part of 114 ½ a. war. 25 Nov 1756 & later surveyed to Henry Johnston. On 27 Apr 1763, Henry Johnston granted the same to Adam Zell.

--By his last will & testament dated 24 May 1777, Adam Zell devised the tract bought of Michael Widware and the timberland bought of Henry Johnston to two of his sons. He ordered his executors to choose from sons Henry Zell, John Zell, Jacob Zell, & Adam Zell [whomever they thought appropriate—reference being made to the "society that I belong"]. The executors have agreed that son John should hold the tracts described above.

16 Jul 1783: Christian Zimmerman & ZD

Y306: Joseph Brubacher, yeoman, & his wife Elizabeth of Manheim tp. enf-rel.to Abraham Myer, yeoman, of same

11a Manheim tp.: HISTORY: Part of a larger tract that John Woolslegle & his wife Anna granted 24 Nov 1752 to Jacob Downer. On 12 Mar 1767, Jacob Downer & his wife Elizabeth granted the same to Michael Gross. On 13 June 1767, Michael Gross granted the same to Joseph Brubacher.

15 June 1767: PZ & GR

Y309: Sheriff Thomas Edwards rel.to James Moorehead of Mount Joy tp.

79a Mount Joy tp.: HISTORY: On 8 Feb 1783, the Court of Common Pleas ordered the sheriff to seize the real estate of Joseph Wolf of Mount Joy tp. & Benjamin Mishey of Rapho tp., yeomen, for unpaid debts owed to Philip Greenewalt. The sheriff duly seized two tracts totaling 110a in Mount Joy tp., late the property to said Joseph Wolf. The sheriff sold one tract, or 79 acres, to James Moorehead at public vendue. Subject to a mortgage given by Joseph Wolf to the General Loan Office in the year 1774.

8 Nov 1783: JJH & JH

Y313: Alexander Wilson, yeoman, & his wife Mary of Earl tp. enf-rel.to Philip Boyer of Salisbury tp.

125a Salisbury tp.: HISTORY: Same tract pat. 18 Jul 1744 to Margaret Anderson (Ref. PB A-11-363). By her last will & testament, Margaret Anderson devised the same to her sons James Anderson & George Anderson. On 27 Sep 1762, James Anderson & his wife Ann granted their right to said George Anderson. By his last will & testament dated 24 Sep 1770, George Anderson ordered his executors [to wit, his wife Rebecca Anderson & John Martin—the latter since resigning] to sell the property if his wife should marry again. Said Rebecca later married John Wallace. On 3 June 1780, Rebecca Wallace (formerly Anderson) granted the tract to Alexander Wilson.

6 Mar 1784: John Sheibly & Nicholas Jund

Y316: John McQuinn (or McQueen) & his wife Susanna of Derry tp. gr.to Josias McQuinn of same

150a Derry tp.: HISTORY: Part of a larger tract pat. 28 Apr 1750 to John McQuinn (Ref. PB A-15-___). This indenture made out of love and affection.

6 Aug 1762: Robert Allison, Patrick Kelley, & William Moore

Y318: Josiah McQuin (or McQueen) & his wife Isabella of Londonderry tp. enf-rel.to Henry Stauffer of York tp., York County

150a Derry tp.: HISTORY: It being the same tract as given in the preceding indenture.

--18 Jan 1783: Frederick Eichelberger, D. Grier, John Tate, & Abraham Scott

Y320: John Leman quitclaims to Henry Stauffer of Londonderry tp.

--His wife's dower in and of 130a Mount Joy tp.: HISTORY: Christian Ebersole, late of Mount Joy tp., died intestate seized in possession of 130a Mount Joy tp. He left a wife Mary (now the wife of said John Leman of Rockenham County, Virginia) and issue sundry children.

17 June 1783: James Bayly & Joseph Work

Y321: John Lardner, gentleman, of Philadelphia [the eldest son of Lynford Lardner by his wife Elizabeth, both deceased] enf-rel.to David Jenkins, ironmaster, of Caernarvon tp.

--His brother James' undivided fifth part of an undivided fourth part of a forge and four tracts of land in Caernarvon tp.: HISTORY: See Deed S101 for the larger history. At the age of 21, the children of Lynford Lardner were to release their claim to the above properties, which they held in right of their late mother Elizabeth. However, son James Lardner, sometime in December 1780, departed as a passenger on board the Ship Shelelah, bound to L'Orient. The ship has never been heard from again, and it is presumed the James Lardner is dead. By his, his right to the property descended to his eldest brother John (the party hereto).

26 June 1783: Ah. Lehre & LW

Y324: Tripartite indenture between the following parties:

1. Benjamin Imoberstag, yeoman, of Lampeter tp.
2. John Burkholder, yeoman, of same
3. Henry Witmer, yeoman, of same

--The first party releases 18a Hempfield tp. to the second party; however, Henry Witmer, the third party, may bring suit to the Court of Common Pleas regarding this property before the end of the February Term.

17 Jan 1784: JY & JH

Y327: Sheriff Thomas Edwards enf-rel.to Ludwick Cassel, the younger, of Mount Joy tp.

61a Mount Joy tp.: HISTORY: On 9 Aug 1783, the Court of Common Pleas ordered the sheriff to seize the real estate of William McCullough & Daniel Brodley, yeoman, of Lancaster County for unpaid debts owed to John Young, "my assignee". The sheriff duly seized 61a Mount Joy tp., which he sold at public vendue to the said Ludwick Cassel.

26 Mar 1784: JH & Andrew Dunlop

Y330: George Cummins (signed "Comming") & his wife Susanna of Manheim tp. enf-rel.to John Swarr, yeoman, of same

6a, 29p Manheim tp.: HISTORY: It being the same tract as given in Deed Y299.

--2 Jan 1784: John Shaffner & CS

Y332: John Swarr of Manheim tp. assigns to George Cummins of same

6a, 29p Manheim tp.: HISTORY: It being the same tract as given in the preceding indenture.

--15 Apr 1784: Jacob Stofft & JH

Y333: Adam Weber, innkeeper, & his wife Rosina of Lancaster Borough enf-rel.to Josiah Kittera, yeoman, of Earl tp.

--Half lot on Orange St. in Lancaster Borough: HISTORY: On 22 June 1741, James Hamilton granted a lot on Orange St. to Michael Shryack. On 3 Nov 1744, Michael Shryock & his wife Maria Catharine assigned the same to Nicholas Kendle. On 7 Nov 1748, Nicholas Kendle granted the same to John Gerr. On 4 Sep 1749, John Gerr & his wife Catharine granted the same to the said Nicholas Kendle. On 20 Mar 1750, Nicholas Kendle & his wife Catharine granted the same to Valentine Hercleroad. Sheriff Joseph Pugh seized the property for unpaid debts and sold the same on 4 Aug 1757 to Isaac Whitelock, gentleman, of Lancaster Borough. On 25 Feb 1758, Isaac Whitelock & his wife Mary assigned the same to Melchior Snyder. On 12 Feb 1767, Melchior Snyder & his wife Margaret granted the same to Michael Shittenhelm (Ref. Deed N213). On 6 Nov 1772, Michael Shittenhelm & his wife Margaret granted half of the said lot to Adam Weber.

8 Apr 1779: ES & CS

Y336: Josiah Kittera, yeoman, & his wife Sarah of Lancaster Borough rel.to John Moore, innholder, of same

--Half lot on Orange St. in Lancaster Borough: HISTORY: It being the same half lot as given in the preceding indenture.

24 Apr 1780: John W. Kittera & Charles Hall

Y338: John Moore, yeoman, & his wife Martha of Lampeter tp. enf-rel.to George Hoofnagle, yeoman, of Lancaster Borough

--Half lot on Orange St. in Lancaster Borough: HISTORY: It being the same half lot as given in the preceding indenture.

2 Nov 1782: Richard Henry & CS

Y341: George Hoofnagle & his wife Magdalena assign to Jacob Stoff (or Stuff), yeoman, of Lancaster Borough

--"within mentioned half lot": HISTORY: Not given, but surely the same half lot as given in the preceding indenture.

30 May 1783: Henry Dering & CS

Y342: John Philip Fernsler assigns to Martin Kendrick of Conestoga

--"the within mentioned lease": HISTORY: No further information.

17 May 1738: William Wright & Hans Kendig

--Philip Fernsler, yeoman, of Lebanon tp. affirms his father's signature on 22 Apr 1784.

Y343: Frederick Struble (or Strubel), yeoman, of Lancaster County assigns to Thomas Cookson, attorney-at-law-, of same

--Two tracts: (1.) lot on Queen St. in Lancaster Borough and (2.) 5a Lancaster tp.: HISTORY: Same two lots that James Hamilton granted to Frederick Struble.

19 Jul 1738: Carl Keller (or Kallar) & Johannes Altenberger

Y344: Henry Fordine, saddler, & his wife Catharine of Lancaster Borough enf-rel.to Christopher Heger, butcher, of same

5a Lancaster tp.: HISTORY: On 20 May 1735, James Hamilton granted 5a Lancaster tp. to Cornelius Verhulst. In Apr 1738, Cornelius Verhulst assigned the same to Michael Bierly. On 9 Jul 1743, Michael Bierly & his wife Catharine assigned the same to Mary Dougherty. On 20 Jan 1754, Mary Dougherty granted the same to John Dougherty. On 28 May 754, John Dougherty granted the same to Michael Fordine. By his last will & testament, Michael Fortine devised the same to Henry Fortine (party hereto).

5 Jan 1782: ES & CS

Y347: Emanuel Carpenter, Esq., & his wife Catharine of Earl tp. enf-rel.to Jacob Shertz, yeoman, of Bart tp.

88a Leacock tp.: HISTORY: Part of 2,300a pat. 6 Nov 1735 to Isaac Lefevre & Daniel Fierree (Ref. PB A-7-319). On 6 Dec 1744, Isaac Lefevre & his wife Catharine and Daniel Fierree & his wife Anna Maria granted 185a to Thomas Faulkner. On 20 June 1746, Thomas Faulkner & his wife Jeane granted the same to Philip Fierree. On 14 & 15 Apr 1748, Philip Fierree & his wife Leah granted the same to their son Joel. On 16 & 17 Apr 1752, Joel Fierree & his wife Mary granted 92 ½ a. to his brother Jacob. On 1 & 2 Aug 1753, Jacob Fierree & his wife Barbara granted 88a to Emanuel Carpenter (Ref. Deed O514 and also E___ [omitted]).

12 June 1775: EG & John Carpenter

Y350: Samuel Leman (or Leaman), yeoman, & his wife Catharine of Toboyne tp., Cumberland County, enf-rel.to Peter Feree & John Shartz [the executors of Daniel Leman, late of Lampeter tp.[

200a Lampeter tp.: HISTORY: Part of 400a Lampeter tp. pat. 26 Mar 1735 to Peter Leman. By his last will & testament, Peter Leman devised the same to his sons Isaac & Daniel. On 23 May 1748, by a deed of partition, Daniel Leman released 200a to his brother Isaac Leman. Said Isaac Leman died intestate leaving a widow named Elizabeth and issue several children. On 2 Dec 1778, the Orphans Court confirmed the 200a tract to his eldest son Samuel Leman (the party hereto). In 1779, Samuel Leman agreed to sell the property to Daniel Leman—money exchanged hands but a deed was never written.

19 Mar 1783: Henry Slaymaker, Christian Denlinger, & Daniel Lefever, Jr.

Y354: John Morgan, miller, & his wife Sarah of Caernarvon tp. enf-rel.to James Old & Henry Weaver, yeomen, both of same

117a Caernarvon tp.: HISTORY: Part of two tracts totaling 248a Caernarvon tp. pat. 18 Aug 1764 to Francis Morgan (Ref. PB AA-5-645). On 30 Jan 1772, Francis Morgan & his wife Jane granted one tract, or 117a, to their son David Morgan. On 10 Oct 1774, David Morgan & his wife Rebecca granted three tracts, including the said 117a tract, to the said Francis Morgan. By his last will & testament dated 21 May 1779, Francis Morgan devised the said tract to his son John Morgan (the party hereto).

26 Mar 1784: Angelhard Brown & John Davis

Y358: Thomas Cookson, gentleman, & his wife Margaret of Lancaster Borough enf.to Francis Fortinee, butcher, of same

--Lot on Queen St. in Lancaster Borough: HISTORY: Same lot that James Hamilton granted 20 May 1735 to Frederick Struble. On 19 Jul 1738, Frederick Struble assigned the same to Thomas Cookson.

7 Nov 1742: Daniel Mackineth & Henrich Bassler

Y359: Frederick Heiss (or Heisz), merchant, & his wife Catharine of Philadelphia enf-rel.to Casper Singer, merchant, of same

---Four tracts and a gristmill, sawmill, and hemp mill: (1.) 53a, 53p Bethel tp.; (2.) 7a, 74p Bethel tp.; (3.) 24a, 15p Bethel tp.; and (4.) 15a Bethel tp.: HISTORY: Not given.

10 Apr 1784: Asheton Humphreys & Charles Jones

Y362: John Hare, yeoman, & his wife Mary of Strasburg tp. enf-rel.to John Howry, yeoman, of same

50a Strasburg tp.: HISTORY: Same tract that John Graff & his wife Barbara granted 19 Mar 1774 to John Hare.

5 Jan 1782: John Lefever, John Hare, & EG

Y364: John Taylor, yeoman, & his wife Margaret of Strasburg tp. enf-rel.to John Howry, yeoman, of same

20a Strasburg tp.: HISTORY: On 6 Oct 1781, Peter Taylor & his wife Anna released 172 ½ a. Strasburg tp. to the heirs of John Taylor, late of Strasburg tp., deceased (Ref. Deed U155). On 6 Sep 1782, the Orphans Court confirmed the property to John Taylor [the eldest son of John Taylor, deceased, & the party hereto]—subject to the widow's dower and paying equal shares thereof to the other children.

14 Dec 1782: Martin Herr, Johannes Miller, & John Stoutzeberger

Y367: William Bowsman, Casper Shaffner Sr., & Margaretha Kuntz, all of Lancaster Borough [the executors of Jacob Kuntz, shopkeeper, late of same] enf.to Henry Brenneman, yeoman, of Manor tp.

166 2/3 a. Manor tp.: HISTORY: Same tract pat. 30 Jul 1741 to Jacob Kuntz (Ref. PB A-10-336). By his last will & testament dated 30 June 1763, Jacob Kuntz ordered his executors to handle the property as they saw fit.

8 May 1765: John Bowman & CS Jr.

Y369: Christian Baughman & Peter Whittmer, both of Manor tp. [the executors of Jacob Martin, late of same] enf-rel.to Isaac Martin, yeoman, of same

139 ½ a., 7p Manor tp.: HISTORY: Part of 163a that Abraham Hare & his wife Anna granted 20 May 1751 to Jacob Martin. By his last will & testament dated 11 Sep 1775, Jacob Martin devised 139 ½ a., 7p to his son Isaac Martin [party hereto].

7 May 1783: CJ & Frederick Ziegler

Y372: Bentz (or Benjamin) Hershy & his wife Magdalena of Lancaster tp. [she being late Magdalena Rhode, the younger daughter of Ulrich Rhode, deceased] quitclaim to Barbara Elleberger [late Barbara Rhode, the eldest daughter of said Ulrich Rhode, deceased]

160a Hempfield & Manor tps.: HISTORY: Part of two tracts: (1.) 232a Hempfield tp. pat. 5 May 1760 to Ulrich Rhode [Ref. PB A-19-530]. (2.) On 26 & 27 Dec 1740, Michael Baughman & his wife Katharine granted 88a Manor tp. to said Ulrich Rhode (adjoining the above tract). // By his last will & testament dated 12 Sep 1763, Ulrich Rhode devised the two above tracts to his daughters Barbara & Magdalena—to be divided equally between them.

4 Feb 1764: Robert Thompson & James Webb Jr.

Y375: John Musser, yeoman, & his wife Susanna of Manor tp. enf-rel.to Benjamin Musser, yeoman, of Manor tp. & John Engel, yeoman, of Donegal tp. in TRUST for the children of Jacob Musser, deceased

32a, 24p Manor tp (Conestoga Manor): HISTORY: On 26 Oct 1772, John Manning & his wife Anna Maria granted 32a, 24p Conestoga Manor to John Musser (Ref. Deed N352). In Nov 1772, John Musser devised the same [with other lands] to his brother Jacob Musser. However, while money exchange hands, a deed was never executed. Said Jacob Musser has since died. By his last will & testament, he named his brother Benjamin Musser (alias Mosser) and John Engel as his executors. Said Jacob Musser left issue three children at the time of his death, to wit, John Musser (since deceased in his infancy), Henry Musser, and Ann Musser (both yet minors). Now, by these presents, the original agreement between John Musser & Jacob Musser is finalized.

17 Apr 1784: EA & WA

Y378: John Mylin (or Myly, or Mily) of Lampeter tp. & Jacob Beam of Conestoga tp. [the guardians of the minor children of Jacob Miller, deceased, late of Conestoga tp.; to wit, Jacob Miller, Elizabeth Miller, Andrew Miller, Henry Miller, Christina Miller, Abraham Miller, & Martin Miller] quitclaim to John Miller of Conestoga tp. [the eldest son of the said Jacob Miller, deceased]

--Two adjoining tracts: (1.) 112 ½ a. Conestoga tp. and (2.) 37 ¼ a. Conestoga tp.: HISTORY: Same tracts of which said Jacob Miller died intestate seized in possession thereof. On 4 Dec 1782, the Orphans Court confirmed the properties to his eldest son John Miller (party hereto).

24 Mar 1784: MH & CJ

Y381: John Miller, yeoman, & his wife Mary of Conestoga tp. enf-rel.to Daniel Breneman, yeoman, of same

--Two adjoining tracts: (1.) 112 ½ a. Conestoga tp. and (2.) 37 ¼ a. Conestoga tp.: HISTORY: They being the same tracts as given in the preceding indenture.

5 Apr 1784: CJ & Valentine Brenneisen

Y384: Daniel Breneman, yeoman, & his wife Barbara of Conestoga tp. enf-rel.to Henry Lighty (or Leighty), yeoman, of Manor tp.

105a, 50p Conestoga tp.: HISTORY: Part of 149 ¾ a. that John Miller & his wife Barbara granted 5 Apr 1784 to Daniel Breneman [see the preceding indenture].

17 Apr 1784: Michael Schreck & CJ

Y387: John Eby, yeoman, & his wife Anna of Rapho tp. enf-rel.to Martin Eby, yeoman, of same

101a, 70p Rapho tp.: HISTORY: Part of 170a, 63p that Christian Huber & his wife Barbara granted 1 May 1772 to John Eby (Ref. Deed P52).

17 Apr 1784: HD & CJ

Y390: Michael Gerber, yeoman, & his wife Magdalena of York Town in York County enf-rel.to John Kauffman, yeoman, of Manheim tp.

--Three tracts: (1.) 31 ½ a. Londonderry tp., (2.) 12a Londonderry tp. and (3.) one-half-acre Londonderry tp.

1. HISTORY: Part of a larger tract pat. 2 Mar 1744 to James Galbreath (Ref. PB A-12-215). On 10 Jul 1757, James Galbreath & his wife Elizabeth granted the same to John Gerber (Ref. Deed D458). On 26 Dec 1770, John Gerber & his wife Elizabeth granted 120a to Michael Gerber (Ref. Deed Q175).
2. HISTORY: Part of 96 ½ a., 30p pat. 14 Oct 1760 to James Galbreath (Ref. PB AA-2-64). On 21 Mar 1761, James Galbreath & his wife Elizabeth granted the same to John Gerber (Ref. Deed G110). On 26 Dec 1770, John Gerber & his wife Elizabeth granted the same to Michael Gerber (Ref. Deed N289).
3. HISTORY: Part of the same 96 ½ a., 30p tract above.

--Certain water rights and privileges are reserved to one Michael Huber.

19 Apr 1784: Daniel Franck & CS

Y393: Charles Klug (or Klugh), baker, & his wife Susanna of Lancaster Borough enf-rel.to Jacob Erisman, yeoman, of Rapho tp.

195a Paxton tp.: HISTORY: Part of 326a that the country sheriff granted 9 Aug 1766 to Charles Klug [it late being the estate of convicted debtor Frederick Stoner]. On 2 Sep 1766, John Potts & his wife Ruth confirmed the same land to Charles Klugh [reason not clear].

17 May 1777: Christian Hershi, Henrich Becker, & CS

Y396: Hans Martin Diller, yeoman, & his wife Christina of Earl tp. enf-rel.to Adam Diller, yeoman, of same

20a Earl tp.: HISTORY: Part of a larger tract in the possession of Hans Martin Diller.

--26 Oct 1754: Jacob Digel & Casper Diller

Y398: Michael Diffederfer, yeoman, & his wife Christina [the late widow & administratrix of Martin Diller, yeoman, late of Lancaster County] rel.to Isaac Richardson

75a Earl tp.: HISTORY: On 1 Dec 1744, Jasper Diller & his wife Barbara granted 75a Earl tp. to his son Martin Diller. On the same date, Jasper Diller & his wife granted another 25a tract in Earl tp. to said Martin Diller. In his lifetime, Martin Diller granted 20a Earl tp. (part of the 75a tract) and 5a Earl tp. (part of the 25a tract) to Adam Diller; however, said Martin Diller died intestate seized in possession of the residue, leaving the said widow and issue several children. On the first Tuesday in March 1762, the Orphans Court ordered the residue to be sold.

5 June 1762: Anthony Ellmaker & Robert McCally

Y401: Isaac Richardson, Esq., & his wife Alice of Lancaster County enf-rel.to Adam Diller, yeoman, of Earl tp.

75a Earl tp.: HISTORY: It being the same tract as given in the preceding indenture [and the same Adam Diller who purchased the other 25 acres].

12 Oct 1762: Anthony Ellmaker & Robert McCally

Y405: Ignatius Zwecker, yeoman, & his wife Elizabeth of Earl tp. enf-rel.to Nicholas Yund, yeoman, of same

--Two contiguous tracts: (1.) 156 ¾ a., 20p Earl tp. and (2.) 81 ¾ a., 3p Earl tp. [excepting certain parcels previously sold by said Ignatius Zwecker: HISTORY: Both part of a larger tract pat. 11 Nov 1741 to Casper Staver (Ref. PB A-9-474). On 5 & 6 June 1743, Casper Staver & his wife Catharine granted the same larger tract to Wendel Zwecker. Said Wendel Zwecker died intestate leaving a widow (since deceased) and issue three children, to wit, Ignatius Zwecker (party hereto), Elizabeth the wife of Michael Oberlee, and Magdalena the wife of Anthony Hinkle. The heirs divided the property into three equal parts, with the second tract above-mentioned being allotted to Anthony Hinkle & his wife and the first to Ignatius Zwecker. On 27 Sep 1764, Anthony Hinkle & his wife Magdalena granted their part to said Ignatius Zwecker (Ref. Deed N446).

18 Mar 1782: JJ & Frederick Seeger

Y408: John Rose [signed Johannes Rose], yeoman, & his wife Eve of Leacock tp. enf-rel.to Adam Brown, yeoman, of Earl tp.

20a, 100p Earl tp.: HISTORY: Part of 310a patented to Jacob Rowland (Ref. PB A-1-292, recorded 20 Mar 1738/39). By his last will & testament dated 2 Sep 1763, Jacob Rowland ordered his executors (to wit, Jonathan Rowland & George Hinkle) to sell his real estate. On 28 Mar 1767, they granted 20a, 100p to Joseph Rowland. On 9 Oct 1778, Joseph Rowland & his wife Barbara granted the same to John Rose.

25 May 1781: Mary Watson, DW, & Johannes Bassler

Y411: Isaac Whitelock & his wife Mary assign to Charles Johnston

--"the within mentioned lot": HISTORY: No further information.

25 Feb 1760: John Craeig & DS

Y412: Charles Johnston, cordwainer, & his wife Elizabeth of Salisbury tp. enf-rel.to Conrad Lind of Lancaster Borough

--"the within mentioned lot": HISTORY: No further information but see the preceding indenture.

4 June 1763: Daniel May & CS

Y413: Conrad Lind & his wife Anna Maria enf-rel.to Leonard May of Manheim tp.

--"the within mentioned lot": HISTORY: Same lot acquired from Charles Johnston [see the preceding indenture].

22 Jul 1763: Christian Shaffer & CS Jr.

Y414: Vincent Meyer, yeoman, & his wife Elizabeth of Earl tp. enf-rel.to his son John Meyer, yeoman, of same

--Three adjoining tracts: (1.) 151a, 90p Earl tp.; (2.) 21a, 31p Earl tp.; and (3.) 9a, 73p Earl tp.

1. HISTORY: Part of three tracts: (a.) plantation in Earl tp. pat. 9 June 1767 to Vincent Meyer [Ref. PB AA-9-352]; (b.) On 24 Jul 1754, Henry End & his wife granted a certain tract in Earl tp. to Vincent Meyer; and (c.) On 10 June 1758, Charles Horlacker & his wife granted a certain tract in Earl tp. to Vincent Meyer.
2. HISTORY: Same history as the first tract.
3. HISTORY: Part of a larger tract that Conrad Breneisen & his wife Maria Elizabeth granted on equal date herewith to Vincent Meyer.

--28 Dec 1782: Conrad Breneisen & Maria Elisabeth Breneisen

Y417: Robert Spear, yeoman, of Hempfield tp. granted the following five slaves their freedom at the age of 30 years:

Ross, born 14 Jan 1770
Philis Fagan (a mulatto), born 11 Apr 1773
Charity Boyla (a mulatto), born in Apr 1775
Adath (a Negro), born in Sep 1777
Sidney (a Negro), born 21 Nov 1779

--23 Apr 1784: HD & CJ

Y418: Barbara Nissly quitclaims to Martin Nissly & John Nissly

--Her dower in and of the real estate of her late husband Martin Nissly: HISTORY: Said Martin Nissly, late of Mount Joy tp., died intestate seized in possession of certain property, leaving a widow named Barbara [the party hereto].

22 Mar 1784: Abraham Risser & J. Stewart

Y419: Jean Renick of Paxton tp. [the widow & executrix of Thomas Renick, late of same] enf-rel.to Henry Ober, yeoman, of Rapho tp.

4 ¼ a Paxton tp.: HISTORY: By his last will & testament, Thomas Renick ordered his executor to sell the said property.

22 Apr 1777: John Clark & CS

Y421: Jean Renick of Paxton tp. [the widow & executrix of Thomas Renick, late of same] enf-rel.to Henry Ober, yeoman, of Rapho tp.

122a. Paxton tp., including a gristmill: HISTORY: Same tract pat. 31 Oct 1771 to Thomas Renick (Ref. PB AA-13-84). By his last will & testament, Thomas Renick ordered his executor to sell the said property.

22 Apr 1777: John Clark, Jacob Kreider, & CS

Y424: John Paul, yeoman, & his wife Catharine of Strasburg tp. enf-rel.to John Bachman (or Boghman, or Boyhman), yeoman, of same

2a, 4p Strasburg tp.: HISTORY: Part of 800a patented to Martin Kendig (Ref. PB A-5-264). One John Newcomer became legally seized in possession of 107 ¾ a. of which he died seized. On 25 Aug 1760, John Newcomer's children [not named] granted the 107 ¾ a. tract to Abraham Newcomer [one of the sons of said John Newcomer, deceased]. On 16 Oct 1769, Abraham Newcomer & his wife Ann granted 2a, 4p to John Paul.

16 Oct 1769: Abraham Newcomer & CS

Y426: Abraham Newcomer, yeoman, & his wife Anna of Strasburg tp. enf-rel.to John Paul (or Pawell) of same

2a, 4p Strasburg tp.: HISTORY: It being the same tract as given in the preceding indenture.

--16 Oct 1769: Johannes Bachman & CS Jr.

Y428: John Senseman, yeoman, & his wife Justina of Cocalico tp. enf-rel.to Christopher Trobinger, weaver, of same

153a Cocalico tp.: HISTORY: Part of six sundry tracts totaling 360a that Jacob Senseman, yeoman, late of Cocalico tp., acquired by sundry conveyances. Said Jacob Senseman died intestate leaving issue the following children: John Senseman (the party hereto) and Rachel the wife of John Balmer. On 11 Sep 1779, John Balmer & his wife Rachel granted their right to the real estate to said John Senseman.

24 Apr 1784: Johannes Small & Conrad Meyer

Y431: Christopher Reehm (or Reem) of the town of Baltimore in Maryland appoints his friend James Bickham as his lawful attorney to sell his right to 62 ¾ a. Bethel tp. [It being the same tract pat. 22 Dec 1764 to Wendle Renninger (Ref. PB AA-10-82). Said Wendel Renninger & his wife granted the same to John Peter Renninger, who granted the same to the said Christopher Reehm & James Bickham.] Said Christopher Reehm is now indebted to the said James Bickham.

23 Jan 1775: David Scott & JMR

Y432: John Michael Schryack & his wife Maria Catharine assign to Peter Gnoble (or Knoble)

--"the within premises": HISTORY: No further information.

13 Feb 1741/42: Daniel Mackineth & John Morris

--John Morris affirms his signature on 5 May 1758.

Y433: Peter Knoble assigns to Hans Michael Byerlie "the within premises" [no further information—but see Deed Y434].

4 May 1784: Daniel Mackineth & John Morris

Y433: Hans Michael Beyerle assigns to George Petz (or Betz) "the within mentioned lot" [no further information--but see Deed Y434].

30 Sep 1742: John Morris & George Honey

Y434: George Petz (or Betz), yeoman, & his wife Anne of Lancaster Borough enf-rel.to Michael Gross (or Crouse), shopkeeper, of same

--Half lot on King St. in Lancaster Borough: HISTORY: On 14 Jan 1740, James Hamilton granted a lot on King St. to Michael Shryack. [The deed then recounts the same transactions as given in the three preceding indentures.]

5 June 1749: EC & David McClure

Y436: Michael Gross & his wife Elizabeth assign to Michael Stump, yeoman, of Lancaster Borough

--"the within mentioned lot": HISTORY: Not given, but see Deed Y438.

11 Dec 1749: Johannes Utzman, MH, & DS

Y437: Michael Stump & his wife Margaretha assign to Lawrence Hoof (or Hoff)

--"the within mentioned half lot: HISTORY: No further information, but see Deed Y438.

18 Dec 1750: MH & Jacob Huble

Y438: Lawrence Hoof, yeoman, & his wife Margaretha of Lancaster Borough enf-rel.to Bernard Hubley, yeoman, of same

--Half lot on King St. in Lancaster Borough: HISTORY: Beginning with Deed Y432, this indenture recounts the full history of this lot.

2 Nov 1752: DS & MH

Y441: Bernard Hubley, shopkeeper, & his wife Eva Magdalena of Lancaster Borough enf-rel.to John Hambright, gentleman, of same

--Half lot on King St. in Lancaster Borough: HISTORY: It being the same half lot as given in the preceding indenture.

17 Sep 1759: Robert Thompson & WA

Y444: Sheriff John Barr gr.to Peter Hallm (or Hallam), baker, of Lancaster County

--Half lot on King St. in Lancaster Borough: HISTORY: On 9 May 1766, the Court of Common Pleas ordered the sheriff to seize the real estate of John Hambright, brewer, of Lancaster Borough for unpaid debts owing to Daniel Wister, the assignee of Alexander Stedman, Esq. The sheriff duly seized a half lot on King St. which he later sold at public vendue to Peter Hallm [subject to a mortgage given to Michael Gross & Ludwig Lauman].

7 Nov 1766: Alexander Wilcocks & Isaac Alexander Ladly

Y446: Peter Halm, baker, & his wife Mary of Lancaster Borough enf-rel.to James Davis, fuller, of Lampeter tp.

--Half lot on King St. in Lancaster Borough: HISTORY: It being the same half lot as given in the seven preceding indentures [the entire history of the property back to James Hamilton is given].

18 June 1772: JB & JH

Y449: James Davis, fuller, & his wife Sarah of Lampeter tp. enf-rel.to Conrad Swartz, saddler, of Lancaster Borough

--Half lot on King St. in Lancaster Borough: HISTORY: It being the same half lot as given in the preceding indenture.

26 Feb 1774: J.J. Loeser & Henrich Losser

Y452: Agreement between George Betz (or Petz), yeoman, & his wife Anna of Lancaster Borough and Michael Gross, innholder, of same

--Said George Betz will sell part of his lot on King St. to Michael Gross. By this indenture, Michael Gross agrees to leave an alleyway between his new building and George Betz's dwelling for their mutual use.

30 May 1749: George Gibson & George Smith

Y453: Isaac Lefever & his wife Eve, Nicholas Mack & his wife Catharine, Henry Eckman (or Hickman) & his wife Esther, George Lefever & his wife Barbara, Henry Christy & his wife Elizabeth, Rudolph Hab (or Hope) & his wife Eve, Adam Lefever & his wife Elizabeth, and Jacob Lefever [they being the children & heirs of Philip Lefever, late of Lancaster County, deceased] enf-rel.to George Betz (or Petz)

--Two lots on King St., one full lot and one half lot: HISTORY: On 3 May 1756, the county sheriff granted the said two lots to Philip Lefever [they late being the estate of convicted debtor George Betz].

23 Aug 1771: Johannes Rohrer, Arnold Bamberger, JR, & GR [also William Hery & Peter Kucher for Jacob Lefever]

Y456: Mary Lefever [the widow of Philip Lefever, deceased, late of Lancaster County] quitclaims to George Betz (or Petz)

--Her dower in two lots on King St., one full lot and one half lot: HISTORY: They being the same lots as given in the preceding indenture.

23 Aug 1771: JR & GR

Y457: George Betz & his wife Anna of Lancaster Borough enf-rel.to Francis Heger, butcher, of same

--Half lot on King St. in Lancaster Borough: HISTORY: Return to Deed Y434. George Betz acquired a full lot on King St. He deeded half to Michael Gross and retained the other half for his own use. Now go to Deed Y453. For unpaid debts, the sheriff seized the property and sold it at public vendue.

19 Feb 1778: L. Herbert & Casper Singer

Y459: Michael Fortinee, butcher, of Lancaster Borough gr.to Valentine Hoffman, blacksmith, of same

--The use of the North Gable on Michael Fortinee's property: HISTORY: Both own adjoining lots on Queen St. in Lancaster Borough.

2 Sep 1755: Hannes Kendig & DS

Y461: Valentine Hoofman assigns to Peter Isch (or Ish), blacksmith, of Lancaster Borough "the within privileges" [see the preceding indenture].

29 Dec 1759: Benjamin Price & WA

Y462: Peter Ish assigns to John Miller, gunsmith, of Lancaster Borough "the within privileges" [see the preceding indenture].

14 Mar 1777: Adam Reigert & CS

Y463: Valentine Hoffman, yeoman, & his wife Anna Maria enf-rel.to Peter Isch (or Ish), blacksmith, of same

--Half lot on Queen St. in Lancaster Borough: HISTORY: On 14 Jan 1740, James Hamilton granted a lot on Queen St. to Anna Maria Hoffman. On 14 Jul 1752, Anna Maria Hoffman granted half of the lot to her son Valentine Hoffman [party hereto].

29 Dec 1759: Benjamin Price & WA

Y465: Nicholas Hoffman, Conrad Hoffman & his wife Charity, Simon Kehrbach & his wife Annotilia, and Valentine Hoffman & his wife Anna Maria [they being the children & heirs of Anna Maria Hoffman, late of Lancaster Borough] enf-rel.to Peter Ish

--Half lot on Queen St. in Lancaster Borough: HISTORY: On 14 Jan 1740, James Hamilton granted a lot on Queen St. to Anna Maria Hoffman. On 14 Jul 1752, Anna Maria Hoffman granted half of the lot to her son Valentine Hoffman; however, she died intestate seized in possession of the other half of the said lot.

13 June 1767: CW & Ferdinand Knay

Y468: Peter Ish, blacksmith, & his wife Philippina of Greenwood tp., Cumberland County enf-rel.to John Miller, gunsmith, of Lancaster Borough

--Lot on Queen St. in Lancaster Borough: HISTORY: It being the same lot acquired by the two preceding indentures.

14 Mar 1777: AR & CS

Y471: Henry Reinael (or Reinail), blacksmith, & his wife Eve of Lebanon tp. enf-rel.to Philip Gloninger, yeoman, of same

--Two tracts: (1.) 28 ¾ a. Lebanon tp. and (2.) 102a Lebanon tp.

1. HISTORY: Part of 30 ¾ a. pat. 22 Feb 1760 to George Reynolds (Ref. PB A-20-466). On 28 Apr 1760, George Reynolds & his wife Eleanor granted 28 ¾ a. to Henry Reinael (Ref. Deed G101).
2. HISTORY: Part of 216 ¾ a. pat. 2 Aug 1760 to George Reynolds (Ref. PB AA-2-19). On 10 Jan 1761, George Reynolds & his wife Eleanor granted 106a [but now computed as 102a] to Henry Reinael (Ref. Deed G99).

--1 May 1767: JT & PM

Y476: Jacob Karch, bookbinder, & his wife Lucina of the town of Lebanon enf-rel.to Philip Gloninger, the younger, yeoman, of Lancaster County

--Lot #151 in the town of Lebanon: HISTORY: It being the same lot as given in Deed X602 and X605.

22 Apr 1784: Frederick Zimmerman & John Rohrer, Jr.

Y479: William Hamilton, Esq., of Philadelphia enf-rel.to Abraham Neaff of Lancaster Borough

--Two lots on Orange St. in Lancaster Borough, numbered 561 and 562 in the town plan: HISTORY: Said William Hamilton is acting in pursuance of powers given to him under the last will & testament of James Hamilton, Esq., deceased.

30 Mar 1784: HD & JY

Y482: Henry Spitzer, yeoman, & his wife Margaret of Lampeter tp. enf-rel.to Christian Hifner, yeoman, of same

5a, 56 ½ p. Lampeter tp.: HISTORY: Part of 100a that Joseph Hains & his wife Elizabeth granted 11 May 1765 to Rudolph Hains (Ref. Deed L85). On 5 Aug 1773, Rudolph Hains granted 10a, 113p to Isaac Hains. On 29 Mar 1777, Isaac Haines & his wife Catharine granted the same to George Nailer. On 23 Jan 1782, George Nailer & his wife Esther granted the same to Henry Spitzer & Bernard Houser, who divided the property between them, with 5a, 56 ½ p. being allotted to Henry Spitzer.

24 Jul 1782: ES & CS

Y484: Henry White, yeoman, of Rapho tp. rel.to Jacob Hiestand, yeoman, of Hempfield tp.

40a Rapho tp.: HISTORY: Warranted to said Henry White and contiguous to other lands that he has sold on this day to Jacob Hiestand.

22 May 1749: John Furry & John Renshaw

--John Furry of Hempfield tp., the son of John Furry, deceased, witness hereto, affirms his father's signature on 26 Apr 1784.

Y486: Tripartite agreement between the following parties:

1. Andrew Hershy, the younger, and Christian Swahr, yeomen, both of Hempfield tp. [the executors of Jacob Histand, yeoman, late of same]
2. Jacob Histand, yeoman, of Hempfield tp.; John Forrer, yeoman, & his wife Elizabeth of Mount Joy tp.; Daniel Erisman, yeoman, & his wife Mary of Lancaster tp.; John Hershy, yeoman, & his wife Catharine of Warwick tp.; and John Stern, yeoman, & his wife Barbara of Mount Joy tp. [the said Jacob, Elizabeth, Mary, Catharine, & Barbara being five children of said Jacob Histand, deceased]
3. Peter Histand, yeoman, of Rapho tp. [the son of said Jacob Histand, deceased]

--131a Rapho tp.: HISTORY: Same tract pat. 10 June 1741 to Henry White (Ref. PB A-10-315). On 22 May 1749, Henry White & his wife Johanna granted the same to Jacob Histand (Ref. Deed A80). Said Jacob Histand died leaving issue three sons and four daughters [the above children plus a son Abraham who has lately died]. By his last will & testament dated 28 Sep 1770, Jacob Histand devised his 131a plantation to his son Peter, subject to certain legacies to be paid to the other heirs. Now, by this indenture, the first & second parties release and quitclaim the said plantation to Peter Histand.

5 Dec 1772: WA & Philip Becker

Y490: David Witmer, miller, of Lampeter tp. gr.to Jacob Feree, yeoman, of Leacock tp.

--Water privileges: HISTORY: On 29 Nov 1777, said Jacob Feree granted a certain water, corn, grist, and merchant mill on the Pequea Creek to said David Witmer. This indenture settles the water rights & privileges.

20 Oct 1778: Jacob Hartman, Samuel Lefever, & J. Gibbons

Y493: William Ritter (or Rutter), yeoman, & his wife Margaret of Leacock tp. rel.to William Crawford, yeoman, of same

52a, 12p Salisbury tp.: HISTORY: Part of 128a Salisbury tp. warranted to Humphrey Fullerton. On 29 Mar 1773, Humphrey Fullerton & his wife Ann granted 52a, 12p [with other lands] to William Ritter. (Note: The tract was resurveyed on 21 Sep 1778, at which time the present acreage was determined.]

____ 178__: ___________ [omitted]

Y495: Humphrey Fullerton, yeoman, of Leacock tp. quitclaims to William Rutter

52a, 12p Salisbury tp.: HISTORY: See the preceding indenture. William Rutter had mortgaged this property (amongst others) to Humphrey Fullerton. Now, by this indenture, Humphrey Fullerton acknowledges satisfaction and releases this (and this only) tract from the mortgage.

19 Sep 1778: SH Jr. & Daniel Herbert

Y497: Francis Fortunee, shopkeeper, & his wife Elizabeth of Lancaster Borough rel.to Jacob Good, yeoman, of Conestoga tp.

--Half lot on Orange St. in Lancaster Borough: HISTORY: On 13 Jul 1745, James Hamilton granted a lot on Orange St. to George Honey. On 9 Jul 1746, George Honey assigned the same to Peter Worrell. On 13 Jul 1747, Peter Worrell & his wife Sarah granted the same to Christopher Trinkle, Ludwig, Stone, & Michael Gross. On 9 Aug 1747, Christopher Trinkle & his wife Ann, Ludwig Stone & his wife Catharine, and Michael Gross & his wife Elizabeth granted the same to Jacob Fortunee. Said Jacob Fortunee died intestate. On 27 June 1751, his children [to wit, Jacob Fortunee (the eldest son), Samuel Fortunee, and David Kuntz & his wife Margaret] granted the same to Francis Fortunee.

23 Mar 1753: GR & Daniel Kinbortz

Y499: Jacob Good, yeoman, & his wife Elizabeth of Conestoga tp. enf-rel.to Jacob Kuntz (or Countz) of Lancaster Borough

--Half lot on Orange St.: HISTORY: It being the same half lot as given in the preceding indenture.

10 Jan 1755: Johannes Mundorph & JB

Y501: William Bowsman, Casper Shaffner Sr., & Margaretha Kuntz, all of Lancaster Borough [the executors of Jacob Kuntz, late of same] enf-rel.to George Moore, mason, of same

--Half lot on Orange St.: HISTORY: It being the same half lot as given in the preceding indenture. By his last will & testament dated 30 June 1763, Jacob Kuntz ordered his executors to sell the said half lot.

29 Mar 1768: John Powell, CS Jr., & Michael Guardner

Y504: George Moore, innkeeper, & his wife Mary of Lancaster Borough rel.to Christophel Ox, yeoman, of same

--Half lot on Orange St.: HISTORY: It being the same half lot as given in the preceding indenture.

29 Oct 1778: WH & PH

Y507: Christopher Ox, yeoman, & his wife Elizabeth of Lancaster Borough enf-rel.to Jacob Ludwig, yeoman, of Strasburg tp.

--Half lot on Orange St.: HISTORY: It being the same half lot as given in the preceding indenture.

25 Mar 1784: Stephen Martin & CS

Y510: Agreement between Jacob Fortinee, yeoman, of Lancaster Borough and Francis Fortinee, yeoman, of same

--Both own adjoining half lots on Orange St. in said borough [said Francis Fortinee had granted Jacob Fortinee his half lot]. This indenture clarifies the rights and privileges concerning a well.

9 Mar 1752: WB, John Gelberth, & DS

--[On 25 June 1753, Francis Fortinee assigned his right to Jacob Good, who on 3 Sep 1753 assigned the right to Daniel Fissel (or Fizle), who on 23 Jul 1754 assigned the right to Jacob Kuntz. On 30 Mar 1768, Jacob Kuntz's executors assigned the right to George Moore, who on 29 Oct 1778 assigned the right to Christopher Ox, who in Mar 1784 assigned the right to Jacob Ludwig. See the preceding indentures. These assignments are located on pages 512-514.]

Y515: Jacob Beyerle & his wife Maria Rosina rel.to Jacob Dewalt

--"within described lot": HISTORY: No further information.

2 May 1749: Margaret Nelson & John Renshaw

Y515: Jacob Dewalt, yeoman, & his wife Margaret of Lancaster Borough enf-rel.to Jacob Rieger, surgeon, of same

--One half lot of the within described lot: HISTORY: No further information but see the preceding indenture.

8 Mar 1755: Benjamin Jones & GR

Y516: Jean Rieger [the widow & executrix of Jacob Rieger, late of Lancaster Borough] rel.to John Shertel (or Shartill) of same

--Half lot on Orange St. in Lancaster Borough: HISTORY: On 20 Jul 1743, James Hamilton granted a lot on Orange St. to Jacob Beyerle. On 2 May 1749, Jacob Beyerle & his wife Maria Rosina assigned the same to Jacob Dewalt. On 8 Mar 1755, Jacob Dewalt & his wife Margaret assigned half of the lot to Jacob Rieger. By his last will & testament, Jacob Rieger ordered his executor to sell the property [see the preceding indentures].

29 June 1761: Stofel Franciscus & Robert Thompson

Y519: John Shertel (or Shartle), pumpmaker, & his wife Christina of Lancaster Borough enf-rel.to John Roberts, hatter, of same

--Half lot on Orange St. in Lancaster Borough: HISTORY: It being the same half lot as given in the preceding indenture.

10 Apr 1784: Polly Shartle & JH

Y522: Sheriff Joseph Pugh, Esq., rel.to Isaac Whitelock, gentleman, of Lancaster Borough

--Lot on Orange St. in Lancaster Borough: HISTORY: Same lot that James Hamilton granted 22 June 1741 to Michael Shryack. On 3 Nov 1744, Michael Shryack & his wife Maria Catharine assigned the same to Nicholas Kindle. On 7 Nov 1748, Nicholas Kindle (or Kendle) granted the same to John Gerr (or Gear). On 4 Sep 1749, John Gerr & his wife Catharine re-conveyed the same to said Nicholas Kindle. On 20 Mar 1750, Nicholas Kindle & his wife Catharine assigned the same to Valentine Hercleroad (Ref. C1). On 7 Aug last, the Court of Common Pleas ordered the sheriff to seize the real estate of Valentine Hercleroad, yeoman, of Tulpehocken in Lancaster County for unpaid debts owing to Dirk Johnson. The sheriff duly seized a lot on Orange St. in Lancaster Borough, which he sold at public vendue to Isaac Whitelock.

4 Aug 1757: WA & CM

Y525: Isaac Whitelock, tanner, & his wife Mary of Lancaster Borough assign to Melchor Snyder

--"the within mentioned & described lot": HISTORY: Not given, but see the preceding indenture.

25 Feb 1758: Joseph Pugh & Joseph Rose

Y526: Melchor Schneider, yeoman, & his wife Margaret quitclaim to John Powell, schoolmaster, of same

--Half lot on Orange St. in Lancaster Borough: HISTORY: Same half lot that Michael Sittehelm & his wife Margaret granted 13 Feb 1767 to John Powell [said Michael Sittehelm owns the adjoining half lot]. See the following indenture.

13 Feb 1767: MH & Caleb Sheward

Y528: Michael Shittenhelm, yeoman, & his wife Margaret of Manheim tp. enf-rel.to John Powell, schoolmaster, of Lancaster Borough

--Half lot on Orange St.: HISTORY: It being part of the same lot assigned to Melchor Snyder in Deed Y525. On 12 Feb 1767, Melchor Snyder & his wife Margaret granted the full lot to said Michael Shittenhelm.

13 Feb 1767: MH & Caleb Sheward

Y531: William Powell, hatter, of Lancaster Borough [the only son of John Powell, deceased, late of same, schoolmaster] enf-rel.to John Roberts, hatter, of same

--Half lot on Orange St.: HISTORY: It being the same half lot as given in the preceding indenture. By his last will & testament dated 11 Feb 1772, John Powell devised the same to his wife Mary until his son William turned age 21 (Reference is made to a burying place on the lot).

14 Apr 1784: Martin Cooper & HD

Y536: Henry Zanck, tanner, & his wife Maria Catharine of Lancaster Borough enf-rel.to Jacob Zanck, tanner, of same

--Two adjoining lots in Lancaster Borough: (1.) lot on Queen St. and (2.) another lot on Queen St. HISTORY: Same lot formerly belonging to Robert Patterson. The country sheriff seized the property due to unpaid debts owed to one Thomas Doyle [the administrator of an unnamed estate]. On 31 Jan 1755, the sheriff granted the property to Isaac Whitelock [the highest bidder at public vendue]. On 8 Feb 1755, Isaac Whitelock & his wife Mary granted the same to Henry Zanck.
HISTORY: Same lot that James Hamilton granted 14 Jan 1740 to Peter Worral. On 7 Dec 1745, Peter Worral & his wife Sarah granted the same to John Aldeberger. On 28 Dec 1748, John Aldeberger & his wife Magdalena granted half of the lot to George Frederick Garvenus. // On 17 Nov 1750, John Aldeberger & his wife Magdalena granted the other half of the lot to Samuel Barr. On 24 Jan 1755, Samuel Barr & his wife Barbara granted their half to the said George Frederick Garvenus. // On 3 Aug 1757, George Frederick Garvenus (alias Calvenus) & his wife Mara granted the whole lot to Michael Bartges (Ref. Deed E473). On 26 Aug 1777, Michael Bartges & his wife Catharine granted the same to George Stehly. On 13 Sep 1777, George Stehly & his wife Dorothea granted the same to Henry Zanck.

--2 Oct 1779: MH & Adam Wilhelm

Y540: Sheriff John Ferree rel.to Casper Singer, tanner, of Lancaster Borough

60a Lancaster tp.: HISTORY: On 5 Feb 1774, the Court of Common Pleas ordered the sheriff to seize the real estate of Frederick Stone, Esq. [the late sheriff] for unpaid debts owing to one Philip Kleiss. The sheriff duly seized the following properties or rights: (1.) lot on King St. in Lancaster Borough on the public square, (2.) estate for life in 60a Lancaster tp. [location once given as Manheim tp., and (3.) estate for life of a lot on Queen St. in Lancaster Borough. At public vendue, the sheriff sold the 60a tract in Lancaster tp. to Casper Singer.

11 Feb 1775: GR Jr. & WA

Y543: George Weiss, yeoman, of Lancaster Borough rel.to Casper Singer, shopkeeper, of Philadelphia

60a Manheim tp.: HISTORY: It being the same tract as given in the preceding indenture. Susanna Weiss, the wife of George Weiss (party hereto), is the daughter of Frederick Stone. By law, she is to receive the said tract when she turns age 21 [said Frederick Stone had only an estate for life in the property]. At present, Susanna Weiss is underage. With this indenture, George Weiss agrees that they will release their claim to the property on the day that Susanna turns 21 [or within 30 days thereafter]; however, if Susanna should die before then—or if a child is born of her body—then this agreement is void.

6 Jul 1779: LW & F. Beates

Y545: George Weiss, yeoman, of Lancaster Borough gr.to Casper Singer, shopkeeper, of Philadelphia
--His estate for life in and of 60a Manheim tp. expectant upon the death of Frederick Stone:
HISTORY: See the preceding indenture.
6 Jul 1779: LW & F. Beates

Y546: Jacob Hartman, yeoman, & his wife Elizabeth of Hempfield tp. rel.to Herman Spohr, yeoman, of Warwick tp.
--Three adjoining tracts: (1.) 1a Hempfield tp., (2.) 3 ¼ a. Hempfield tp., and (3.) 44p Hempfield tp.

1. HISTORY: Part of 219a Hempfield tp. pat. 27 Feb 1760 to George Smith (Ref. PB A-20-486). On 1 Oct 1764, George Smith granted 1a Hempfield tp. to Jacob Hartman.
2. HISTORY: Part of the same 219a tract above. On 9 Feb 1767, George Smith granted 3 ¼ a. to Jacob Hartman.
3. HISTORY: Part of the same 219a tract above. On 1 Dec 1767, the executors of George Smith granted part of the tract to George Mummert. On 12 Sep 1771, George Mummert & his wife Barbara granted 44p to Jacob Hartman.

--2 Sep 1772: Jacob Shaffer & EM

Y550: Henry Herman, yeoman, & his wife Anna Eva of Hempfield tp. enf-rel.to Herman Spohr (or Spore), innkeeper, of same
--Two tracts: (1.) 2a Hempfield tp. and (2.) 33 1/3 p. Hempfield tp.

1. HISTORY: Part of 219a Hempfield tp. pat. 27 Feb 1760 to George Smith (Ref. PB A-20-486). On 9 Feb 1767, George Smith granted 2a to Henry Herman.
2. HISTORY: Part of the same 219a tract above. On 1 Dec 1767, the executors of George Smith granted a part of the tract to George Mumma. On 12 Sep 1771, George Mumma & his wife Barbara granted 33 1/3 p. to Henry Herman.

--12 Dec 1780: Jacob Stoltz & Johannes Hougentobler

Y553: The Supreme Executive Council appoints Henry Slaymaker, Esq., as Justice Elect for the Districts of Lampeter & Strasburg townships, to serve as a Justice of the Peace, on 24 June 1784.

Y554: The Supreme Executive Council appoints Michael Hubley, Esq., as Justice Elect for Lancaster Borough, to serve as a Justice of the Peace, on 7 Jul 1784.

Y554: The Supreme Executive Council appoints John Miller, Esq., as High Sheriff of Lancaster County on 18 Oct 1785.

Y555: John Miller, Esq., the newly appointed sheriff of Lancaster County, with Adam Reigart & Adam Weaver, innkeepers, of Lancaster Borough, are bound to the President of the Supreme Executive Council, contingent on said Miller faithfully serving his duties as county sheriff.
21 Oct 1785: GR & JH

Y557: The Supreme Executive Council appoints John Offner, gentleman, as the coroner of Lancaster County on 17 Oct 1785.

Y557: James Crawford, merchant, & his wife Ann of Philadelphia enf-rel.to William McCausland, yeoman, of Leacock tp.
54 ¾ a., 20p Leacock tp.: HISTORY: Same tract that said William McCausland & his wife Elizabeth granted 16 June last to James Crawford (Ref. Deed AA-351).

Y559: The Supreme Executive Council appoints John Luther, Esq., as Justice Elect for the District of Earl tp., to serve as a Justice of the Peace, on 8 Apr 1786.

Y559: The Supreme Executive Council appoints John Luther, Esq., to the Lancaster County Court of Common Pleas on 8 Apr 1786.

Abstracts of Lancaster County Deed Book Z

Z1: Christian Burkholder, yeoman, & his wife Ann of Earl tp. enf-rel.to John Grove, yeoman, of same

10a Earl tp.: HISTORY: Same tract that John Bitzer & his wife Mary granted 28 Apr 1770 to Christian Burkholder (Ref. Deed P338).

23 Mar 1782: Martin Hoover, Marcus Martin, & Daniel Grof

Z3: Henry Gochenouer, yeoman, and Joseph Gochenouer, yeoman, & his wife Catharine of Hempfield tp. enf-rel.to John Kneissly, yeoman, of Manheim tp.

200a Hempfield tp.: HISTORY: Part of 403a pat. 16 Apr 1740 to Joseph Gochenouer, alias Coghennouer. By his last will & testament, Joseph Gochenouer devised 200a to Henry Gochenouer & Joseph Gochenouer [the parties hereto], ordering his executors, to wit, John Coffman & John Huber, to make a deed good for the same (which they did on 16 Sep 1768). This indenture includes certain water rights that John Newcomer & his wife Elizabeth granted 27 Jul 1765 to Henry & Joseph Gochenouer.

1 May 1783: Christian Schenck, CS, & John Shaffner

Z6: Adam Simon Kuhn & his wife Mary of Lancaster Borough enf-rel.to Abraham Kobach (or Kabagh) of same

--Lot #45 in Lancaster Borough: HISTORY: Part of a larger tract partly in Lancaster Borough pat. 16 Nov 1737 to John Musser (Ref. PB A-8-314). On 7 Sep 1744, John Musser & his wife Fronica granted a certain parcel to Adam Simon Kuhn. On 7 Sep 1744, Adam Simon Kuhn & his wife Mary granted the major part of this parcel to James Hamilton, reserving a lot on ground on the east end of King St. for themselves—it now being Lot #45 in the town plan.

29 Oct 1765: JB & FK

Z8: Abraham Kobach (or Gobat), yeoman, & his wife Maria Magdalena of Derry tp. enf-rel.to Frederick Sheffer, waggoner, of Lancaster Borough

--Lot #45 in Lancaster Borough: HISTORY: It being the same lot as given in the preceding indenture.

6 Oct 1770: AH & JH

Z10: Christian Muma of Rapho tp. mort.to Stephen Wenger, yeoman, of Lancaster County

--Sundry items (no land).

7 Jan 1784: Jacob Misser, Jr., & Noah Ceasey

--Stephen Wenger ack.sat. 22 May 1786.

Z11: Esther McConnell & William Dickey [the administrators of Robert McConnell, yeoman, late of Paxton tp.] gr.to Peter Babb

172a Paxton tp.: HISTORY: Same tract war. 21 Apr 1775 to Bartram Galbreath & surveyed on 1 May 1775 to Robert McConnell. Said Robert McConnell died intestate leaving a widow [the said Esther, party hereto] and issue several children. On 10 Apr 1776, the said administrators petitioned the Orphans Court, requesting permission to sell the property in order to pay debts. The court granted their request.

21 May 1776: James Cowden & Thomas McArthur, Jr.

Z15: John Rauch, yeoman, & his wife Catharine of Derry tp. rel.to Michael Brown of Lebanon tp.

148a Hanover tp.: HISTORY: Same tract war. 11 Apr 1750 & later surveyed to John Moyer. On 1 Apr 1761, John Moyer granted the same to John Rauch. Said John Rauch received a patent for the land on 7 Jan 1768 (Ref. PB AA-10-220).

12 Mar 1770: Henrich Ziegler, Mathew Carother, & James McCreight

Z17: Michael Brown & his wife Anna of Hanover tp. rel.to George Minnich of Bethel tp., Berks County

148a Hanover tp.: HISTORY: It being the same tract as given in the preceding indenture.

--1 Apr 1774: Johannes Rauch, Johannes Gungrich, & James McCreight

Z20: Robert Huey, yeoman, & his wife Agnes of Salisbury tp. rel.to Hugh Robison, yeoman, of Paxton tp.

242a Salisbury tp.: HISTORY: Part of 430a pat. 25 Apr 1744 to Robert Hughey (Ref. PB A-12-100). By his last will & testament, Robert Hughey (or Huey) devised 242a to his grandson Robert Huey (the party hereto). On 3 May 1783, by a tripartite agreement, Samuel Hughes & John Wilson confirmed the property to said Robert Huey (Reference is made to May Term proceedings in the Court of Common Pleas).

30 Mar 1784: John Robinson & Margaret Boyd

Z22: Evan Evans, yeoman, & his wife Jane of Earl tp. enf-rel.to Nathan Evans, yeoman, of same

--Nathan Evans, late of Earl tp., the father of the above parties, died seized in possession of the following properties:

200a Earl tp.: HISTORY: Same tract pat. 5 Feb 1753 to John Evans (Ref. PB A-17-254). On 9 Nov 1753, John Evans & his wife Anne granted the same to Nathan Evans [father of the parties hereto] (Ref. Deed G287)—excepting one acre previously granted to Joshua Evans and 152 perches previously granted to James Douglass.

296a Earl tp.: HISTORY: Same tract pat. 3 Feb 1762 to Nathan Evans [father of the parties hereto] (Ref. PB AA-2d-489).

128a, 123p Earl tp. & 52a Earl tp.: HISTORY: Same tracts both pat. 3 Feb 1762 to Nathan Evans [father of the parties hereto] (Ref. PB AA-2d-489).

51 ¾ a. Earl tp.: HISTORY: Same tract that Henry Stouffer & his wife Elizabeth granted 5 Mar 1770 to Nathan Evans [father of the parties hereto].

15a, 8p Caernarvon tp.: HISTORY: Part of 200a Caernarvon tp. pat. 31 Dec 1733 to Nathan Evans Sr. (Ref. PB A-6-364). On 2 Apr 1761, Nathan Evans & his wife Susanna granted 15a, 8p to Nathan Evans Jr. [father of the parties hereto] (Ref. Deed G286).

--Said Nathan Evans [the father] died intestate seized in possession of all the above properties, leaving issue two sons, Evan & Nathan (the parties hereto). The two sons partitioned the properties, with the following tracts being allotted to Nathan: (1.) 130a [from tract #1 above], (2.) 133a [from tracts #3 and #4 above] and (3.) 52a [from tract #1 and #2]. Now, by this indenture, Evan Evans & his wife release any claim to the properties allotted to said Nathan Evans by division.

4 Aug 1782: Emanuel Newswanger & ZD

Z28: Jacob Weaver, the younger, yeoman, & his wife Mary of Earl tp. enf-rel.to Nathaniel (Nortz) Zwecker, yeoman, of same

37a, 50p Caernarvon tp., including a gristmill & sawmill: HISTORY: Same tract that said Henry Weaver & his wife Fronica granted to said Jacob Weaver (Ref. Deed X435), including certain water rights acquired in Deed Q195.

16 Mar 1784: CS, PH, Henry Peters, & John Morgan

Z31: Martin Bowman, millwright, & his wife Elizabeth of Earl tp. enf-rel.to Michael Altz, blacksmith, of same

48a, 134p Earl tp.: HISTORY: Part of 313a pat. 8 June 1749 to Conrad Holtzbaum (Ref. PB A-15-102). On 9 & 10 Jul 1749, Conrad Holtzbaum & his wife Susanna granted the same to Valentine Ente. On 25 Dec 1745, Valentine Ente & his wife Susanna granted the same to Weireck Bence. On 27 Nov 1762, Weireck Bence & his wife Mary granted 162a to Jacob Bence. On 1 May 1771, Jacob Bence & his wife Margaret granted 48a, 134p to Martin Bowman.

12 May 1772: JJ & George Wiler

Z34: George Dietrich, carpenter, & his wife Dorothea of Earl tp. enf-rel.to Michael Altz, blacksmith, of same

24a, 66p Earl tp.: HISTORY: Part of 313a pat. 8 June 1749 to Conrad Holtzbaum (Ref. PB A-15-102). On 9 & 10 Jul 1749, Conrad Holtzbaum & his wife Susanna granted the same to Valentine Ente. On 25 Dec 1745, Valentine Ente & his wife Susanna granted the same to Weireck Bence. On 27 Nov 1762, Weireck Bence & his wife Mary granted 162a to Jacob Bence. On 1 May 1771, Jacob Bence & his wife Margaret granted 24a, 66p to John Alter. On 20 June 1771, John Alter & his wife Ann granted the same to Martin Bowman. On 12 May 1772, Martin Bowman & his wife Elizabeth granted the same to George Dietrich.

26 Apr 1784: Hannes Bender & EC

Z37: Martin Hoe, yeoman, & his wife Elizabeth of Cocalico tp.; George Hoe, yeoman, & his wife Magdalena of Cocalico tp.; Michael Stephen, yeoman, & his wife Mary of Cocalico tp.; Jacob Haushalter, yeoman, & his wife Margaret, of Heidelberg tp.; and Adam Nees [the guardian of Barbara Reitter] quitclaim to Michael Reitter

100a Cocalico tp.: HISTORY: Jacob Reitter, late of Cocalico tp., died intestate seized in possession of 100a Cocalico tp. He left issue the said Michael Reitter and five daughters, to wit, the said Elizabeth Hoe, Magdalena Hoe, Mary Stephen, Margaret Houshalter, and Barbara Reitter. On 2 Mar 1768, the Orphans Court confirmed the real estate to the said Michael Reitter, the only son—subject to paying the other heirs their equal share thereof. Now, with this indenture, the other heirs acknowledge having received their due share with the exception of a certain sum to be paid after the death of Mary Geibe, late Mary Reitter, the widow.

24 Apr 1770: EC Jr., Maria Zimmerman, George Himwill & Michael Meyer

Z39: Christian Lang (or Long), yeoman, & his wife Margaret of Lancaster County enf-rel.to Michael Greybill, yeoman, of same

150a on Mill Creek: HISTORY: Part of 500a pat. 15 June 1733 to Amos Lewis, then of Haverford in Chester County (Ref. PB A-6-180). On 27 & 28 May 1738, Amos Lewis granted 250a to Christian Long [recorded in Philadelphia County].

31 Aug 1741: Will Richardson & Thomas Cookson

--Margaret Long affirms her signature on 9 June 1772.

Z41: Martin Huber (or Hoober), yeoman, & his wife Magdalena of Earl tp. enf-rel.to Michael Krebil, miller, of same

13a, 1r Earl tp.: HISTORY: Part of 159a Earl tp. pat. 22 Apr 1761 to Martin Huber (Ref. PB AA-2-233).

--15 Mar 1784: Christian Huber, Joseph Huber, & David Huber

Z44: Michael Diffederfer (or Diefenderfer), merchant, & his wife Christina of Lancaster County enf-rel.to Christian Primer, shoemaker, of Earl tp.

9a, 33p Earl tp.: HISTORY: Part of 268a pat. 19 June 1760 to Michael Diffederfer (Ref. PB A-19-609).

--7 Apr 1783: Johannes Krim & MH

Z46: Jacob Mayer & Martin Bare [the executors of John Bare, late of Conestoga tp.] rel.to John Bare of same [the son of said John Bare, deceased]

216a Conestoga tp.: HISTORY: Part of two larger tracts, to wit, 126a and 350a, that Patrick Carrigan & his wife Margaret granted 2 May 1751 to John Bare (Ref. Deed C79). By his last will & testament, John Bare devised (1.) 150a Conestoga tp. [the residue of a larger 250a tract] and (2.) 30a Conestoga tp. [the residue of a larger 230a tract] to his son John, ordering his executors to make a deed good for the same.

14 Apr 1783: ES & CS

Z49: Jacob Mayer & Martin Bare [the executors of John Bare, late of Conestoga tp.] rel.to Jacob Bare of same [the son of said John Bare, deceased]

200a Conestoga tp.: HISTORY: By his last will & testament, John Bare devised 200a Conestoga tp. [part of a larger 230a tract] to his son Jacob, ordering his executors to make a deed good for the same.

14 Apr 1783: ES & CS

Z52: Nathaniel (or Nartz) Zwecker, yeoman, & his wife Elizabeth of Earl tp. rel.to James McConnel, shopkeeper, of same

--Lot #1 in the town of New Design in Earl tp.: HISTORY: On 28 Aug 1760, Michael Diffenderfer & his wife Christina granted the same said lot to Laurence Olvart. On 17 Jan 1763, Laurence Olvart & his wife Barbara granted the same to Peter Gander. On 19 Jan 1763, Peter Gander & his wife Barbara granted the same to John Sensnich. On 5 Feb 1764, John Sensnich & his wife Mary granted the same to Christian Stoutsberger. On 14 Feb 1765, Christian Stoutsberger & his wife Elizabeth granted the same to George Kinzer. On 6 Apr

1773, George Kinzer & his wife Charlotte granted the same to Daniel Magee. On 20 Jul 1778, Daniel Magee granted the same to Nathaniel Zwecker.

13 Oct 1778: Peter Baker & Conrad Laub

Z54: John Scott of Allen tp., Cumberland County, enf-rel.to George Ross, Jr., Esq., of Lancaster Borough

127a, 5p Leacock tp.: HISTORY: Part of 150a Leacock tp. war. 24 May 1737 to Christian Krebs, then of Leacock tp., yeoman, who had been settled on the land 18 months prior to the warrant. On 18 Aug 1739, Christian Krebs assigned the same to William Beard of Leacock tp. By divers conveyances, the right to the property came to the said John Scott, who had the property resurveyed in pursuance to a new warrant issued 26 Sep 1761, which found the property to actually contain 156 acres. Said John Scott received a patent for the same on 8 Mar 1762 (Ref. PB AA-2d-528).

7 June 1779: William Scott & Henrich Witmer

Z57: William Shields, yeoman, & his wife Eleanor of Drumore tp. enf-rel.to William Nelson, fuller, of same

21 ¾ a. Drumore tp.: HISTORY: Part of a larger tract that Jehu Howel & his wife Margery granted 7 June 1779 to Henry Bowman. On 14 Mar 1783, Henry Bowman granted 21 ¾ a. to William Shields (Ref. Deed U384).

20 Nov 1783: James Knox, Joseph Shields, & Moses Irwin

Z60: Jacob Holtzinger, yeoman, of Antrim tp., Cumberland County, and George Bentz, yeoman, & his wife Anna Maria of York tp., York County [the said Jacob & Anna Maria being two children of Jacob Holtzinger, deceased, late of Earl tp., yeoman] quitclaim to Conrad Holtzinger & Engelhart Holtzinger [two sons of the said Jacob Holtzinger, deceased]

180a Earl tp.: HISTORY: By his last will & testament dated 27 Oct 1760, Jacob Holtzinger devised his plantation to his son Conrad & Engelhart when they come of age. The property is subject to the dower of the widow Veronica, who is now the wife of Peter Becker.

2 May 1775: Peter Bender (Becker?) & WA

Z62: Frances Lardner enf-rel.to David Jenkins

--His undivided fifth part of an undivided fourth part of Windsor Forge: HISTORY: Not given; however, said Frances Lardner has recently reached the age of 21.

9 Feb 1774: Catharine Lardner & LW

Z64: Hannah Lardner enf-rel.to David Jenkins

--Her undivided fifth part of an undivided fourth part of Windsor Forge: HISTORY: Not given; however, said Hannah Lardner has recently reached the age of 21.

22 May 1778: Joseph Jenkins & John Lardner

Z65: William Lardner enf-rel.to David Jenkins

--His undivided fifth part of an undivided fourth part of Windsor Forge: HISTORY: Not given; however, said William Lardner has recently reached the age of 21.

29 May 1782: Andrew Douglass & LW

Z66: Christopher Wegman, storekeeper, & his wife Eva Maria of Lebanon tp. enf-rel.to Albright Swinefort, yeoman, of Lancaster County

--Two contiguous lots in Middletown in Paxton tp.: HISTORY: Same two lots that the country sheriff seized and granted 9 Aug 1766 to Christopher Wegman.

22 Mar 1773: Casper Jost & JT

Z68: Alexander Jamison & his wife Isabella of Middletown in Paxton tp. rel.to William Crabb & Thomas Crabb, both of same

--Two contiguous lots in Middletown in Paxton tp.: HISTORY: They being the same two lots as given in the preceding indenture. On 6 Mar 1778, Albright Swinefort & his wife Margaret granted the same to Alexander Jamison.

22 Feb 1779: Johannes Backenstoss & H. Davis

Z70: William Crabb of Paxton tp. rel.to Thomas Crabb of same

--His moiety of two contiguous lots in Middletown in Paxton tp.: HISTORY: They being the same two lots as given in the preceding indenture.

31 Jan 1780: Joshua Elder & Nicholas Grossman

Z73: Thomas Crabb, yeoman, & his wife Mary of Paxton tp. enf-rel.to Peter Grubb, Esq., of Hopewell Forge

--Two contiguous lots in Middletown in Paxton tp., numbered 21 & 22 in the town plan: HISTORY: Not given, but review the preceding indentures—perhaps the same lots.

25 May 1780: Thomas Minshall & James Burd

Z75: Peter Grubb, Esq., of Hopewell Forge in Warwick tp. enf-rel.to John Fritz of Paxton tp.

--Two contiguous lots in Middletown in Paxton tp., numbered 21 & 22 in the town plan: HISTORY: They being the same two lots as given in the preceding indenture.

6 May 1784: Timothy Green & John Gilchrist Younger (the younger?)

Z78: Timothy Shaw of Paxton tp. gr.to Joseph Shaw of same

217a Paxton tp.: HISTORY: Same tract war. 14 Mar 1748 & later surveyed to Timothy Shaw [resurveyed on 14 Mar 1768].

15 June 1768: John Collier & Margaret Collier

Z80: Sheriff Frederick Stone gr.to Eve Catharine Rieger

--Lot #248 on Prince St. in Lancaster Borough: HISTORY: On 10 Nov 1770, the Court of Common Pleas ordered the sheriff to seize the real estate of John Held, yeoman, late of Lancaster County, for unpaid debts owing to said Eve Catharine Rieger [the administratrix of Bartholomew Rieger, deceased]. The sheriff duly seized the above-described lot on Prince St., which he sold at public vendue to the said Eve Catharine Rieger.

9 May 1771: JH & CW

Z82: Eve Catharine Rieger assigns to Mathias Zahneisen, carpenter, of Lancaster Borough

--"the within mentioned lot": HISTORY: Not given but see the preceding indenture.

24 Nov 1783: WH

Z83: James Ewing, yeoman, & his wife Patience of Hallam tp., York County enf-rel.to Christian Hershey, yeoman, of Manor tp.

--Two tracts: (1.) 200a Donegal tp. and (2.) 230a Donegal tp.

1. HISTORY: Same tract pat. 15 Mar 1737 to Thomas Ewing (Ref. PB A-8-347).
2. HISTORY: Same tract pat. 29 May 1733 to Joseph Borton (Ref. Phil. Book F-6-176). On 16 Apr 1734, Joseph Borton granted the same to John Ross (Ref. Deed L315). Said John Ross mortgaged the property to the General Loan Office; however, he later defaulted and the trustees of the General Loan Office seized the property. On 3 May 1738, the trustees granted the same to Thomas Ewing (Ref. Deed A37).

--Said Thomas Ewing died intestate leaving issue four children: James Ewing (party hereto), John Ewing, William Ewing, & Samuel Ewing. Both William & Samuel Ewing died intestate in their minority, unmarried & without issue. On 31 Dec 1764, John Ewing granted his right to his brother James Ewing (Ref. Deed M388), giving said James Ewing full right to both properties.

22 Nov 1768: Jacob Eresman & William A. Atlee

Z88: Henry Schneider & his wife Elizabeth, John Schneider & his wife Esther, Philip Reyer & his wife Elizabeth, Jacob Kintzi (or Kintzy) & his wife Margaret, Esther Hollinger, & Susanna Sigrist quitclaim to Peter Schneider [the said Henry, John, Elizabeth, Margaret, Esther, Susanna, & Peter being the seven children of Henry Schneider, deceased, late of Warwick tp.]

193a Warwick tp.: HISTORY: Part of two tracts pat. 17 Dec 1751 to Henry Schneider (Ref. PB A-16-125). Said Henry Schneider died intestate leaving issue the above seven children; however, in his lifetime, he had allotted the said land to his son Peter. The other heirs now legally confirm the late father's intentions.
11 Nov 1780: ES, CS, John Ricksecker, & Christian Reist

Z91: Jacob Carpenter, yeoman, of Lancaster County enf-rel.to Joseph Haynes, yeoman, of same
3a Lampeter tp.: HISTORY: Part of a larger tract that Daniel Carpenter & his wife Magdalena granted in 1759 to Jacob Carpenter.
9 May 1760: Rudolph Haines & DS

Z93: Christina Meyer, widow, of Paxton tp. rel.to John Meyer, yeoman, of Derry tp.
25a Derry tp.: HISTORY: Part of 120a Derry tp. pat. 16 Dec 1772 to John Meyer of Derry tp. (Ref. PB AA-13-301). By his last will & testament, John Meyer directed his wife Christina (party hereto) to either reserve the property for his youngest son Samuel Meyer or sell for the best price. John Meyer, the other party hereto, is another son of the said John Meyer, deceased.
23 Jan 1783: John Laning & James Russel, Jr.

Z95: George Heft, yeoman, & his wife Dorothea of Brecknock tp. rel.to Christopher Heft, yeoman, of same
160a Brecknock tp.: HISTORY: Part of 257a pat. 2 June 1768 to George Heft (Ref. PB AA-10-381).
--1 Apr 1779: AN & John Smuller

Z97: Thomas & John Penn, the Governors & Proprietors of the Province of Pennsylvania gr.to Nathaniel Stevenson
323 ½ a. Donegal tp.: HISTORY: Same tract war. 11 Aug 1749 & later surveyed to James Stevenson. Said James Stevenson later devised the same to his son Nathaniel Stevenson (party hereto).
15 Mar 1775: (Seal)

Z99: Philip Hefft gr.to John Musselman
--Water rights: HISTORY: This indenture is written in German—no history appears to be given, rather only details of the agreement.
18 Nov 1772: Johannes Rim & Peter Hafft

Z100: Abraham Bower, yeoman, & his wife Elizabeth of Cocalico tp. enf-rel.to Philip Heft, hatter, of Cocalico tp.
109a Cocalico tp.: HISTORY: On ___ 177__, John Istand & his wife Elizabeth granted 109a Cocalico tp. to Abraham Bower.
16 Nov 1778: Samuel Gut & Hannes Mohler

Z102: John Brackbill & Benjamin Brackbill, both of Strasburg tp. [the administrators of George Weaver, yeoman, late of Caernarvon tp.] enf-rel.to Henry Weaver, yeoman, of Caernarvon tp.
246a Caernarvon tp.: HISTORY: On 17 Feb 1774, said Henry Weaver & his wife Fronica granted 230a Caernarvon tp. to said George Weaver (Ref. Deed Q195). A resurvey found the property to actually contain 246 acres. Said George Weaver died intestate seized in possession thereof. On 4 June 1782, the Orphans Court ordered his administrators to sell the property.
30 Dec 1783: James Old & James Webb, Jr.

Z107: George Michael Rank of Surry County, North Carolina [the eldest son of Michael Rank, deceased, late of Earl tp., yeoman] appoints Philipp Grosch, yeoman, of Lancaster County as his lawful attorney to handle his share of his late father's 420-acre plantation in Earl tp.
11 Feb 1784: John Conrad, George Hauser J.P., Jacob Blum J.P. & Peter Hauser

Z108: John Rank of Surry County, North Carolina [son of Michael Rank, deceased, late of Earl tp., yeoman] appoints Philipp Grosch, yeoman, of Lancaster County as his lawful attorney to handle his share of his late father's 420-acre plantation in Earl tp.

11 Feb 1784: John Conrad, George Hauser J.P., Jacob Blum J.P. & Peter Hauser

Z110: Philip Fassnacht (or Fastnaught) & his wife Juliana of Earl tp. and David Ream, taylor, of Lancaster County [the said Juliana & David being two children of Elizabeth Ream, deceased] enf-rel.to Michael Reiter, yeoman, of Cocalico tp.

43a Cocalico tp.: HISTORY: By his last will & testament dated 8 June 1757, Michael Reiter [grandfather of Michael Reiter, party hereto] devised his plantation to his wife Agnes Reiter, his son Jacob Reiter, & his daughter Elizabeth wife of Nicholas Ream. A 48-acre tract was allotted to Elizabeth Ream as her equal share. She died intestate seized in possession thereof leaving issue the said David & Juliana and six other children. // Said Michael Reiter (the party hereto) now holds a part of this 48a tract, containing about 43a (which he purchased from Adam Bower). Now, by this indenture, Philip Fassnacht & his wife Juliana and David Ream released their right, claim, and interest in and of the said 43a parcel bought from Adam Bower.

16 Jan 1782: Adam Bower & AN

Z112: Philip Fassnacht (or Fastnaught) & his wife Juliana of Earl tp. and David Ream, taylor, of Lancaster County [the said Juliana & David being two children of Elizabeth Ream, deceased] enf-rel.to John Martin, yeoman, of Cocalico tp.

43a Cocalico tp.: HISTORY: By his last will & testament dated 8 June 1757, Michael Reiter [grandfather of Michael Reiter, party hereto] devised his plantation to his wife Agnes Reiter, his son Jacob Reiter, & his daughter Elizabeth wife of Nicholas Ream. A 48-acre tract was allotted to Elizabeth Ream as her equal share. She died intestate seized in possession thereof leaving issue the said David & Juliana and six other children. // Said John Martin (the party hereto) now holds a part of this 48a tract, containing about nine or ten acres (which he purchased from Adam Bower). Now, by this indenture, Philip Fassnacht & his wife Juliana and David Ream released their right, claim, and interest in and of the said nine or ten-acre parcel bought from Adam Bower.

16 Jan 1782: Adam Bower & AN

Z115: George Weiss, innholder, & his wife Susanna of Philadelphia enf-rel.to Christopher Baker, conveyancer, of same

--Their undivided fifth part of the real estate of John Dehuff: HISTORY: Said John Dehuff died seized of divers property. He left issue five children, including a daughter Susanna who married Frederick Stone. Said Susanna died intestate on 30 Jan 1761. They had issue four children, but three died in their minority unmarried and without issue. The surviving child, Susanna, married George Weiss (the parties hereto).

6 May 1784: Henry Tremps & Richard Taylor

Z118: Christopher Baker & his wife Catharine enf-rel.to George Weiss

--Their undivided fifth part of the real estate of John Dehuff: HISTORY: See the preceding indenture.

7 May 1784: Henry Tremps & Richard Taylor

Z119: Jacob Funck, yeoman, & his wife Fronica of Manheim tp. rel.to John Snably (or Snevely), yeoman, of same

301 ½ a. on a branch of the Conestoga Creek: HISTORY: Same tract pat. 15 May last to Jacob Funck (Ref. PB A-7-176).

5 June 1735: John Naglee, John Lesher, C. Brockden, Johann Shenck, Johann Herbert Weber

Z121: Christian Hershy & his wife Barbara, Abraham Hershy & his wife Elizabeth, Peter Reesher (or Riesser), Samuel Heir & his wife Anna, Abram Neeff & his wife Mary, David Heir & his wife Barbara, Henry Heir & his wife Hester, and Jacob Errisman & his wife Addah [they being the surviving heirs of Christian Hershy, or Hersha, deceased, late of Manheim tp.] enf-rel.to Benjamin Hershy [another son of the said Christian Hershy, deceased]

305a Manheim tp.: HISTORY: Same tract pat. 15 May last to Jacob Funck (Ref. PB A-7-176). On 5 June 1735, Jacob Funck & his wife Fronica granted the same to John Snably (Ref. Phil. Deed F-8-249). On 4 & 5 May 1743, John Snably & his wife Ann granted the same to Christian Hershy [excepting four acres]. Said

Christian Hershy died intestate seized in possession of the property [now revised as containing 305a], leaving issue the above-named three sons & six daughters [daughter Elizabeth, not named above, is/was the wife of Peter Reesher].

___ Nov 1762: JB, Wilton Atkinson, & Herman Long

Z125: Benjamin Landis, yeoman, & his wife Anna of Manheim tp. enf-rel.to Benjamin Hershy, yeoman, of same

7a, 105p Manheim tp.: HISTORY: Part of 276a that John Jacob Snevely & his wife Barbara, Andrew Hershy & his wife Mary, John Long & his wife Ann, and Jacob Kaufman & his wife Eve granted 23 Mar 1752 to Benjamin Landis (Ref. Deed D72).

12 May 1783: MH & CJ

Z127: Benjamin Hershy, yeoman, & his wife Catharine of Manheim tp. enf-rel.to Samuel Myers, yeoman, of same

--Two tracts: (1.) 145 ½ a. Manheim tp. and (2.) 7a, 105p Manheim tp.

1. HISTORY: Part of the same 305a tract acquired by Benjamin Hershy in Deed Z121.
2. HISTORY: It being the same tract as given in the preceding indenture.

--1 May 1784: HD & CJ

Z131: James Reed, yeoman, & his wife Jenney of Drumore tp. enf-rel.to his brother John Reed of same

40a, 28p Drumore tp. [excepting four acres that James Reed previously granted to William Aulls]: HISTORY: Part of a larger tract war. 15 Mar 1753 to James Maxwell. On 24 Nov 1763, James Maxwell granted the same larger tract to said John Reed. On 14 Dec 1773, John Reed granted the same to said James Reed.

9 Aug 1783: Thomas Clark & Moses Irwin

Z133: Abraham Stoner, yeoman, & his wife Ann of Manor tp. enf-rel.to Christian Stoner, yeoman, of same

83 ½ a. Manor tp.: HISTORY: On 8 May 1762, Abraham Stoner & his wife Salome granted 112 ¼ a. Manor tp. to John Stoner. Said John Stoner died intestate leaving a widow named Elizabeth and issue the following children: Abraham Stoner (the eldest son & party hereto), Christian Stoner, John Stoner, Jacob Stoner, & Elizabeth Stoner. On 4 June 1782, the Orphans Court confirmed the real estate to the said Abraham, the eldest son.

8 May 1784: CJ & HD

Z137: George Matter, yeoman, & his wife Catharine of Earl tp. rel.to Leonard Stone, yeoman, of same

89a Earl tp.: HISTORY: Part of 165a, 27p Earl tp. pat. 17 Oct instant to George Matter (Ref. CB A-4-172).

--26 Oct 1776: EC Jr. & Jacob Carpenter

Z138: Leonard Stone (or Stein), yeoman, & his wife Mary of Earl tp. enf-rel.to George Martin, yeoman, of same

89a Earl tp.: HISTORY: It being the same tract as given in the preceding indenture.

--13 Mar 1783: Michael Marti & ZD

Z141: John Robeson (or Robinson), yeoman, & his wife Jean of Hanover tp. enf-rel.to Robert Robeson of Mount Joy tp.

149a Donegal & Mount Joy tps.: HISTORY: Part of 461 ½ a. in Donegal & Mount Joy tps. patented to Andrew Robinson by two separate acts, one dated 26 Nov 1745 (Ref. PB A-12-273) and the other 17 Feb 1764 (Ref. PB AA-4-481). On 2 May 1783, Andrew Robinson & his wife Agnes granted two parcels, one containing 43 ½ a. and the other 105 ½ a., to John Robinson/Robeson.

8 Apr 1784: Timothy Green, Thomas Robinson, & John Thompson

Z144: Andrew Grocknow (or Groknow), yeoman, & his wife Maria of Londonderry tp. rel.to George Goepfert, weaver, of Mount Joy tp.

140a Londonderry tp.: HISTORY: Same tract war. 11 May 1768 to John Dirr (Ref. Application #3291). On 12 Nov 1769, John Dirr & his wife Maria granted the same to Andrew Grocknow.

7 Apr 1783: Elizabeth Herr & Christian Herr

Z145: John Foster, yeoman, of Londonderry tp. enf-rel.to William Hay, yeoman, of same

--His undivided fifth part of two adjoining tracts, (1.) 250a Londonderry tp. and (2.) 150a Mount Joy tp.: HISTORY: Late the estate of John Foster, the elder, who died intestate leaving issue the following children: David Foster (since deceased), John Foster (the party hereto), Catharine Foster (now wife of John Davis), and Margaret Foster (now wife of Samuel Millegan).

31 Aug 1778: William Leaver & PM

Z147: Samuel Millegan, yeoman, & his wife Margaret of Armaugh tp., Cumberland County enf-rel.to William Hay, yeoman, of Londonderry tp.

--Their undivided fifth part of two adjoining tracts, (1.) 250a Londonderry tp. and (2.) 150a Mount Joy tp.: HISTORY: See the preceding indenture.

25 Nov 1778: PG & PM

Z149: Mathew Hay & his wife Mary and John Hay, all of Londonderry tp., enf-rel.to William Hay of same

250a Londonderry tp.: HISTORY: On 6 Apr 1779, James Hay & his wife Sarah granted 250a Londonderry tp. to Mathew Hay & John Hay, subject to the directions given under the last will & testament of John Hay, deceased.

15 Apr 1784: Jacob Cooke & Thomas Robinson

Z151: James Hay, Mathew Hay & his wife Mary, Jonathan McClure & his wife Sarah, John Hay, David Hay, Samuel Hay, & Margaret Hay rel.to their brother William Hay, Esq., of Londonderry tp.

--The two within described tracts [not identified]: HISTORY: By his last will & testament, John Hay, Esq., of Londonderry tp. devised the said two tracts to his wife and eight children [presumably the eight parties hereto].

15 Apr 1784: Jacob Cooke & Thomas Robinson

Z153: Philip Heft, hatter, & his wife Sarah of Cocalico tp. enf-rel.to John Ream, yeoman, of same

25a, 29p Cocalico tp.: HISTORY: Part of two tracts: (1.) 389a pat. 28 June 1734 to Eberhard Ream [Ref. PB A-8-96] and (2.) 113a patented to the said Eberhard Ream [Ref. PB A-15-542, recorded 13 Nov 1750]. On 15 Feb 1759, by their two separate indentures, Eberhard Ream & his wife Elizabeth granted 60a (part of the 389a) and 62a (part of the 113a) to their son Nicholas Ream. On 20 Aug 1768, Nicholas Ream granted 25a, 29p to Philip Heft.

10 Sep 1774: Hannes Keil & ZD

Z156: James Old, yeoman, & his wife Margaret of Caernarvon tp. enf-rel.to John Diller, blacksmith, of same

31a Caernarvon tp.: HISTORY: Part of the 246a tract given in Deed Z102. On 30 Dec 1783, Henry Weaver granted 90a Caernarvon tp. to James Old.

30 Dec 1783: John Brackbill, William Smith, James Webb Jr., & Hannah Mendenhall

Z159: George Heft, yeoman, & his wife Dorothea of Brecknock tp. rel.to John Lutz, yeoman, of same

48a Brecknock tp.: HISTORY: Part of 257a pat. 2 June 1768 to George Heft (Ref. PB AA-10-381).

--1 Apr 1779: AN & John Smuller

Z161: Philip Ranck, cordwainer, & his wife Magdalena of Brecknock tp. enf-rel.to Valentine Ranck, yeoman, of Caernarvon tp.

105a, 71p Earl tp.: HISTORY: Same tract pat. 9 Oct 1760 to Philip Ranck (Ref. PB AA-1-112).

--4 Mar 1763: Hannes Wenger & ZD

Z164: Mary Plumstead (widow), Archibald McCall (merchant), & Judah Foulke (merchant), all of Philadelphia [the executors of William Plumstead, Esq., late of same] rel.to Valentine Rank, yeoman, of Caernarvon tp.

253a Salisbury tp.: HISTORY: Same tract pat. 7 Feb 1739 to John Denniston of Salisbury tp. (Ref. PB A-10-5). On 14 Feb 1739, John Denniston mortgaged the same to the General Loan Office. He defaulted on his payments and the property was seized. On 14 Apr 1752, the trustees of the General Loan Office granted the same to William Plumstead. By his last will & testament dated 24 Oct 1760, William Plumstead ordered the property sold.

6 May 1772: PMR & Samuel Gilaspy

Z167: The trustees of the General Loan Office rel.to William Plumstead, Esq., of Philadelphia

253a Salisbury tp.: HISTORY: It being the same tract as given in the preceding indenture.

--14 Apr 1752: Benjamin Chapman, Josiah Dyer, & James Johnston

Z169: Samuel Boude, yeoman, & his wife Mary of Lancaster Borough enf-rel.to John Utzman, yeoman, of same

--Lot on Duke St. in Lancaster Borough: HISTORY: Not given.

16 Jul 1750: John O'Nell & Johannes Fuchs

Z171: John Utzman, yeoman, & his wife Albertina of Lancaster Borough gr.to Dietrich Benedict, yeoman, of same

--Two tracts: (1.) lot on Duke St. in Lancaster Borough and (2.) 146a in York County

1. HISTORY: It being the same lot as given in the preceding indenture.
2. HISTORY: Same tract warranted to Zachery Shugart & Conrad Holtzbaum. On 28 Aug 1753, they granted the same to John Utzman.

--19 Sep 1753: Peter Pritz & Joseph Rose

Z173: Jacob Hostetter, yeoman, & his wife Anna; Abraham Hostetter & his wife Catharine; John Brubacher & his wife Anna; Christian Hershy (or Hirshi) in right of his late wife Barbara, deceased; Christian Bomberger & his wife Elizabeth; John Greiter (or Crydor) & his wife Margaret; and Catharine Hostetter [all women nee Hostetter] rel.to John Hostetter

150a [location not given]: HISTORY: Same tract pat. 5 June 1734 to Jacob Hostetter, yeoman (Ref. PB A-6-339). By his last will & testament dated 16 Jan 1756, Jacob Hostetter devised the same to his son John (the party hereto), subject to him paying the other heirs their equal share. [Ed. Note: Though not stated as such, the grantors hereto must be the other children of said Jacob Hostetter, deceased.]

1 Oct 1761: DS & ASK

Z175: Martin Bowman, yeoman, & his wife Susanna of Earl tp. enf-rel.to Martin Bowman, Sr., yeoman, of same

45a, 36p Earl tp.: HISTORY: Same tract pat. 15 Apr 1774 to John Ream (Ref. PB AA-14-250). On 22 Apr 1782, John Ream & his wife Margaret granted the same to Martin Bowman, Jr. On 22 Apr 1782, Martin Bowman & his wife Susanna granted the same to Martin Bowman [sic].

20 Sep 1782: John Bowman & Juliana Bowman

Z178: Martin Bowman, yeoman, & his wife Elizabeth of Earl tp. enf-rel.to Christopher Deetrick, miller, of same

45a, 36p Earl tp.: HISTORY: It being the same tract as given in the preceding indenture.

--18 May 1784: Martin Frey & Abraham Graff

Z180: John Klein, yeoman, of Warwick tp. rel.to Christian Kreiss (or Crise), yeoman, of same

30a Warwick tp.: HISTORY: Same tract that Conrad Glassbrenner granted 6 May 1756 to Peter Klein & his wife Barbara (Ref. Deed Q416). Said Peter Klein died leaving issue the said John Klein, to whom the property descended.

8 May 1784: CJ & HD

Z181: John Witmer, the younger, gentleman, & his wife Mary of Radnor tp., Chester County enf-rel.to John Burkholder, yeoman, of Lampeter tp.

100a Lampeter tp.: HISTORY: Part of 200a pat. 3 Nov 1738 to Martin Cryder (Ref. PB A-1-131). On 11 Jan 1758, Martin Cryder & his wife Barbara granted ____ [not given] to Tobias Cryder (Ref. Deed D456). On 18 May 1775, Tobias Cryder & his wife Anna granted _____ to Martin Cryder, John Cryder, Jacob Cryder, & Henry Cryder. On 19 May 1775, Martin Cryder & his wife Elizabeth, John Cryder, Jacob Cryder, and Henry Cryder & his wife Magdalena granted ____ to John Witmer, Jr. (Ref. Deed S284).

8 Apr 1783: N. Lee & James Woods

Z184: John Brubacher, yeoman, & his wife Ann of Manheim tp. enf-rel.to Christian Bamberger, yeoman, of same

127a, 80p Manheim tp.: HISTORY: Part of three tracts: (1.) 50a taken from a larger tract pat. 22 Jan 1740 to Peter Schwar [Ref. PB A-9-278]. On 30 Mar 1742, Peter Schwar granted 50a to John Brubacher. (2.) 44a taken from a larger tract pat. 15 Feb 1738 to Roger Hunt (Ref. CB A-1-202). On 9 May 1747, Roger Hunt & his wife Esther granted the same to John Mayer. On 22 Nov 1748, John Mayer & his wife Maria granted 44a to John Brubacher. (3.) Being the residue of a larger tract pat. 18 Nov 1762 to John Brubacher (Ref. PB AA-4-101).

26 Apr 1784: John Shaffner & CS

Z187: John Brubacher, yeoman, & his wife Ann of Manheim tp. enf-rel.to John Brubacher, Jr., yeoman, of same

99a Manheim tp.: HISTORY: Part of a larger tract pat. 18 Nov 1762 to John Brubacher (Ref. PB AA-4-101).

26 Apr 1784: John Shaffner & CS

Z189: Henry Kring, yeoman, & his wife Elizabeth of Heidelberg tp. enf-rel.to Peter Spengler, yeoman, of same

250a Heidelberg tp.: HISTORY: Same tract war. 14 Oct 1747 to Sebastian Rudy, who died intestate seized in possession thereof. On the first Tuesday in March 1761, the Orphans Court confirmed the real estate to his son Abraham Rudy. On 20 Mar 1765, Abraham Rudy granted the same to Henry Kring.

11 May 1784: Henry Mayer & Henry Sheffer

Z192: Tripartite agreement among the heirs of Jacob Kauffman, deceased, late of Hempfield tp.; to wit:

1. Jacob Kauffman, yeoman, & his wife Barbara of Manheim tp.
2. Andrew Kauffman, yeoman, & his wife Magdalena of Hempfield tp.; Peter Bachman, yeoman, & his wife Mary of Manheim tp.; Benedict Eshelman, yeoman, & his wife Elizabeth of Hempfield tp.; Anna Brubaker, widow, of Rapho tp.; and Eve Kauffman, widow, of Hempfield tp. [the widow of the said Jacob Kauffman, deceased]
3. Isaac Kauffman, yeoman, of Hempfield tp.

--198 ¾ a Hempfield tp.: HISTORY: Part of 231a Hempfield tp. pat. 24 Oct 1743 to Jacob Kauffman, alias Koffman [Ref. PB A-12-169]. Said Jacob Kauffman intended the land for his son Johannes; however, son Johannes died in his minority, unmarried and without issue during the lifetime of his father. By agreement, the property reverted as part of the estate of Jacob Kauffman, the father. By his last will & testament dated 14 May 1767, Jacob Kauffman devised 200a [part of the above tract] to his son Isaac—subject to certain legacies paid to the other heirs; to wit, his widow Eve and his children Jacob (the eldest son), Andrew, Mary, Elizabeth, and Anna [the grantors above]. (It is further noted that Jacob Kauffman, the father, purchased the land from one Martin Kauffman prior to obtaining the patent.)

13 Sep 1771: WA, Jacob Neff, & WC

Z196: Philip Royer, yeoman, & his wife Elizabeth of Manheim tp. enf-rel.to Michael Kremer of Lancaster Borough

--Half lot on Queen St. in Lancaster Borough: HISTORY: On 13 Jul 1745, James Hamilton granted a full lot on Queen St. to Jacob Regree. On 27 Oct 1748, Jacob Regree & his wife Jane granted the same to

John Shriber & John Shankmeyer, who partitioned the lot between them. On 14 Feb 1748/49, John Shankmeyer & his wife Elizabeth released half of the lot to John Shriber. On 4 May 1750, John Shriber & his wife Maria granted their said half lot to John Schneider, who died intestate seized in possession thereof. In pursuance to an Orphans Court order, his administrators (Christian Buch & Magdalena Schneider) granted the same to Christian Voght on 5 Feb 1770. On 6 Feb 1770, Christian Voght & his wife Elizabeth granted the same to John Schneider [a different one]. On 3 Nov 1774, John Schneider granted the same to said Michael Kremer. The county sheriff seized the property due to unpaid debts owed by the said Michael Kremer. On 8 Sep 1774, the sheriff granted the said half lot to Jacob Dickert. On 24 Nov 1774, Jacob Dickert & his wife Johanna granted the same to Philip Royer.

26 May 1784: Johannes Kramer & CS

Z199: John Smith & Catharine May (the widow of Philip May) rel.to Philip Smith & William Smith, yeomen, both of Hempfield tp.

125a Hempfield tp.: HISTORY: Same tract pat. 19 May 1769 to Henry Smith. By his last will & testament, Henry Smith devised the same to his sons Philip Smith & William Smith, subject to legacies to be paid to his son John Smith & his daughter Catharine, wife of Philip May [the said four children being the parties hereto].

19 Apr 1784: PG & John Huber

Z201: Peter Baker, the younger, yeoman, & his wife Christina of Earl tp. enf-rel.to George Hildebrand, yeoman, of same

158a Earl & Leacock tps.: HISTORY: Same tract pat. 4 June 1735 to Thomas Small (Ref. PB A-7-207). On 12 Apr 1748, Thomas Small & his wife Mary Ann granted the same to Peter Summy. On 26 Dec 1748, Peter Summy & his wife Margaret granted the same to Peter Baker. On 28 Oct 1765, Peter Baker, Sr., granted the same to his son Peter Baker, Jr. (the party hereto).

8 May 1784: James Crawford & JJ

Z204: Martin Leviston (or Lowigston), yeoman, of Earl tp. enf.to Alexander Martin, yeoman, of Lancaster County

248a Earl tp.: HISTORY: Same tract war. 27 Feb 1734 to Martin Leviston.

--10 Feb 1736: David Edwards & Thomas Edwards

--Gabriel Davis on his oath affirms Thomas Edwards' signature on 1 June 1784.

Z205: Alexander Martin, yeoman, of Lebanon tp. enf-rel.to James Martin, yeoman, of Earl tp.

100a Earl tp.: HISTORY: Part of the same 248a tract as given in the preceding indenture. By his last will & testament dated 9 June 1769, Alexander Martin devised 200a Earl tp. to his son Alexander. By his last will & testament dated 20 Aug 1778, Alexander Martin devised 100a to his nephew Alexander Martin (party hereto).

3 Dec 1778: Susanna Jones & JJ

Z207: Tripartite agreement between:

1. Elizabeth Lightfoot, widow, of Reading in Berks County [the widow of Benjamin Lightfoot, gentleman, late of same]
2. Elizabeth Biddle, widow, of Reading in Berks County [the widow & executrix of Edward Biddle, gentleman, late of same] & James Biddle, Esq., of Reading [the executor of said Edward Biddle, deceased]
3. John Jenkins, miller, of Caernarvon tp.

--93a Caernarvon tp. war. 6 Feb 1769 to Daniel Levan, the younger (Ref. Application #3824). On 28 Dec 1769, Daniel Levan granted the same to Benjamin Lightfoot & Edward Biddle. By his last will & testament dated 21 Apr 1777, Benjamin Lightfoot devised his real estate to his wife. By his last will & testament dated 27 Jul 1779, Edward Biddle ordered his executors to sell his share of the property. Now, by this indenture, the parties of the first and second part grant their respective shares of the said 93a tract to John Jenkins.

2 Dec 1783: James Shoemaker & James Scull

Z210: Sheriff Thomas Edwards rel.to Martin Shenk, yeoman, of Elizabeth tp.

38a, 10p Warwick tp.: HISTORY: On 9 Aug 1783, the Court of Common Pleas ordered the sheriff to seize the real estate of Peter Weiland, yeoman, of Warwick tp. for unpaid debts owed to one Abraham Graff. The sheriff duly seized 50a Elizabeth tp. [sic], which he later sold at public vendue to Martin Shenk.

1 June 1784: JH & PH

Z212: Frederick Anspach, butcher, & his wife Elizabeth of Lancaster Borough enf-rel.to John Bonnet, yeoman, of same

--Lot #24 on High St. in Lancaster Borough: HISTORY: Same lot that Samuel Bethel & his wife Susanna granted 10 Aug 1762 to George Kester. On 4 May 1778, George Kester & his wife Margaret granted the same to Frederick Anspach.

13 Feb 1782: John Offner & CS

Z214: John Bonnet & his wife Magdalena assign to Christina Razor, spinster, of Lancaster Borough

--"the within mentioned & described lot": HISTORY: Not given but see the preceding indenture.

14 Feb 1783: AR & Abraham Dehuff

Z216: Sheriff Thomas Edwards gr.to Nathaniel Ellmaker

61a, 66p Earl tp.: HISTORY: The County Commissioners ordered the sheriff to seize the body and lands of Valentine Kinser of Earl tp., tax collector for Earl tp. in 1781 and 1782, who kept part of the taxes illegally for himself. The sheriff duly seized the above-described tract, which he sold at public vendue to Nathaniel Ellmaker.

2 June 1784: JJ & CS

Z218: Christian Kreiss (or Creist, or Kreis) & his wife Elizabeth of Frederick County, Maryland, enf-rel.to George Sahm (or Sham), yeoman, of Warwick tp.

182a, 130p Warwick tp.: HISTORY: Part of two adjoining tracts: (1.) 110a, 90p Warwick tp. pat. 1 Jul 1766 to John Creist [Ref. PB AA-7-95]. (2.) 77 ¼ a. Warwick tp. pat. 10 Nov 1774 to John Creist [Ref. PB AA-14-743]. // Said John Creist, or Kreiss, died intestate leaving a widow named Barbara and issue six children, to wit, Christian Kreiss (the eldest son & party hereto), Henry Kreiss, Frederick Kreiss, Elizabeth Kreiss, Catharine Kreiss, & Susanna Kreiss. On 2 Mar 1784, the Orphans Court confirmed the real estate to the said eldest son, Christian.

3 June 1784: HD & CJ

Z221: John Lecky, yeoman, of Bart tp. enf-rel.to John Graff & Jacob Graff, yeomen, both of Martic tp.

173a Bart tp.: HISTORY: Same tract that Thomas Lecky granted 10 Mar 1769 to John Lecky (Ref. Deed N91).

4 Mar 1780: John Groft & EG

Z223: John Graff, yeoman, of Martic tp. rel.to John Hare, yeoman, of Strasburg tp.

--One undivided moiety of 173a Bart tp.: HISTORY: It being the same larger tract given in the preceding indenture. [Added history: Same tract warranted & surveyed to Thomas Lecky in pursuance of application #1589.]

30 May 1784: Bentz Groff & EG

Z225: Benjamin Graff, yeoman, of Strasburg tp. [the surviving executor of Jacob Graff, yeoman, late of Martic tp.]; Jacob Niessle (or Nessly, or Nissle), yeoman, & his wife Elizabeth of Lancaster County [she being a granddaughter of said Jacob Graff, deceased]; and Abraham Graff, yeoman, of Lancaster County [he being a grandson of said Jacob Graff, deceased] quitclaim to John Graff, yeoman, of Lancaster County [he being another grandson of said Jacob Graff, deceased]

153a Martic tp.: HISTORY: By his last will & testament dated 15 Mar 1760, Jacob Graff devised his 300a plantation that he lived on to his grandchildren John Graff & Jacob Graff—conditional on them paying his other grandchildren, Abraham Graff & Elizabeth Graff, their equal share when his grandson Jacob Graff reaches age 21. [Note: Grandson Jacob Graff is identified as the son of John Graff, deceased.]

30 Aug 1782: Adam Kindig & EG

Z229: Benjamin Graff, yeoman, of Strasburg tp. [the surviving executor of Jacob Graff, yeoman, late of Martic tp.]; Jacob Niessle (or Nessly, or Nissle), yeoman, & his wife Elizabeth of Lancaster County [she being a granddaughter of said Jacob Graff, deceased]; and Abraham Graff, yeoman, of Lancaster County [he being a grandson of said Jacob Graff, deceased] quitclaim to Jacob Graff, yeoman, of Lancaster County [he being another grandson of said Jacob Graff, deceased]

150a Martic tp.: HISTORY: By his last will & testament dated 15 Mar 1760, Jacob Graff devised his 300a plantation that he lived on to his grandchildren John Graff & Jacob Graff—conditional on them paying his other grandchildren, Abraham Graff & Elizabeth Graff, their equal share when his grandson Jacob Graff reaches age 21. [Note: Grandson Jacob Graff is identified as the son of John Graff, deceased.]

30 Aug 1782: Adam Kindig & EG

Z233: Sheriff Thomas Edwards gr.to Frederick Fenstermacher

--Lot #71 in Millersburg in Manor tp., containing five acres: HISTORY: On 9 Aug 1783, the Court of Common Pleas ordered the sheriff to seize the real estate of John Kennet, yeoman, of Manor tp. for unpaid debts owing to one John Grove. The sheriff duly seized the above-described lot, which he sold at public vendue to Frederick Fenstermacher.

3 June 1784: JH & J. Hubley

Z235: Abraham Steiner, blacksmith, & his wife Salome of Bethlehem tp., Northampton County, rel.to Henry Schneider, turner, of Warwick tp.

300a Warwick tp.: HISTORY: Contains parts of the following three tracts: (1.) 292a on a branch of the Conestoga pat. 7 Oct 1736 to Abraham Steiner [Ref. PB A-7-95] and (2.) 57a Lebanon tp. pat. 12 Dec 1739 to Abraham Steiner (Ref. PB A-10-23d). Said Abraham Steiner died intestate seized in possession of both tracts. By an order of the Orphans Court, the tracts were confirmed to Abraham Steiner, his eldest son; however, since Abraham, the father, was an alien at the time of both patents, Abraham, the son, took out a new patent for both properties on 27 Feb 1762 (Ref. PB AA-3-197). (3.) 87a, 47p Warwick tp. pat. 29 Apr 1761 to Abraham Steiner, the son (Ref. PB AA-1-269).

6 May 1762: George Klein & James Webb, Jr.

Z239: Henry Schneider & his wife Elizabeth, Peter Schneider & his wife Susanna, Philip Reyer & his wife Elizabeth, Jacob Kintzi (or Kintzy) & his wife Margaret, Esther Hollinger, & Susanna Sigrist quitclaim to John Schneider [the said Henry, John, Elizabeth, Margaret, Esther, Susanna, & Peter being the seven children of Henry Schneider, deceased, late of Warwick tp.]

183a, 145p Warwick tp.: HISTORY: Part of a larger tract that Abraham Steiner & his wife Salome granted 6 May 1762 to Henry Schneider (see the preceding indenture). Said Henry Schneider died intestate leaving issue the above seven children; however, in his lifetime, he had allotted the said land to his son John. The other heirs now legally confirm the late father's intentions.

11 Nov 1780: ES & CS

Z242: John Sneider, yeoman, & his wife Esther of Warwick tp. enf-rel.to Arnold Becker, yeoman, of same

183a, 145p Warwick tp.: HISTORY: It being the same tract as given in the preceding indenture.

--7 Feb 1784: John Huber & CS

Z244: Melchior Brenneman, yeoman, & his wife Anna of Donegal tp.; Christian Graff, yeoman, & his wife Fronica of York County; and John Steman (or Stoneman), yeoman, & his wife Mary of Donegal tp. [the said Anna, Fronica, & Mary being three daughters of Jacob Snevely, yeoman, late of Lampeter tp., deceased] quitclaim to John Snevely (or Sneably)

200a Lampeter tp.: HISTORY: Same tract that John Houser granted 3 Sep 1766 to Jacob Snevely (Ref. Deed M379). By his last will & testament dated 6 May 1776, Jacob Snevely devised 200a Lampeter tp. to his son John Snevely (party hereto), subject to certain legacies to be paid to his above-named three daughters.

1 May 1781: Johannes Meylin & Henry Hartman

Z248: John Shreiber, yeoman, & his wife Mary of Lancaster Borough enf-rel.to Christopher Breidenhart, gunsmith, of same

--Half lot on Queen St. in Lancaster Borough: HISTORY: On 13 Jul 1745, James Hamilton granted a lot on Queen St. to Michael Hubley. On 20 June 1746, Michael Hubley & his wife Rosina granted the same to Jacob Hoover. On 11 Jul 1748, Jacob Hoover assigned the same to Frederick Hoover. On 27 Dec 1750, Frederick Hoover & his wife Barbara assigned the same to John Snevely. Said John Snevely died intestate without making disposition of the northern moiety, or half lot. The right descended to his sister Hannah, the wife of Benjamin Landus. On 11 Mar 1752, Benjamin Landus & his wife Hannah granted the said half lot to John Shreiber.

10 June 1757: Peter Pritz & CM

Z251: Christopher Breitenhardt, gunsmith, & his wife Dorothea of Lancaster Borough enf-rel.to Lodwick Stone, yeoman, of same

--Half lot on Queen St. in Lancaster Borough: HISTORY: Not given but see the preceding indenture.

7 Sep 1763: Robert Thompson & DS

Z253: Lodwick Stone, yeoman, & his wife Catharine of Lancaster Borough enf-rel.to John Spore, yeoman, of same

--Half lot on Queen St. in Lancaster Borough: HISTORY: It being the same half lot as given in the preceding indenture.

1 Nov 1763: Christian Voght, Francis Sanderson, & JH

Z254: John Spore, yeoman, & his wife Mary of Lancaster Borough enf-rel.to Jacob Dickert, gunsmith, of same

--Half lot on Queen St. in Lancaster Borough: HISTORY: It being the same half lot as given in the preceding indenture.

4 Jan 1768: Anthony Snyder & William A. Atlee

Z257: George Hoofnagle, innkeeper, & his wife Magdalena of Lancaster Borough enf-rel.to James Davis, yeoman, of Lampeter tp.

--Lot on Queen St. in Lancaster Borough: HISTORY: Same lot that James Hamilton granted 1 Mar 1744 to Michael Fordine. On 3 May 1756, Michael Fordine & his wife Margaret granted the same to Joseph Simons. On 9 June 1756, Joseph Simons assigned the same to Isaac Levy. On ___ Dec 1756, Isaac Levy re-conveyed the same to said Joseph Simons. On 20 Dec 1756, Joseph Simons & his wife Rose. granted the same to John Spore (Ref. Deed G11). The county sheriff then seized the property from John Spore due to unpaid debts. On 5 Dec 1769, the sheriff granted the same to George Hoofnagle (Ref. Deed N144).

24 Dec 1777: Henry Keppele Jr. & CS

Z259: John Meyer (or Meier) & his wife Margaret of Upper Paxton tp.; Joseph Brubacher & his wife Elizabeth; and Christian Brubacher & his wife Elizabeth of Manheim tp. rel.to George Kline of Manheim tp.

300a Upper Paxton tp.: HISTORY: Same tract war. 4 Apr 1769 and later surveyed to said John Meyer, "or for me." [A bit confusing.]

8 June 1784: CJ & Daniel Franck

Z261: Sheriff John Barr rel.to Charles Klugh, baker, of Lancaster Borough

--Three tracts: (1.) 326a Paxton tp., (2.) 210a Paxton tp., including a ferry, and (3.) one moiety 28a Paxton tp.—it being an island in the Susquehanna River opposite to the first described tract.

1. HISTORY: Same tract pat. 19 Mar 1747 to Richard Peters (Ref. PB A-14-89).
2. HISTORY: Same tract that William Richey granted 30 May 1744 to Richard Peters (Ref. Deed B254).
3. HISTORY: Part of 28a Paxton tp. pat. 19 Mar 1747 to Richard Peters (Ref. PB A-14-89).

--On 10 Sep 1756, Richard Peters of Philadelphia granted all three described tracts to John Potts, Esq., of Manatawny tp. in Philadelphia County. On 17 Feb 1762, John Potts granted the first two described tracts and one moiety of the third to Frederick Stoner, then of Philadelphia County but now of Lancaster County. On 11 May 1765, the Court of Common Pleas ordered the sheriff to seize the real estate of said Frederick Stoner, yeoman, of Paxton tp. The sheriff duly seized the above-described three tracts, which he sold at public vendue to Charles Klugh.

9 Aug 1766: Robert Magaw & William A. Atlee

Z266: John Potts, Esq., & his wife Ruth of Pottsgrove in Philadelphia County enf-rel.to Charles Klugh, baker, of Lancaster Borough

--Three tracts: (1.) 326a Paxton tp., (2.) 210a Paxton tp., including a ferry, and (3.) one moiety 28a Paxton tp.—it being an island in the Susquehanna River opposite to the first described tract: HISTORY: See the preceding indenture. Said John Potts never executed a deed to Frederick Steiner for the above lands. Now, to better confirm the title to Charles Klugh, he formally releases any claim to the above properties.

2 Sep 1766: John Epple & Isaac Potts

Z269: Susanna Klug, Charles Klug, & Frederick Frick [the administrators of Charles Klug, late of Lancaster Borough] enf-rel.to John Epply & Sophia Epply of same

--Two tracts: (1.) 144a, 136p Paxton tp., including a ferry, and (2.) 8 ¾ a. Paxton tp., located on an island opposite of the first tract: HISTORY: They being part of the same tracts as given in Deed Z261. Said Charles Klug died intestate. On 3 Dec last, his administrator petitioned the Orphans Court to sell part of his real estate in order to pay estate debts.

22 Mar 1783: MH & CS

Z273: Henry Martin, yeoman, & his wife Anna of Earl tp. enf-rel.to their son Henry Martin, yeoman, of same

153a Earl tp.: HISTORY: Same tract pat. 6 Nov 1747 to Henry Martin (Ref. PB A-12-551).

--19 Oct 1765: SH & George Hoffman

Z275: Benjamin Landis, Sr., yeoman, of Lampeter tp. rel.to his son Henry Landis

--Two tracts: (1.) 44a Lampeter tp. and (2.) 6a Lampeter tp.: HISTORY: Same tracts that Abraham Musgrave & his wife Mary granted 24 May 1746 to Benjamin Landis.

2 Jan 1762: Hannes Witmer & Hannes Histandt

Z276: Ignatius (or Nartz) Zwecker, yeoman, & his wife Elizabeth of Earl tp. enf-rel.to Henry Steinbring, yeoman, of same

95p Earl tp.: HISTORY: Part of 325a [then 295a] pat. 11 Nov 1741 to Casper Staver (Ref. PB A-9-474). On 5 & 6 June 1743, Casper Staver & his wife Catharine granted the same to Wendel Zwecker. Said Wendel Zwecker died intestate leaving issue three children: Ignatius Zwecker (party hereto), Elizabeth the wife of Michael Oberlee, and Magdalena the wife of Anthony Hinkle. The heirs partitioned the property, with an 81 ¾ a. parcel being allotted to said Anthony Hinkle in right of his wife. On 27 Sep 1764, Anthony Hinkle & his wife Magdalena granted the same parcel to the said Ignatius Zwecker (Ref. Deed N446).

18 Mar 1782: JJ & Frederick Seeger

Z279: Jacob Brua, yeoman, & his wife Jane of Strasburg tp. enf-rel.to Catharine Reser, single woman, of same

--1a lot in the Village of Strasburg: HISTORY: Same lot that Benjamin Graff & his wife Elizabeth granted 28 Jul 1764 to Jacob Brua.

11 Apr 1783: John Brua & EG

Z282: Benjamin Landis, yeoman, of Lampeter tp. rel.to his son Jacob Landis

200a Lampeter tp.: HISTORY: Part of 5,553a pat. 25 June 1718 to Tobias Collet and others. The said 200a tract, being part thereof, has since become vested in Benjamin Landis.

25 Aug 1761: Jacob Hartman & Hannes Witmer

Z283: John Musser (or Mosser) & his wife Christina of Conestoga tp. enf-rel.to Henry Miller, taylor, of same

68a Conestoga tp.: HISTORY: Part of a larger tract pat. 11 May 1768 to Henry Kaigey (Ref. PB AA-10-352). On 28 May 1768, Henry Kaigey & his wife Barbara granted the same to John Musser. On 6 May 1769, John Musser & his wife Christina granted part thereof to Henry Miller; however, neither party was satisfied by the arrangement. Thus, that indenture was voided and this one takes its place.

6 May 1773: George Bickham & JB

Z285: Lazarus Stewart of Hanover tp. enf-rel.to John Stewart (or Stuart) of Mount Joy tp.

100a Hanover tp.: HISTORY: Not given.

--19 Oct 1762: James Cunningham & Robert Mountgomery

Z287: John Stewart assigns to Joseph Berky

100a Hanover tp.: HISTORY: It being the same tract as given in the preceding indenture.

--4 Nov 1763: Hannes Seiler & Hans Kieffer

Z287: Peter Brubaker, yeoman, & his wife Anna of Lancaster County enf-rel.to Christian Stevens, yeoman, of same

18a Hempfield tp.: HISTORY: Part of 90 ½ a. pat. 29 May 1761 to Peter Brubaker (Ref. PB AA-1-282).

--21 Jul 1761: WJ & DS

Z289: Sheriff Thomas Edwards gr.to Francis Shopp (or Shole?)

18a Hempfield tp.: HISTORY: On 7 Feb 1784, the Court of Common Pleas ordered the sheriff to seize the real estate of Benjamin Imoberstag, yeoman, of Lampeter tp., for unpaid debts owed to one Henry Whitmer. The sheriff duly seized 18a Hempfield tp., which he later sold at public vendue to the said Francis Shopp.

3 June 1784: JH & J. Hubley

Z292: Wendel Loudermilk, yeoman, of Heidelberg tp. enf-rel.to his son Melchior Loudermilk, yeoman

--Two tracts: (1.) 48 ¼ a. Heidelberg tp. and (2.) 115a Heidelberg tp.

1. HISTORY: Part of 456a pat. 25 Jan 1755 to Richard Tea (Ref. PB A-19-58). On 27 Jan 1755, Richard Tea granted 48 ¼ a. to Wendel Loudermilk (Ref. Deed F256).
2. HISTORY: Part of 278a pat. 4 May 1750 to Wendel Loudermilk (Ref. PB A-15-432).

--8 June 1772: Michael Cab & Michael Bright

Z295: Wendel Loudermilk, widow, of Heidelberg tp. enf-rel.to his son Melchior Loudermilk, yeoman, of same

163a Heidelberg tp.: HISTORY: Part of 278a pat. 4 May 1750 to Wendel Loudermilk (Ref. PB A-15-432).

--6 Apr 1773: Jost Hoffman & Michael Breght

Z298: Melchior Loutermilch, yeoman, & his wife Catharine of Earl tp. enf-rel.to Henry Kring, yeoman, of Heidelberg tp.

--Two tracts: (1.) 278a Heidelberg tp. and (2.) 48 ¼ a. Heidelberg tp.: HISTORY: They being the same tracts as given in the two preceding indentures.

6 May 1784: Christian Staufer & MH

Z302: Lazarus Stewart & his wife Ann of Hanover tp. rel.to Daniel Ludwick of Heidelberg tp., Berks County

240a Hanover tp.: HISTORY: Same tract war. 20 Oct 1743 and later surveyed to Lazarus Stewart.

--21 Oct 1779: Johannes Fuchs, Jacob Schnebele, & Johannes Becker

Z304: Daniel Ludwig rel.to Jacob Loos, yeoman, of Tulpehocken tp., Berks County

240a [location not given]: HISTORY: Not given, but see the preceding indenture.

--24 Dec 1779: Henry Spyker & Peter Spycker

Z305: David Stewart (or Steuart) & Margery Young, both of Hanover tp., quitclaim to Daniel Ludwig of Tulpehocken tp., Berks County

--Their two undivided eighth parts of their father's real estate: HISTORY: Lazarus Stewart, late of Hanover tp., died intestate leaving issue seven children [including the two grantors above] and seized in possession of a certain plantation (no further information).

18 May 1784: Sara Jones, David Young, & Samuel Jones

Z306: George Lightner, carpenter, & his wife Catharine of Lancaster Borough enf-rel.to John Light, late of the Army

--Lot on Middle St. in Adams Town in Lancaster Borough: HISTORY: Same lot that Jacob Loeser & Anna Catharine Deemer [the executors of Jacob Deemer] granted 29 Apr 1762 to Benedict Spitzfaden. On 8 Feb 1765, Benedict Spitzfaden & his wife Mary granted the same to Martin Cryder, John Cryder, & Jacob Cryder. On 25 Mar 1767, Martin Cryder & his wife Elizabeth granted their part to said Jacob Cryder. On 14 Apr 1767, John Cryder & his wife granted their part to said Jacob Cryder. On 22 June 1780, Jacob Cryder & his wife Ann granted the full lot to George Lightner.

15 Mar 1784: WH & Peter Shindel

Z308: Joseph Gibbons, yeoman, & his wife Hannah of West Town in Chester County enf-rel.to his son Abraham Gibbons, yeoman, of Leacock tp.

277a Leacock tp.: HISTORY: Part of 1,000a pat. 14 Oct 1733 to Joseph Gibbons (Ref. PB A-6-273).

--18 Feb 1769: James Gibbons & Moses Brinton

Z311: Jacob Line, yeoman, of Manheim tp. [the eldest son of Jacob Line, formerly Jacob Line, Jr., yeoman, late of same] quitclaims to John Meister, yeoman, of same

--His undivided moiety of two adjoining tracts: (1.) 230a Manheim tp. and (2.) 19a Manheim tp.: HISTORY: 230a Manheim tp. pat. 2 Dec 1748 to Jacob Line, Jr. (Ref. PB A-14-152). Said Jacob Line died leaving a widow Catharine [now the wife of John Meister, party hereto] and issue several children. By his last will & testament dated 15 Mar 1762, Jacob Line devised his plantation to his wife until 15 Mar 1774 in order to maintain his children—then the property should be transferred to his two eldest sons. The heirs have since found that part of the plantation was omitted in the original survey. On 2 June 1768, an adjoining 19a parcel was patented to said John Meister, alias Masters, in trust for the heirs of Jacob Line (Ref. PB AA-7-397). // On 26 Mar last, Jacob Sherrer [who married Elizabeth, a daughter of Jacob Line, deceased] and John Mixell [who married Catharine, another daughter] petitioned the Orphans Court for their shares of the property. On 1 June last, the Orphans Court confirmed the land to the said two sons [not named]—one moiety to each.

5 Jul 1774: William A. Atlee & Christian Wirtz

Z315: Jacob Sharer (or Sherrer), yeoman, & his wife Elizabeth and John Meixel, yeoman, & his wife Catharine, all of Leacock tp. [the said Elizabeth & Catharine being daughters of Jacob Line, deceased] quitclaim to John Meister, yeoman, of Manheim tp.

--Their right, claim, interest, & title to two adjoining tracts: (1.) 230a Manheim tp. and (2.) 19a Manheim tp.: HISTORY: See the preceding indenture. The two eldest sons of Jacob Line, deceased, are Jacob Line & John Line [see the following indenture].

5 Nov 1774: Jacob Lein & William A. Atlee

Z321: John Lein (or Line), yeoman, of Manheim tp. [the second son of Jacob Line, deceased, late of same] quitclaims to John Meister, yeoman, of same

--His undivided moiety of two adjoining tracts: (1.) 230a Manheim tp. and (2.) 19a Manheim tp.: HISTORY: See the preceding two indentures.

30 Sep 1778: PH, Philip Reyer, & Henrich Franck

Z326: George Franciscus, yeoman, & his wife Barbara of Leacock tp. [she being a daughter of Jacob Line, deceased, late of Manheim tp.] quitclaim to John Meister, yeoman, of Manheim tp.

--Their right, claim, interest, & title to two adjoining tracts: (1.) 230a Manheim tp. and (2.) 19a Manheim tp.: HISTORY: See the preceding three indentures.

13 Dec 1782: George Moore & PH

Z332: John Graham, yeoman, & his wife Rachel of West Nantmeal tp., Chester County rel.to the Honorable Frederic Eugene Baron de Beelen Bertholf, Esq., & his wife Lady Joanna Maria Theresia, now adjourning at or near the City of Philadelphia

--200a in Lancaster & Chester counties, including 23a, 89p Salisbury tp. [the grantor's brother, Abraham Graham, is identified as an adjacent landowner in the metes & bounds]: HISTORY: Said John Graham holds 212a in West Nantmeal tp., Chester County, and Salisbury tp., Lancaster County, under the last will & testament of his late father. Said John Graham & his wife Rachel have already granted the land in Chester County to the said Frederick Bertholf. [Reference is made to proceedings in the May Term of 1783 in the Chester County Court of Common Pleas. Further reference is made to a tripartite agreement between said John Graham, Samuel Boyd, Esq., and John Jordan—the latter whom appears to be a tenant on part or all of the property.]

22 Apr 1784: LW & Frederick ________

Z335: James Hamilton, Esq., of Philadelphia gr.to Peter Worrall, Isaac Whitelock, & Thomas Poultney [the trustees of the Society of People called Quakers in Lancaster Borough]

--Lot on Queen St. in Lancaster Borough: HISTORY: Not given, but the lot adjoins the Quaker burying ground.

1 May 1754: Calvin Cooper & Mathias Sandham

Z338: James Hamilton, Esq., of Philadelphia gr.to Peter Worrall, Isaac Whitelock, & Thomas Poultney [the trustees of the Society of People called Quakers in Lancaster Borough]

--Lot on Queen St. in Lancaster Borough: HISTORY: Not given, but another lot in the possession of the said Quaker society.

1 May 1754: Calvin Cooper & Mathias Sandham

Z339: Jacob Frank & his wife Catharine enf-rel.to John Everman, blacksmith, of Lancaster Borough

--"within described lot": HISTORY: Not given.

--10 June 1745: Youst Shider & John Morris

Z340: Gabriel Lemble (or Lemle) & his wife Klarin enf.to John Eberman, smith, of Lancaster County

--"within mentioned lot": HISTORY: Not given.

7 May 1744: Sebastian Groffe & Stephen Mann

--Frederick Mann, son of Stephen Mann, deceased, affirms his father's signature on 23 June 1784.

Z342: John Eberman, smith, & his wife Juliana enf.to George Carl Meyer, joiner, of Lancaster County

--"within mentioned lot": HISTORY: Not given.

16 Jan 1744/45: Jos. Henrich Sturtzenacker & John Adam Bossler

Z343: Daniel Debus (or Davis), blacksmith, & his wife Barbara, formerly of Lancaster Borough but now of the Province of Maryland, rel.to Lodowick Franciscus, yeoman, of Lancaster Borough

--Half lot on King St. in Lancaster Borough: HISTORY: On 14 Jan 1740, James Hamilton granted a full lot on King St. to Gabriel Emble. By sundry conveyances [see the preceding indentures], one moiety of the lot came into the possession of Charles Meyer [the other moiety being in the possession of George Appleman]. By court order, the county sheriff seized the real estate of George Carl Meyer, including the said half lot. On 26 Mar 1751, the sheriff granted the half lot to Daniel Debus. The property is subject to two mortgages, one owed to George Coalridge and the other to Michael Crouse.

27 Nov 1751: MH & CM

Z346: Ludwick Franciscus, yeoman, & his wife Elizabeth of Augusta County, Virginia, rel.to Jacob Metzger, yeoman, of Lancaster Borough

--Half lot on King St. in Lancaster Borough: HISTORY: It being the same half lot as given in the preceding indenture.

17 June 1761: DS & Robert Thompson

Z349: Henry Musser (or Musier), yeoman, of Lancaster County gr.to Frederick Doughterman of Lancaster Borough

--Lot #56 on High St. near Lancaster Borough in Lancaster tp.: HISTORY: Not given.

8 Apr 1762: Henrich Lichty & James Webb, Jr.

Z352: Frederick Dochterman & his wife Susanna enf-rel.to Jacob Metzger, weaver, of Lancaster Borough

--Lot #56 on High St. near Lancaster Borough: HISTORY: It being the same lot as given in the preceding indenture.

24 Mar 1773: Philip Thomas & J. F. Loeser

Z353: Henry Musser, yeoman, & his wife Ann of Lancaster Borough rel.to Jacob Metzger, weaver, of Lancaster Borough

--The yearly rent charges for Lot #56 on High St. near Lancaster Borough: HISTORY: See the two preceding indentures.

19 Oct 1782: ES & CS

Z355: Godfry Gretchner (or Kretchner) & his wife Mary of Philadelphia [she late being the widow of Dietrich Benedict] appoints her son George Benedict, yeoman, of Middletown in Paxton tp. as their lawful attorney to recover monies owed to them out of the estate of said Dietrich Benedict, which are to be paid by Leonard Benedict, weaver, of Lancaster Borough.

7 June 1784: PMR & H. Beyerle

Z356: George Benedict, yeoman, of Middletown in Paxton tp. acknowledges that he has received certain sums from Leonard Benedict [the eldest son of Dietrich Benedict, deceased]. Said Leonard Benedict holds the real estate of his late father [see the preceding power of attorney].

25 June 1784: Richard Shott & J.J. Henry

Z357: Casper Persinger (or Bersinger) & his wife Addalheyk of Lancaster Borough rel.to Joseph Thomas, yeoman, of Lancaster County

--Half lot on King St. in Lancaster Borough: HISTORY: On 14 Jan 1740, James Hamilton granted a lot on King St. to Andrew Miller. On 16 May 1744, Andrew Miller & his wife Margaret granted the same to Andrew Bather, butcher. On 19 Aug 1746, Andrew Bather & his wife Elizabeth granted the full lot to said Casper Persinger.

5 Nov 1747: DS & Jorg Ritles

Z360: Joseph Thomas, taylor, & his wife Mary of Lancaster County enf.to John Mesencope, blacksmith, of same

--Half lot on King St. in Lancaster Borough: HISTORY: It being the same lot as given in the preceding indenture.

23 Aug 1748: Margaret Stout & DS

Z362: John Messencope (or Mesenkob), blacksmith, & his wife Elizabeth of Lancaster Borough enf-rel.to Valentine Weaver, turner, of same

--Half lot on King St. in Lancaster Borough: HISTORY: It being the same half lot as given in the preceding indenture.

26 Dec 1758: Margaret Stout & DS

Z364: Valentine Weber & his wife Philippina assign to Jacob Yantz, slaughterer, of Lancaster Borough
--Half lot on King St. in Lancaster Borough: HISTORY: It being the same half lot as given in the preceding indenture.
20 Dec 1767: Jacob Weaver & JY

Z365: Henry Musser, yeoman, & his wife Anna of Lancaster tp. enf-rel.to John Eppele, yeoman, of Lancaster Borough
2a, 17p Lancaster tp.: HISTORY: Part of 130a that Jacob Hostater [the surviving executor of John Musser, father of the said Henry Musser] granted 25 Feb 1761 to Henry Musser (Ref. Deed H177).
11 June 1764: WJ & Joseph Boude

Z368: John Eppelee & his wife Sophia enf-rel.to Jacob Jentz (or Yentz), butcher, of Lancaster Borough
2a, 17p Lancaster tp.: HISTORY: Not given, but see the preceding indenture.
--1 Feb 1775: JB & J.F. Loeser

Z369: Nicholas Dello, yeoman, & his wife Catharine of Hempfield tp. enf-rel.to Jacob Yentz (or Wentz), butcher, of Lancaster Borough
6 ¾ a., 15p in Lancaster Borough: HISTORY: Part of 95a, 25p that John Leman & his wife Anna granted 2 Mar 1771 to Nicholas Dello (Ref. Deed Q390).
24 Dec 1772: James Wright & Samuel Bethel

Z372: Henry Musser, yeoman, & his wife Anna of Lancaster tp. enf-rel.to Jacob Jentz, butcher, of Lancaster Borough
--The yearly ground rents for eight lots in Lancaster Borough: HISTORY: (1.) On 20 Mar 1762, said Henry Musser grants lots 79-82 on High St. & South St. in Lancaster tp. to William White. On 20 Nov 1771, William White assigned the same four lots to Nicholas Boass. (2.) On 2 Jul 1763, said Henry Musser granted lots 97-100 on South St. in or near Lancaster Borough to said Nicholas Boass. // On equal date herewith, said Nicholas Boass granted all eight lots to said Jacob Jentz.
11 May 1776: Nicholas Boass & J.F. Loeser

Z375: William Branson, merchant, of Philadelphia gr.to Robert Boyd of Lancaster County
175a Sadsbury tp.: HISTORY: Same tract that Lancaster County Sheriff Andrew Work granted 3 May 1749 to Bernard Vanleer in trust for the said William Branson.
27 Apr 1750: Thomas Cookson & Andrew Work

Z376: Rudy Sheffer, yeoman, & his wife Maria Barbara of Earl tp. enf-rel.to John Winger, yeoman, of same
50a Earl tp.: HISTORY: Part of 173 ½ a. pat. 1 May 1761 to Philip Sheffer (Ref. PB AA-2-249). Said Philip Sheffer died intestate leaving issue eight children. On 4 May 1773, the Orphans Court confirmed the said 173 ½ a. tract to his son Rudy Sheffer (party hereto).
7 June 1784: Conrad Merck & ZD

Z379: Hugh Gilleland, yeoman, of Hanover tp. enf-rel.to Peter Wallmer, Jr., yeoman, of same
117a Hanover tp.: HISTORY: Part of 234a Hanover tp. war. 16 Feb 1744 to Hugh Gilleland. By his last will & testament dated 11 Mar 1750/51, Hugh Gilleland devised the same to his two sons, Robert Gilleland [the eldest son] and Hugh Gilleland [party hereto]—one moiety to each.
22 Mar 1771: Thomas Clark & Timothy Green

Z381: The heirs of Hugh Gilleland, deceased [see below] quitclaim to Peter Wallmer (or Wellmer, or Walmore), the younger, of Hanover tp.
117a Hanover tp.: HISTORY: It being the same tract as given in the preceding indenture. Said Hugh Gilleland, the elder, died leaving issue the following children: Robert Gilleland, Hugh Gilleland, Mary [now wife of William McCullough], Eleanor [now wife of Andrew Berryhill], Anne [now wife of John Graham], Elizabeth [now wife of William Craig], and Agnes [now wife of Robert Hill]. Son Robert Gilleland has since died. Under the last will & testament of their father, his 234-acre plantation was divided between his two

sons, one moiety to each, subject to equal shares of the valuation being paid to the other heirs. Now, with this indenture, the other heirs release their claim to son Hugh's moiety, which he has conveyed to the said Peter Walmer, Jr.

23 Oct 1771: Margaret Martin, Timothy Green, Samuel Brown, & A. Berryhill

Z384: Sheriff John Ferree gr.to Frederick Heyl, yeoman, of Lancaster County

4 ¾ a. Lancaster tp.: HISTORY: On 7 May last, the Court of Common Pleas ordered the sheriff to seize the real estate of Mathias Rosh, yeoman, late of Lancaster County, deceased [in the hands of his administrator Henry Rosh, yeoman ("unadministered by Catharine Rosh")] for unpaid debts owed to one Paul Zantzinger. The sheriff duly seized 4 ¾ a. Lancaster tp., which he later sold at public vendue to Frederick Heyl.

8 Dec 1774: Samuel F. Atlee & JR

Z387: Frederick Heyl & his wife Ursula assign to John Schwenck, yeoman, of Lancaster tp.

4 ¾ a. Lancaster tp.: HISTORY: Not given, but see the preceding indenture.

--5 Oct 1779: Kasper Schnebli & CS

Z388: James Crawford, yeoman, & his wife Ann of Earl tp. rel.to Melchor Loutermilch, yeoman, of same

150a Earl tp., including a gristmill: HISTORY: On 25 Nov 1780, Joseph Reed, the late President of the Supreme Executive Council, granted the said tract and mill to James Crawford [it being late the estate of attainted traitor George Ryne] (Ref. Deed Q518).

15 June 1784: JJ & DW

Z391: Isaac Whitelock, tanner, & his wife Mary of Lancaster Borough and Bernard Hubley, merchant, & his wife Magdalena of same enf-rel.to Ann Thompson [the widow & devisee of Robert Thompson, practitioner of physick, late of same]

10a [location not given]: HISTORY: Part of 400a pat. 31 Dec 1717 to Michael Shank & Henry Pare (Ref. PB A-5-275). On 2 & 3 Sep 1728, Michael Shank & Henry Pare granted 200a to Peter Beller, yeoman. On 12 Jul 1729, said Michael Shank granted an additional 1 ¾ a. tract to said Peter Beller. // On 19 & 20 Dec 1731, Peter Beller & his wife Elizabeth granted two tracts, 100a (part of the 200a) and 1 ¾ a., to John Lane. On 9 & 10 June 1740, John Lane & his wife Mary granted the same two tracts to Roger Hunt. On 11 & 12 June 1740, Roger Hunt & his wife Esther granted the same two tracts to Francis Fortinee, butcher. On 22 & 23 Jan 1740 [sic], Francis Fortinee & his wife Elizabeth granted the same two tracts to John Gristy. On 28 & 29 May 1742, John Gristy & his wife Anna granted the same two tracts to Jacob Tombaugh. By his last will & testament dated 5 Mar 1758, Jacob Tombaugh ordered his executors (to wit, Bernard Hubley & Melchior Snyder) to sell the properties. On 12 Jul 17__, they granted the same two tracts to Isaac Whitelock (reserving a one-quarter-acre burying ground for the use of Peter Beller's heirs and five acres previously granted by Jacob Tombaugh in his lifetime to Frederick Tombaugh & Conrad Bott). On 21 Jul 1758, Isaac Whitelock & his wife Mary granted one moiety of both tracts to Bernard Hubley.

20 Apr 1765: Christian Wertz & Christoph Breitenherdt

Z397: John Nixon, John Maxwell Nesbitt, George Clymer, Robert Morris, John Wilcocks, John Ross, Richard Bache, Thomas Lawrence Jr., & John Shea, merchants, all of Philadelphia, and Alexander Wilcocks, Esq., attorney-at-law, of the same, enf-rel.to Walter Shee (or Shea), merchant, of Philadelphia

--Lots #19 & 24 in Lancaster Borough: HISTORY: Same two lots that said Walter Shee & his wife Ann granted 17 June 1774 to the above-named parties [it being part of ten acres laid out into lots by the said Walter Shee & his wife [see the following indenture].

23 Feb 1779: Thomas Clarkson, Samuel Story, & Richard Humphreys

Z399: Walter Shee, merchant, & his wife Ann (late Ann Thompson) of Philadelphia

10a near Lancaster Borough: HISTORY: It being the same tract as given in Deed Z391.

--26 Feb 1779: William Webb & John Ord

Z401: George Line, yeoman, & his wife Salome of Leacock tp. enf-rel.to Martin Heller (or Hiller), blacksmith, of same

50a Leacock tp.: HISTORY: Part of 300a pat. 4 May 1736 to said George Line (Ref. PB A-9-123). On 22 Mar 1745, George Line & his wife Salome granted part thereof to Emanuel Carpenter, Esq. (Ref. Deed B271). On 16 Apr 1770, Emanuel Carpenter & his wife Catharine re-conveyed the same to George Line (Ref. Deed N211).

21 Mar 1778: David Bender & James Gibbons

Z404: Philip Sheffer, yeoman, & his wife Elizabeth of Earl tp. enf-rel.to Peter Reitenbach, yeoman, of same

143a Earl tp.: HISTORY: Same tract pat. 8 Dec 1746 to William Shearer (Ref. PB A-14-36). On 19 Nov 1748, William Shearer & his wife Sarah granted the same to Paul Gunkle. The county sheriff later seized the property due to unpaid debts. On 30 Nov 1756, the sheriff granted the same to Joseph Paxton & his wife Sarah. On 17 Apr 1760, Joseph Paxton & his wife Sarah granted the same to John Martin. On 28 Mar 1767, John Martin & his wife Barbara granted the same to Philip Sheffer. Said Philip Sheffer died intestate leaving issue several children. On 4 May 1773, the Orphans Court confirmed the property to his son Philip (the party hereto).

31 Aug 1782: Jonathan Roland & HR

Z407: Rebecca Ashbridge [the widow & administratrix of John Ashbridge, joiner, late of Lancaster Borough] rel.to Jacob Schaeffer, tobacconist, of same

--Half lot on Queen St. in Lancaster Borough: HISTORY: On 13 Jul 1745, James Hamilton granted a full lot on Queen St. to John Hart. On 14 Jul 1749, John Hart & his wife Margaret granted half of the lot to Jacob Hoofman & David Razor (alias Debus Roeser). On 19 Nov 1750, Debus Roeser & his wife Margaret granted their right to said Jacob Hoofman. On 29 Mar 1751, Jacob Hoofman & his wife Elizabeth assigned the said half lot to Susanna Connally. By her last will & testament, Susanna Connally ordered her executors [to wit, James Wright & Arthur Patterson] to sell the property. On 24 Dec 1759, they granted the same to David Stout. Said David Stout died intestate leaving a nuncupative will. Letters of Administration were granted to Margaret Stout (the widow) and Isaac Whitelock. In pursuance to an Orphans Court order dated 19 Jul 1764, they granted the said half lot on 21 Jan 1765 to John Ashbridge. Said John Ashbridge died intestate seized in possession thereof. On 8 Jan 1774, the Orphans Court ordered his said widow & administratrix to sell the property.

10 May 1774: Charles Hall & CJ

Z410: Tripartite agreement between the following parties:

1. Christian Swar (or Shwar), yeoman, & his wife Elizabeth of Hempfield tp. and Andrew Hershy, yeoman, & his wife Mary of same
2. David Musselman, yeoman, of same
3. Alexander Lowry, yeoman, of Lancaster Borough; Jacob Neave, yeoman, of Hempfield tp.; and John Hoover, yeoman, of Hempfield tp.

--On 12 Feb 1784, said David Musselman & his wife Barbara granted 260a Hempfield tp. to the said Lowry, Neave, & Hoover in trust. They were given the authority to sell & dispose of the said property in order to discharge debts owing by the said David Musselman. // On 13 June 1783, David Musselman & his wife Barbara granted 51a Hempfield tp. to said Swar & Hershy (Ref. Deed X251). This 51a tract is part of the aforementioned 260a tract. It was understood between both parties that said Swar & Hershy would re-convey the property to David Musselman once he had satisfied debts that he owed them. // Now, by this indenture, the party of the third part pays the debts owed to the party of the first part, who now re-convey the 51a tract to the party of the third part under the conditions of the agreement between the second and third parties.

22 Mar 1784: WH & William A. Atlee

Z415: Tripartite agreement between the following parties:

1. Alexander Lowry, yeoman, of Lancaster Borough; Jacob Neave, yeoman, of Hempfield tp.; and John Hoover, yeoman, of Hempfield tp.
2. David Musselman, yeoman, of Hempfield tp.
3. Martin Cryder, yeoman, of Hempfield tp.

--The parties of the first & second part release the following properties to the party of the third part: (1.) 194a Hempfield tp., (2.) 51a Hempfield tp., and (3.) 15a Hempfield tp.

1. HISTORY: Same tract pat. 16 Jan 1744 to David Musselman (Ref. PB A-11-491). Said David Musselman died intestate leaving issue two sons, David Musselman (party hereto) and Christian Musselman, to whom the property descended. On 2 Mar 1773, Christian Musselman released his right to the property to his said brother David (Ref. Deed U134).
2. HISTORY: Same tract that Adam Tate, late of Hempfield tp., granted 1 Aug 1780 to David Musselman (Ref. Deed U132).
3. HISTORY: Same tract that John Weller, yeoman, & his wife Mary of Hempfield tp. granted 18 Mar 1780 to David Musselman.

--On 12 Feb 1784, said David Musselman & his wife Barbara granted the said three properties (totaling 260a Hempfield tp.) to the said Lowry, Neave, & Hoover in trust. They were given the authority to sell & dispose of the said property in order to discharge debts owing by the said David Musselman. The said party of the first part has recently sold the same at public vendue to the party of the third part. Now, with this indenture, title to the same is officially transferred.
22 Mar 1784: WH & William A. Atlee

Z423: John Woolslegle, yeoman, & his wife Anna of Lancaster County enf-rel.to Jacob Downer, tanner, of same

204a Manheim tp.: HISTORY: Part of a larger tract pat. 4 Aug 1741 to John Woolslegle (Ref. PB A-9-408).

24 Nov 1752: George Murray, John Correll, & DS

Z425: Sheriff John Bear gr.to Michael Gross

205a Manheim tp.: HISTORY: On 11 May 1765, the Court of Common Pleas ordered the sheriff to seize the real estate of Jacob Downer, yeoman, late of Lampeter tp., for debts owed to Isaac Whitelock & Benjamin Davis. The sheriff duly seized the following properties: (1.) 500a Lampeter tp., (2.) 190a Manheim tp., and (3.) 700a Donegal tp. [on which stands May Town]. The sheriff has since sold the 190a (or 205a) tract in Manheim tp. at public vendue.

6 Feb 1767: Richard Peters, Jr. & E. Biddle

Z430: Michael Gross, merchant, & his wife Elizabeth of Lancaster Borough enf-rel.to Abraham Myer, yeoman, of Lancaster tp.

205a Manheim tp.: HISTORY: It being the same tract as given in the preceding indenture.

--30 Sep 1767: PZ & WA

433: Elizabeth Seger (or Seiger) of Lampeter tp. enf-rel.to Luke Romer, blacksmith, of same

6a Lampeter tp.: HISTORY: Part of 96a Lampeter tp. that Mary Seger granted 20 Oct 1783 to Elizabeth Seger (Ref. Deed X267).

4 May 1784: JJACK & CJ

Z436: Thomas Small, gunsmith, & his wife Mary Ann of Earl tp. rel.to Peter Summy, yeoman, of same

158a on Mill Creek: HISTORY: Same tract pat. 4 June 1735 to Thomas Small (Ref. PB A-7-207).

--12 Apr 1748: Simeon King & James Whitehill

Z437: John Getz, yeoman, & his wife Anna Maria of Lancaster tp. enf-rel.to John Fisher, shoemaker, of Lancaster Borough

--Lot on Orange St. in Lancaster Borough: HISTORY: Same lot that the county sheriff granted 7 Feb 1755 to David Stout. On 8 Feb 1755, David Stout & his wife Margaret granted the same to Martin Lowman. On 5 Oct 1759, Martin Lowman & his wife Anna granted the same to John Getz.

22 Mar 1777: Bitter Sipe & CS

Z440: Daniel Fleming, yeoman, of Salisbury tp. rel.to Amos Slaymaker of same

--His undivided moiety of two adjoining lots: (1.) 151 ¾ a, 25p Salisbury tp. and (2.) 50a Salisbury tp.

1. HISTORY: Same tract that the county sheriff granted 20 Aug 1771 to James Fleming (Ref. Deed N401).
2. HISTORY: Same tract that the county sheriff granted 5 Sep 1775 to James Fleming (Ref. Deed S353).

--Said James Fleming died intestate seized in possession of both properties. On the first Tuesday in June 1782, the Orphans Court confirmed both properties to his eldest son Daniel Fleming (party hereto).

13 Sep 1782: Henry Slaymaker, Jacob McDill, & Hannah Slaymaker

Z442: Daniel Izron, weaver, & his wife Margaret of Lancaster Borough rel.to George Swartz (or Swates), saddler, of same

--Half lot on King St. in Lancaster Borough: HISTORY: On 14 Aug 1740, James Hamilton granted a full lot on King St. to George Notterman. On 2 May 1748, George Notterman assigned the same to Bartholomus Izron. On 2 May 1748, Bartholomus Izron granted the same to his son Daniel (party hereto).

28 Mar 1749: Hannah Young, Jacob Muller, & Edward Smout

Z443: Sheriff William Smith enf.to Peter Denich

--Half lot on King St. in Lancaster Borough: HISTORY: On _____ [omitted], the Court of Common Pleas ordered the sheriff to seize the real estate of Sigmond Basserman, baker, & Jacob Gallentine, taylor, of Lancaster Borough for debts owed to George Snevely. The sheriff duly seized the said half lot on King St. and sold it at public vendue to said Peter Denich. [Note: The property description appears similar to the preceding indenture.]

7 Aug 1760: Robert Magaw & DS

Z446: Michael Shryack assigns to John Emich, nailsmith, of Lancaster Borough

--"the within lot of ground": HISTORY: Not given, but subject to a yearly rent to be paid to James Hamilton.

15 Feb 1741/42: HISTORY: George Honey & John Morris

Z447: John Ehmig assigns to Henry Walter, locksmith, of Lancaster Borough

--"the within lot": HISTORY: Not given, but probably the same lot as given in the preceding indenture.

19 Mar 1742/43: Margaret Fox & James Fox

Z448: Henry Walter & his wife Charlotte assign to George Metzger, weaver, of Lancaster Borough

--the within mentioned lot": HISTORY: Not given, but the property description is the same as given in the preceding indenture.

10 Sep 1748: John Kehler & John Bruneberger

--Martha Weaver [the husband of Jacob Weaver] affirms her late father Henry Walter's signature on 3 Jul 1784.

Z449: Andrew Miller, yeoman, & his wife Margaret of Lancaster tp. assign to Andrew Bawder (or Bathur), butcher, of Lancaster Borough

--Lot on King St. in Lancaster Borough: HISTORY: Same lot that James Hamilton granted to the said Andrew Miller.

16 May 1744: John Heneberger & Ja. Fox

Z451: Andrew Bawder, butcher, & his wife Elizabeth of Lancaster Borough enf.to Casper Persinger (or Persinghan), yeoman, of Lancaster County

--Lot on King St. in Lancaster Borough: HISTORY: It being the same lot as given in the preceding indenture.

19 Aug 1746: Edmund Acworth

--Abraham Dehuff affirms Edmund Ackworth's (deceased, late of Lancaster Borough) signature on 3 Jul 1784.

Z452: Casper Shaffner, Jacob Hollinger, & Jacob Metzger, yeomen, all of Lancaster County, rel.to Martin Bamberger & William Bowsman, yeomen, of same

--Half lot on King St. in Lancaster Borough: HISTORY: By his last will & testament dated 29 May 1750, Casper Persinger, yeoman, late of Lancaster Borough, devised the use of the said half lot to his wife Audelcheit for the rest of her natural life—then to the above grantors in trust for the use of the Reformed Calvinist Church in Lancaster.

5 Feb 1760: John Barr, John Hopson, & DS

Z454: Martin Bomberger & William Bowsman, yeomen, of Lancaster Borough enf-rel.to Valentine Weaver, yeoman, of Lancaster County

--Half lot on King St. in Lancaster Borough: HISTORY: It being the same half lot as given in the preceding indenture.

12 May 1760: ASK & DS

Z457: Valentine Weaver & his wife Philippina of Lancaster Borough enf-rel.to Melchor Rudisill of same

--Half lot on King St. in Lancaster Borough: HISTORY: It being the same half lot as given in the preceding indenture.

31 Jul 1766: Brohard Burdik & JB

Z459: Henry Zell, Samuel Stouffer & his wife Elizabeth, John Houston & his wife Barbara, the said John Houston as guardian of Jacob Zell, Daniel Stieber & his wife Ann, the said Daniel Stieber as guardian of Adam Zell, Morgan Evans & his wife Susanna, and Amos Evans as guardian of Margaret Zell [the said Henry, Elizabeth, Barbara, Jacob, Ann, Adam, Susanna, & Margaret being the children & heirs of Adam Zell, deceased, late of Caernarvon tp.] enf-rel.to Joseph Horst of Earl tp.

HISTORY: By his last will & testament, Adam Zell devised his lands bought of Henry Johnson & Michael Widware to two of his following four sons: Henry, John, Jacob, & Adam Zell. At their discretion, his executors were to make the decision. On 16 Jul 1783, his executors granted (1.) 100a Caernarvon tp. [land bought of Michael Widware] and (2.) 57 ¼ a. Caernarvon tp. [being one moiety of the land bought of Henry Johnson] to John Zell, son of said Adam Zell, deceased. On 17 Jul 1783, John Zell granted the same two tracts to said Joseph Horst (party hereto). Now, by this indenture, the other heirs of Adam Zell, deceased, formally release their claim to the property.

28 Apr 1784: William Boyd, Daniel Diller, Samuel Elliot, & William Smith

Z462: Tripartite agreement between the following parties:

1. Henry Line & his wife Anna of East Pennsborough tp., Cumberland County
2. George Gantz, yeoman, of Rapho tp.
3. George Bard (or Beard), yeoman, of Leacock tp.

--By his last will & testament dated 26 Feb 1755, John Line devised 250a Leacock tp. to his son Henry Line (party hereto. Previously, Henry Line granted the same to George Gantz (party hereto); however, there exists a dispute regarding the property. Now, by this indenture, the party of the first part grants the said property to the party of the second part; however, the party of the third part has legal right to bring forth a lawsuit in the Court of Common Pleas before the end of the May Term next ensuing.

20 Apr 1784: Stephen Chambers & JY

Z466: William Reynolds, yeoman, & his wife Prudence of West Nottingham tp., Chester County; Jacob Hains, Jr., & his wife Mary of the same; Henry Reynolds, Jr., & his wife Mary of Little Britain tp.; and Samuel Brown & his wife Sarah of West Nottingham tp., Chester County [the said Prudence, Jacob, Mary, & Sarah being four children of Jacob Hains, deceased, late of West Nottingham tp., Chester County] rel.to Joshua Hains [another son of said Jacob Hains, deceased]

--One moiety of 350a Salisbury tp.: HISTORY: On 8 June 1734, Richard Eavenson & his wife Jemima granted 350a Salisbury tp. to Jacob Haines (Ref. Deed H310). By his last will & testament dated 24

May 1742 (proved in Chester County), Jacob Haines devised the tract to his eldest son Joshua Haines & his youngest son Stephen Haines.

18 Apr 1770: William Haines & Job Haines

Z469: Jesse Reynolds & his wife Sarah of West Nottingham tp., Chester County enf.to William Haines of same

--Three tracts: (1.) plantation in Little Britain tp., (2.) 234a [location not given], and (3.) 31a [location not given].

1. HISTORY: Not given.
2. HISTORY: Part of 464a surveyed to Henry Reynolds Sr. [the said 234a now being in the possession of James Burford]. On 15 2mo. 1775, Henry Reynolds Sr. granted 234a to Jesse Reynolds.
3. HISTORY: Same tract surveyed to the said Henry Reynolds in pursuance to application #2518 dated 21 Apr 1767. On 15 2mo. 1775, Henry Reynolds Sr. granted the same to Jesse Reynolds.

--17 3mo. 1777: David Cope & John Scott

Z471: Jacob Meyer, yeoman, & his wife Ann of Manheim tp. enf-rel.to Richard Henry, taylor, of Lancaster Borough

--Two lots on Queen St. in Lancaster Borough: HISTORY: The first being the same lot that Samuel Bethel & his wife Susanna granted 26 May 1769 to said Jacob Meyer. The second being the same lot that said Samuel Bethel & his wife Susanna granted 10 Aug 1763 to Abel Reese. On 30 Mar 1779, Abel Reese & his wife Catharine granted the same to Jacob Meyer.

26 Jul 1783: ES & CS

Z474: Benjamin Mischi (or Meeshy) & John Mischi, both of Rapho tp., mort.to Baltzer Shellhorn of same

--Certain articles & crops on their plantation as given in an annexed list [not copied on the record].

3 Jul 1784: Sebastian Kelb & Noah Ceasey

--Baltzer Shellhorn ack.sat. 6 May 1785.

Z476: Alexander Benjamin, yeoman, & his wife Elizabeth of the town of Lebanon enf-rel.to Mathias Primmer, taylor, of same

56a Lebanon & Bethel tps.: HISTORY: It being part of two contiguous tracts: (1.) 56a Lebanon & Bethel tps. war. 19 Oct 1756 to Herman Orndorff. The right to this land came into the possession of John Altick, who had the tract surveyed. (2.) 20a, 128p Lebanon & Bethel tps. war. 6 Oct 1773 to the children & heirs of said John Altick, deceased. // By his last will & testament, John Altick ordered that his lands were to be sold when his son Michael reached age 21, with the profits to be divided equally among his four children, to wit, Michael Altick, Catharine Altick, Elizabeth Altick, & Barbara Altick. By their several indentures, the said heirs, to with Michael Altick, Catharine now wife of John Kuns, and Barbara now wife of Frederick Helm released their shares to Alexander Benjamin [the husband of Elizabeth Altick, the other daughter of said John Altick, deceased].

29 Dec 1783: PM & JT

Z479: John Dickinson, Esq., & his wife Mary of Kent County, Delaware, enf-rel.to Robert Coleman, ironmaster, of Elizabeth Furnace in Lancaster County

--His undivided third part of 10,000in Lancaster County, including a mine or iron ore and Elizabeth Furnace: HISTORY: On 2 Nov 1774, the county sheriff granted the same third part to said John Dickinson, who had brought a lawsuit against the previous owner, Alexander Stedman & his wife Elizabeth of Philadelphia, for failure to pay debts owed to him (Ref. Deed S57).

30 Dec 1780: Nicholas Van Dyke & Isaac Norris

Z482: Charles Stedman, Esq., & his wife Margaret of Philadelphia enf-rel.to Robert Coleman, ironmaster, of Lancaster County

--His undivided third part of 10,000in Lancaster County, including a mine or iron ore and Elizabeth Furnace: HISTORY: Not given, but the properties include lands in Elizabeth, Heidelberg, Lebanon, Cocalico,

& Warwick tp. Said Robert Coleman now holds two-thirds of Elizabeth Furnace [see the preceding indenture]; the remaining one-third belongs to Daniel Benezet, Esq.

25 Feb 1784: Joseph Work, Esq., of Donegal tp. and Samuel Nicholas, innholder, of Philadelphia

Z484: John Steiner (or Stoner), yeoman, & his wife Barbara of Lancaster County gr.to Frederick Taxes, yeoman, of Lancaster Borough

--Lot on Orange St. in Lancaster Borough: HISTORY: Same lot that James Hamilton granted 14 Aug 1751 to Mauritz Pfund. On 15 Oct 1754, Mauritz Pfund granted the same to said John Steiner. On 20 Mar 1755, John Steiner granted the same to Jacob Immell. On 23 Feb 1758, James Immell re-conveyed the lot to John Steiner.

9 Jul 1761: Henry Neff, John Brubaker, & Joseph Rose

Z487: Frederick Taxes [German signature] & his wife Christina assign to Henry Rung, shoemaker, of Lancaster Borough

--"the within mentioned lot": HISTORY: Not given, but see the preceding indenture.

20 Feb 1764: Henry Kreybill & CS

Z488: Johanna Sophia Junghausin of Ober Eula in the Electorate of Saxony in Germany [the only sister & heir of John Christopher Hayne, pewterer, of Lancaster Borough, deceased] quitclaims to John Frederick Steinman, pewterer, of Lancaster Borough [the stepson of the said John Christopher Hayne, deceased]

--Lot on King St. in Lancaster Borough: HISTORY: On 22 June 1767, Joseph Simons & his wife Rose granted a lot on King St. to John Christopher Hayne (Ref. Deed P391). Said John Christopher Hayne died intestate leaving a widow but no children. By law, his only sister has legal right to his real & personal estate.

25 Apr 1783: John Frederick Moering & George Sponer

--John Frederick Moering appeared in Lancaster on 21 June 1784 [presumably he witnessed this indenture in Germany].

Z492: Johanna Sophia Junghausin of Ober Eula in the Electorate of Saxony in Germany [the only sister & heir of John Christopher Hayne, pewterer, of Lancaster Borough, deceased] quitclaims to John Frederick Steinman, pewterer, of Lancaster Borough [the stepson of the said John Christopher Hayne, deceased]

--Her right & claim to the personal estate of her late brother: HISTORY: Said John Christopher Hayne died intestate leaving a widow but no children. By law, his only sister has legal right to his real & personal estate.

25 Apr 1783: John Frederick Moering & George Sponer

--John Frederick Moering appeared in Lancaster on 21 June 1784 [presumably he witnessed this indenture in Germany].

Z494: Christian Swartz, weaver, & his wife _______ [omitted] of Brecknock tp. enf-rel.to Robert Mathers, weaver, of Salisbury tp.

55a, 62p Brecknock tp.: HISTORY: It being the total of four contiguous parcels, all part of 177a Brecknock tp. pat. 21 Jan 1768 to William Morris (Ref. PB AA-10-237). // On 19 Feb 1768, William Morris & his wife Ann granted 18a, 147p and an additional 15a, 7p to Christopher Keck. On 12 Oct 1771, Christopher Keck & his wife Margaret granted the same two tracts to Christian Swartz. // On 24 Feb 1768, William Morris & his wife Ann granted 20a, 22p and an additional 168p to Joseph Wanger (Ref. Deed O188). On 23 Nov 1773, Joseph Wanger & his wife Catharine granted the same to Christian Swartz.

22 Jul 1783: George Hober & ZD

Z497: Samuel Boude, practitioner of physick, of Lancaster Borough mort.to Joseph Simons, merchant, of same

--His undivided moiety of a lot on Chestnut St. in Lancaster Borough: HISTORY: Same lot that James Hamilton granted 6 Sep 1757 to said Samuel Boude & Joseph Simons.

23 Sep 1758: William A. Atlee & Daniel East

Z501: Thomas Mitchel, yeoman, & his wife Margaret of Donegal tp. enf-rel.to David Franks, Jeremiah Warder, Edward Shippen, & Thomas Lawrence, merchants, all of Philadelphia & Joseph Simons, merchant, of Philadelphia

294a Donegal tp.: HISTORY: Same tract (amongst others) pat. 10 Aug 1745 to James Mitchel (Ref. PB A-11-542). By his last will & testament dated 17 Feb 1746/47, James Mitchel of Donegal tp. devised the said tract to his son William Mitchel & his son-in-law Thomas Mitchel—one moiety to each. On 12 Mar 1747, William Mitchel & his wife Esther granted their moiety to said Thomas Mitchel, giving him full right to the entire tract.

1 Nov 1758: John Daubenheim & William A. Atlee

Z506: Samuel Boude, practitioner of physick, & his wife Mary of Lancaster Borough enf-rel.to Joseph Simons, merchant, of same

--One undivided moiety of a lot on Chestnut St. in Lancaster Borough, including tools for making pot ash or pearl ash: HISTORY: On 6 Sep 1757, James Hamilton granted a lot on Chestnut St. to Samuel Boude & Joseph Simons. The said Boude & Simons have agreed to partition the lot. Now, by this indenture, Samuel Boude & wife release their claim to Joseph Simons part of the lot.

17 Apr 1759: Mathias Book & William A. Atlee

Z509: Mary Dougherty assigns the "within indenture" over to Alexander Gibbony, mason, of Lancaster Borough [no further information].

3 Nov 1742: David Jones & Robert Thompson

Z510: Alexander Gibbony & his wife Mary assigned the "within written indenture" over to Edward Smout, gentleman, of Lancaster Borough [no further information].

8 Jul 1747: George Gibson & L.T. Nyberg

Z511: Mary Test [the daughter of Thomas Test, test, and devisee under the last will & testament of Edward Smout, Esq., deceased] enf-rel.to Conrad Swartz, saddler, of Lancaster Borough

--Lot on Vine St. in Lancaster Borough: HISTORY: Same lot that James Hamilton granted 13 Aug 1740 to Mary Dougherty. On 3 Nov 1742, Mary Dougherty assigned the same to Alexander Gibbony. On 8 Jul 1747, Alexander Gibbony & his wife Mary assigned the same to Edward Smout. By his last will & testament, Edward Smout devised the property to Mary Test, the youngest daughter of Thomas Test.

18 Feb 1772: Michael Haberstich, John Bickham, & JB

Z514: Thomas Krauter, yeoman, & his wife Elizabeth of Manor tp. enf-rel.to Jacob Koser of Greenwich tp., Berks County

--Two five-acre lots in the town of Millersburg in Manor tp., numbered 36 & 37 in the town plan. HISTORY: On 1 May 1764, John Miller & his wife Elizabeth granted Lot #36 to George Moore. On 19 Sep 1766, George Moore granted the same to Philip Frick. On 4 Aug 1773, Philip Frick & his wife Margaret assigned the same to Thomas Krauter.

HISTORY: On 24 June 1765, John Miller & his wife Elizabeth granted Lot #37 to Michael Haberstich. On 30 June 1766, Michael Haberstich & his wife Salome assigned the same to Philip Frick. On 4 Aug 1773, Philip Frick & his wife Margaret assigned the same to Thomas Krauter.

--12 Apr 1783: ES & CS

Z517: Jacob Kosser & his Margaret assigned to Andrew Shrenck, taylor, of Lancaster tp.

--Two five-acre lots in the town of Millersburg, numbered 36 & 37 in the town plan: HISTORY: Not given, but clearly the same lots as given in the preceding indenture.

13 Mar 1784: CS Jr. & CS

Z518: Salome Hains, widow, of Lampeter tp. enf-rel.to John Boham, yeoman, of Strasburg tp.

--Lot #8 in Hains Town in Lampeter tp., containing four acres: HISTORY: Part of 50a Lampeter tp. that Christian Furrer granted on 25 Mar 1774 to Francis Smith. On equal date herewith, Francis Smith granted the same [with another 18a, 42p tract] to Salome Hains.

1 Apr 1783: JK & James Smith Jr.

Z520: Elizabeth Seger (or Seiger) of Lampeter tp. enf-rel.to John Boham, yeoman, of same

6a Lampeter tp.: HISTORY: Part of 96a Lampeter tp. that Mary Seger granted 20 Oct 1783 to Elizabeth Seger (Ref. Deed X267).

4 May 1784: JJACK & CJ

Z522: John Brown, mason, & his wife Dorothea of Lancaster Borough enf-rel.to Michael Halman of Fermanaugh tp., Cumberland County

--Lot #553 on Prince St. in Lancaster Borough: HISTORY: Same lot that James Hamilton granted 1 May 1761 to Peter Hesler (Ref. Deed I32). On 2 Dec 1763, Peter Hesler assigned the same to John Brown.

28 Apr 1784: Henry Gross & MH

Z525: Michael Holman & his wife Susanna assign to Henry Gross of Lancaster Borough

--"the within mentioned lot": HISTORY: Not given, but see the preceding indenture.

29 Apr 1784: MH & JH

Z526: Elizabeth Seger (or Seiger) of Lampeter tp. enf-rel.to Adam Mellow (or Mallow) of same

--6a Lampeter tp.: HISTORY: Part of 96a Lampeter tp. that Mary Seger granted 20 Oct 1783 to Elizabeth Seger (Ref. Deed X267).

4 May 1784: JJACK & CJ

Z529: Tripartite agreement between the following parties:

1. Magdalena Henneberger of Lancaster Borough [the widow of John Henneberger, yeoman, late of same]
2. George Stricker, yeoman, & his wife Catharine of Frederick County, Maryland, and Eberhart Michael, yeoman, & his wife Mary of Elizabeth tp. [the said Catharine & Mary being the two daughters of said John Henneberger, deceased]
3. Christopher Reem, mason, of Lancaster Borough

--Said John Henneberger died intestate seized in possession of a half lot on King St. in Lancaster Borough. He left the said widow Magdalena and issue two daughters, to whom the property descended. Now, by this indenture, the parties of the first and second part grant the said half lot to Christopher Reem, the party of the third part.

18 Nov 1760: Daniel May & Michael Diffenderfer

Z532: Christopher Ream (or Reehm) & his wife Catharine assign to John Maurer of Lancaster Borough

--"the within written indenture": HISTORY: Not given, but see the preceding indenture.

20 Jan 1775: Henry Zank & EM

Z534: John Maurer, yeoman, of Lancaster Borough enf-rel.to Jacob Maurer, yeoman, of same

--Half lot on King St. in Lancaster Borough: HISTORY: On 15 Aug 1740, James Hamilton granted a full lot on King St. to John Henneberger. In his lifetime, John Henneberger granted half of the lot to Jacob Fetter on 2 Jan 1751; however, he died intestate in regards to the other half lot. [Now see the two preceding indentures.]

13 Nov 1776: Henry Helm & EM

Z537: John Witmer, the younger, & his wife Mary of Lancaster Borough enf-rel.to John Witmer, the elder, of Lampeter tp.

150a Lampeter tp.: HISTORY: Part of 1,000a Strasburg tp. pat. 16 Dec 1716 to John Evans of London (Ref. PB A-5-203). On 5 Mar 1716 [sic], John Evans granted the same (amongst other lands) to John Moore (Ref. Phil. Deed E7-10-374). On 3 & 4 Sep 1730, John Moore granted the same to William Evans. // On 24 & 25 Dec 1731, William Evans granted 100a to Daniel Herman. // On 30 & 31 Jan 1731, William Evans granted 300a to James Webb. On 16 & 17 Jul 1735, James Webb granted 50a to said Daniel Herman. // On 15 Feb 1739, Daniel Herman granted both tracts, or 150a, to his son Emanuel (Ref. Deed B589). On 6

May 1754, Emanuel Herman & his wife Mary granted the same [now located in Lampeter tp.] to Daniel Herman, the younger. By his last will & testament dated 3 Oct 1757, Daniel Herman, the younger, devised the same to his daughter Mary [the land at the time being leased to John Young]. Said Mary has since married John Witmer, the younger [the party hereto]. On 10 Sep instant, said Mary reached the age of 21. On that day, said John Witmer & Mary granted the 150a tract to Benjamin Witmer. On 11 Oct 1771, Benjamin Witmer & his wife Ann re-conveyed the same tract to said John Witmer, the younger.

22 Sep 1779: Elizabeth Gross & CJ

Z542: David Musselman, yeoman, & his wife Barbara of Hempfield tp. enf-rel.to Alexander Lowrey of Lancaster Borough and Jacob Neave & John Hoover, millers, both of Hempfield tp. in TRUST

260a Hempfield tp.: HISTORY: The said Lowrey, Neave, & Hoover are granted the land in trust to use and/or sell as necessary to satisfy the debts owing by the said David Musselman.

12 Feb 1784: Henry Broobaker, Samuel Neff, JY, Sophia Kauffman, & Frederick Berg

Z547: Roger Hunt, yeoman, of Chester County [the administrator of Henry Hunt, late of Lancaster County] rel.to George Sanderson, innholder, of Lancaster Borough

--Two tracts: (1.) five-acre lot near Lancaster Borough and (2.) lot on King St. in said borough: HISTORY: Same lots that James Hamilton granted 20 May 1735 to Henry Hunt, who died seized in possession thereof. On 24 Dec 1742, the Orphans Court ordered the said lots to be sold in order to pay estate debts.

11 Nov 1743: Arthur Buchanon & Thomas Worrall

Z549 & Z551: John Lane (Leane), yeoman, & his wife Mary of Lancaster County lease & release to Roger Hunt, yeoman, of Chester County

--Two tracts: (1.) 100a and (2.) 1 ¾ a. [location not given]: HISTORY: Both part of 400a pat. 31 Dec 1717 to Michael Shank & Henry Pare (Ref. PB A-5-275). On 2 & 3 Sep 1728, Michael Shank & Henry Pare granted 200a to Peter Beller. On 19 & 20 Dec 1731, Peter Beller & his wife Elizabeth granted two parcels, 100a and 1 ¾ a., to John Lane.

9 & 10 June 1740: John Dehuff & Daniel Mackineth

Z555 & Z556: Roger Hunt, yeoman, & his wife Esther of Chester County lease & release to Francis Fortiney, butcher, of Lancaster County

--Two tracts: (1.) 100a and (2.) 1 ¾ a. [location not given]: HISTORY: They being the same tracts as given in the preceding indenture.

11 & 12 June 1740: John Dehuff, Daniel Mackineth, & Samuel Deceney

Z560: Thomas Houston, yeoman, of Strasburg tp. enf-rel.to Daniel Houston (or Huston), yeoman, of Leacock tp.

50a Strasburg & Leacock tps.: HISTORY: Part of 190a that Thomas Cookson & his wife Mary of Lancaster Borough granted 10 June 1752 to John Houston. By his last will & testament dated 10 Aug 1769, John Houston devised the same to his son Thomas [party hereto].

8 Dec 1785: John W. Kittera & John Jago

Surname Index to Lancaster County Deed Books W, X, Y, Z

Please be advised that a surname may appear more than once on a page. Further be advised that all surnames are spelled as given in the record. It is strongly suggested that you check for all phonetic spelling variations. It also must be noted that vowels are frequently interchangeable

H

L

M

O

P

Q

R

S

T

Y

Z